John A. John Alfred Poor, Laura Elizabeth Poor

The First International Railway And the Colonization of New England

John A. John Alfred Poor, Laura Elizabeth Poor

The First International Railway And the Colonization of New England

ISBN/EAN: 9783744723862

Printed in Europe, USA, Canada, Australia, Japan

Cover: Foto ©ninafisch / pixelio.de

More available books at **www.hansebooks.com**

THE

FIRST INTERNATIONAL RAILWAY

AND

THE COLONIZATION OF NEW ENGLAND

LIFE AND WRITINGS OF

JOHN ALFRED POOR

EDITED BY

LAURA ELIZABETH POOR

"PEACE HATH HER VICTORIES
NO LESS RENOWNED THAN WAR"

G. P. PUTNAM'S SONS
NEW YORK   LONDON
27 WEST TWENTY-THIRD STREET   24 BEDFORD STREET, STRAND
The Knickerbocker Press
1892

"Imagination is, in the popular mind, obstinately connected with poetry and romance. When the attempt is made to extend the application of the creative energy of the imagination to business and politics, the sentimental outcry against such a profanation of the term becomes almost deafening. Every poetaster is willing to admit that Newton is one of the few grand scientific discoverers that the world has produced; but he still thinks that, in virtue of versifying some commonplaces of emotion and thought, he is himself superior to Newton in imagination. In fact, it is the direction given to the creative faculty, and not the material on which it works, that discriminates between Fulton and Bryant, Whitney and Longfellow, Bigelow and Whittier, Goodyear and Lowell. Descending from the inventors, it would be easy to show that, in the conduct of the every-day transactions of life, more quickness of imagination, subtlety and breadth of understanding, and energy of will have been displayed by our men of business than by our authors."

—E. P. WHIPPLE, on American Literature.

CONTENTS.

	PAGE
THE LIFE OF JOHN ALFRED POOR	1
LIST OF PUBLISHED WRITINGS	136
FIRST ARTICLE ON THE ST. LAWRENCE AND ATLANTIC RAILWAY. FOR THE "SHERBROOKE GAZETTE"	142
FIRST ARTICLE ON THE ATLANTIC AND ST. LAWRENCE RAILWAY. FOR THE "PORTLAND ADVERTISER"	147
PLAN FOR SHORTENING THE TIME OF PASSAGE BETWEEN NEW YORK AND LONDON	154
THE NORTHEASTERN BOUNDARY. REPORT OF THE SELECT COMMITTEE OF THE HOUSE OF REPRESENTATIVES	176
AN AMERICAN ZOLL-VEREIN. LETTER TO THE SHIP-CANAL CONVENTION	211
THE TRANSCONTINENTAL RAILWAY. ADDRESS DELIVERED AT RUTLAND, VERMONT, JUNE, 1869	218
A NATIONAL HIGHWAY. MEMORIAL TO THE CONGRESS OF THE UNITED STATES	264
A BILL TO SECURE CHEAP TRANSPORTATION OF BREADSTUFFS AT UNIFORM RATES	275
THE FATHER OF ENGLISH COLONIZATION IN AMERICA: A VINDICATION OF THE CLAIMS OF SIR FERDINANDO GORGES. DELIVERED BEFORE THE HISTORICAL SOCIETIES OF MAINE AND NEW YORK, 1859	282
THE FIRST COLONIZATION OF NEW ENGLAND. AN ADDRESS DELIVERED AT FORT POPHAM, MAINE, 1862	353
APPENDIX	397

FIRST INTERNATIONAL RAILWAY.

THE LIFE OF JOHN ALFRED POOR.

The following pages will try to depict a hero of commerce. Mr. Poor's name is well known, yet few persons have any adequate idea of the toil which filled up and shortened his years; of the vastness of the schemes carried out by his instrumentality; and of the patriotism which impelled him to devote his life to that cause which he perpetually pursued, and which underlaid his every thought. Mr. Poor's opinions and character can best be shown from his writings; yet his writings serve only to illustrate his actions. More than with most men, his thoughts and his deeds went together; it is impossible to separate them. The simplest narrative therefore will connect them, and show the gradual but steady development, till the day of his death, of the ideas which had inspired his youth.

Although Mr. Poor was considered to have the genius of a worker, and really wrote only to express his conception of what should be done, few professedly literary men can show a style of more force and clearness. When he leaves his marshalling of hard facts and gives free play to his imagination and enthusiasm, his stately sentences are not unworthy of that Webster whose style he so much admired.

From a list of his published writings a selection has been made, as they involve necessarily some repetitions; but the list itself is far from complete. Mr. Poor himself said: "The list herewith submitted embraces only such papers as contain original suggestions, or the record of important proceedings. The bulk of my writings have been occasional contributions to the newspapers of Portland, Bangor, Montreal, Washington, Boston, and the lower British Provinces, advocating the various measures in which I have been engaged." In addition to this Mr. Poor edited, for six years, the daily newspaper which he owned, and there are few of its issues which do not contain some article by him; and himself drew up the different railway bills presented by him to Congress, and the Legislatures of Maine and Massachusetts.

"William the Conqueror's third and youngest son Prince Henry, was rather snubbed by his older brothers, and lived a jovial life in Normandy. One morning, as he was riding at the head of his mounted men-at-arms, in the vicinity of the city of Caen, he approached a small chapel—of the Roman Catholic faith, of course — just as its bell rang forth the call, to matin prayers. The gay yet devout young prince halted his men, dismounted, and entered the humble sanctuary, where the parish priest, a gaunt, spare man, known as Father Roger, at once recognized him.

The priest, recollecting doubtless that soldiers do not like long prayers, and being, perhaps, himself more anxious for favor on earth than in heaven, despatched the morning service with extraordinary rapidity. 'Whereat,' says the historian, 'they were so well pleased that the prince said to him, "Follow my camp," which he did.' Soon afterwards the prince went to England to join his brother, King William Rufus, and he took the Caen priest as his chaplain. On crossing the Channel, every Norman assumed a surname, and the lean chaplain became Roger Poor. The nomenclature of that day was based, as in this case, on personal characteristics or local habitations. The families of Short, Long, Black, White, Brown, Gray, and Head, with many others, thus obtained their surnames.

"In the year 1100, King William Rufus, while hunting in the New Forest, was accidentally killed by an arrow which was fired at a buck, but which glanced from a tree and pierced the monarch's heart. His younger brother, Prince Henry, who was hunting with him, no sooner witnessed his death, than he hastened to London and seated himself on the throne of England, regardless of the claims of the elder brother, Duke Robert, who was making love in Italy.

"Roger Poor thus became his Majesty's chaplain. He kept up his Norman reputation for short prayers, and soon became such a favorite that the king made him his private secretary, although the historians say—alas, that I must repeat it in this presence—'he was rather illiterate.' As a courtier, however, Roger Poor excelled, and he was generally liked, although perhaps not much respected. His faculties expanded with his good fortune, and while exercising his religious duties he supported the royal prerogative with such zeal, and displayed such submission to the royal will that King Henry appointed him Bishop of Sarum.

"Bishop Roger Poor was in due time promoted to the office of Chief Justiciar, or Lord High Chancellor, which made him in reality Prime Minister, and during the king's visits to Normandy, sometimes extending over a year, he governed England as regent. Up to this time the crown of England had only descended in the male line, for although Queen Boadicea had ruled over the Britons, no female had ever sat on the Anglo-Saxon throne. Bishop Roger Poor (to please King Henry, who had no legitimate sons, and who desired to leave his crown to his daughter Matilda) laid it down as incontrovertible doctrine 'that the crown, like a private inheritance, should descend to the daughter of the person last seized.' He was also greatly instrumental in obtaining from the barons of England, as well as those of Normandy, a recognition of the Princess Matilda as the successor to her father in both countries. Under this decree, promulgated by Bishop Poor, Queen Victoria now occupies the English throne, and it was the origin of what are now termed 'Woman's Rights.'

To the favor of King Henry, Bishop Roger Poor owed a privilege, eagerly coveted by the turbulent nobility of the times, when the consequence of individuals was estimated by the strength and splendor of their fortified residences. He built a castle at Devizes, which was considered as one of the most sumptuous and stately edifices in England; and a second at Sherborne, little inferior; and he repaired the castle of Sarum, which was entrusted to his custody. He also expended large sums in completing and embellishing the cathedral of Sarum, which had been injured by a storm soon after its dedication. Indeed some of the old English chroniclers distinguish him by the title of 'the great builder of churches and castles.'

"In addition to Bishop Roger Poor's vast wealth, which flowed from his numerous places and preferments, his great influence enabled him to bring from Normandy several of his relations, and to obtain for them honorable positions. One of his nephews, Alexander, was first made Archdeacon of Sarum, next Chancellor, and finally, in 1123, Bishop of Lincoln. Another nephew, Nigellus, was appointed a prebend in the church of St. Paul's, and, in 1133, Bishop of Ely. King Henry, late in life, quarrelled with Bishop Roger Poor, and dismissed him from civil office. For this the bishop revenged himself after the king's death in 1135, by forgetting his sworn allegiance to the Princess Matilda, and aiding in giving the crown to Stephen, Earl of Blois. He defended himself by asserting that circumstances had changed, but that he remained consistent to his principles, and he was rewarded by a restoration to his position as Chief Justiciar. The Bishop of Ely, his nephew, was appointed Treasurer of the realm, and his son, Roger Poor, was made Chancellor.

"King Stephen also gave Bishop Roger Poor extensive landed possessions, yielding large revenues, and when asked by an attendant if he was not displaying too much generosity towards his favorite, the monarch replied: 'By the Nativity, I would give him half of England if he had asked for it. He shall sooner be tired of asking than I of giving.' The bishop obtained a grant of the burgh of Malmesbury, and displayed his characteristic fondness for building by commencing a stately castle there, like those at Devizes and Sherborne.

"Fortune—fickle jade,—after a long attendance on Bishop Poor, at last deserted him, and pierced him with scorpion's sting.

"King Stephen's jealousy was inflamed by the insinuation of some of his courtiers, and he determined to stop the further erection of the castles which were being erected all over England, commencing with that of Bishop Poor at Malmsbury. Summoning the bishop to a great council at Oxford, he received him with marked respect, but his retinue was involved in a quarrel with the attendants of the Earl of Brittany, in which one of the latter was killed and another dangerously wounded. This affray was made the pretext for ordering Bishop Poor and his connections to deliver up their castles. They complied, with the exception of Nigellus Poor, Bishop of Ely, who fled to the castle of Devizes, and prepared for resistance.

"Enraged at this contumacy, King Stephen marched with a body of troops to Devizes, carrying with him Bishop Poor and his son as prisoners. Bishop Nigellus, refusing to surrender, King Stephen ordered a gallows to be erected, and informed Bishop Roger Poor that his son Roger, to whom he was much attached, should be hung unless the castle was surrendered to him. The aged prelate supplicated for mercy, and with difficulty prevailed upon his nephew to open the gates of the castle. The bishop's sacred office protected him from violence, but the treasures which he had accumulated during long years of prosperity were seized by King Stephen, and the old man sank under his troubles, dying in December, 1139—an example of that instability of power and caprice of fortune which Shakespeare has so feelingly described.

"Alexander Poor, Bishop of Lincoln, succeeded his uncle as Lord Chancellor, but died when on a mission to the Pope in 1147. The great seal was then entrusted to Bishop Roger Poor's son Roger, who possessed neither the ability nor the pliancy of his father. Taking part with the barons who held out their castles against the king, he was made prisoner, and refused to take the oath of submission, even when threatened with the penalties of treason. As a singular favor he was allowed to abjure the realm, and he died in exile.

"Another nephew of Bishop Roger Poor, Richard Poor, located himself in Gloucestershire, and brought up three sons, Herbert, Richard, and Philip. The two first named were educated for the Church, and were advanced by old friends of their great uncle, Bishop Roger.

"Herbert Poor was made Archdeacon of Canterbury, and in 1194 was consecrated Bishop of

Sarum. In 1194 he appears on the rolls as one of the king's justices, and in 1199 he attended at the coronation of King John. He had great trouble, however, at Sarum, the soldiers of the garrison not agreeing with the priests at the cathedral.

"Bishop Richard Poor, brother of his predecessor, was first Dean of Sarum, consecrated Bishop of Chichester in 1215, and removed to Sarum in 1217. His first care was to have the new cathedral at Salisbury commenced, and the stately Gothic pile soon rose in all its fair proportions. In unity of design and as a specimen of old English ecclesiastical architecture, it is unequalled, and its elegant spire, 406 feet high, the loftiest in England, though added in the reign of Edward the Third, is in perfect harmony with the rest of the edifice.

"Bishop Richard Poor was translated to the see of Durham before the cathedral was completed. 'He was,' says Godwin, 'a man of rare learning in those times, and of notable integrity for his life and conversation.' Matthew Paris says that perceiving the approach of death he caused the people to be assembled, and from the pulpit addressed them in a pious discourse, desiring them to mark well his exhortations, as he was shortly to be taken from them. The next day he did the same, bidding them farewell, and requesting the prayers and forgiveness of those whom he had offended. The third day he sent for his particular acquaintances; and calling together his family and servants, distributed among them his last benefactions. He then tenderly dismissed each individual, and having arranged his temporal affairs, betook himself to prayer, in which act of devotion he gave up the ghost, on the fifteenth day of April, 1237.

"Salisbury Cathedral contains the monument of Bishop Roger Poor, brought from Sarum, and of Bishop Richard Poor. In the library are manuscripts of the Old and New Testaments, transcribed under the auspices of Bishop Poor, and also his seal. Philip Poor of Amesbury, from whom I believe that we are all descended, was the brother of Bishops Herbert and Richard Poor, and the Poors still live in Wiltshire."

The preceding account of the rise of the family was made by Major Ben: Perley Poore for a gathering of the Poors at Newburyport, Massachusetts. The name of the three bishops is Poor on their tombstones at Salisbury Cathedral; but a Roger obtained the title of Sir Roger le Poer; settled in Ireland; from him descended the family name of the Marquis of Waterford, De le Poer. From the county of Hampshire and the town of Andover, Daniel Poor, a Puritan, came to New England in 1638. His name is on the town records of Andover, Massachusetts; and for nearly two hundred years the Poors lived and died in Essex County, Massachusetts. Finally the land grew too straitened for them, and in 1790 three brothers of the name went down into the wilderness of Maine. In a beautiful mountain valley in the northern part of what is now Oxford County, Maine, they found Deacon Ezekiel Merrill, its first settler, descendant of Nathaniel Merrill, who came to Ipswich, Massachusetts, from England in 1633. The Poors joined him; a few other families followed ; all men of force and also of an intelligence and education far above those of the average pioneer; and all of pure English stock. The town received the name of East Andover; which it retained till the separation of Maine from Massachusetts in 1820.

It seems impossible that only a hundred years have passed since the conditions described by Mr. Poor, as follows:

"Died, in Andover, Me., in 1848, Sarah Merrill, relict of the late Deacon Ezekiel Merrill, aged ninety-three years and eight months. She was a daughter of Moses Emery, of Newbury, Mass., and was born 1753; at nineteen, married, and soon after with her husband united with the church in their native place. Apprehensive, with others in the vicinity of the sea-coast, of the danger to which the outbreak of the American Revolution exposed them, they removed to Pelham, N. H., where they lived until after the peace of 1783. As their pecuniary means had become reduced, they concluded to remove to Maine, where land was cheap; and in March, 1788, with seven children—the eldest a son fourteen years old, the youngest a daughter about four—they started for Sudbury-Canada, now Bethel. At Fryburg their road terminated. There Mr. Merrill employed men with snow-shoes, and sixteen sleds drawn by their own hands, to carry the family and movable articles to Sudbury-Canada, a distance of about thirty miles. There was then no house or inhabitant on their route. They threw up a camp for the night about midway between Fryburg and Bethel; and the second day reached the first house. In this place they remained about fifteen months, when with a small company in Andover, Mass., he became a purchaser from Massachusetts of the township on Ellis River, now called Andover. From their residence in Sudbury-Canada to this place the distance was about thirteen miles by land, and three times as far by water.

"Having procured boats of the Indians, in the month of May, 1789, the family, nine in all, embarked and sailed easily down the Androscoggin to the mouth of Ellis River, whence they stemmed the current. They supped and rested for the night under a large pine. Early the next morning they re-embarked, and proceeded up the river to the Forks, where they were received by some Indian families, from whom they had procured their boats, into their cabins, and treated with much hospitality for the night.

"The year before, Mr. Merrill and his sons had felled some trees, and made a slight camp about two miles from the Indian cabins. The third morning, Mrs. Merrill with one son and a guide walked through the woods to this place, and the other children in the boat were pushed up the stream against the camp. It was towards noon, and they now prepared what has been called their Thanksgiving Dinner. Their present situation is thus described:

"'The cabin they had built was so small that very little could be put into it; therefore some of the men felled a few trees and stripped off the bark; they set up four crotched stakes, and laid on saplings, and spread bark overhead so as to keep off sun and rain. Under this shelter they put the articles which the weather would injure. They then drove stakes into the ground, and laid wicker brush for their bed-steads, to keep their beds from the ground, —they having no floor, and there being no boards nearer than twenty-five miles, nor any road by which they could be brought. The children pulled up the small bushes, and wet and trod the ground so as to make it hard. This finished the third day from Bethel. The next day their companions from Bethel returned.'

"They soon sowed some grain, and planted some potatoes; after which they built a log-house, containing one room; this they covered with bark, and made doors of bark, and laid round saplings overhead for chamber floor. They were now twelve miles from any white inhabitants; they, however, received great kindness from the Indians; not only in supplies of food from their hunting, but especially when the next year, in July, 1790, in this solitude, another daughter was added to the family.

"In the year 1791 many beginnings of settlements were made by proprietors. The next year one more family came into town; and in 1793-4 three or four females. In May of 1793 their oldest daughter, not fifteen years old, was married. In October of the same year their house and most of its contents were burned. The children sleeping overhead were awakened by the fire in the roof, and barely escaped, losing all but the clothes in which they slept. This was a heavy loss; they were able, however, to erect a frame house before winter,—a saw-mill having been erected a year or two earlier,—and thenceforward, with their neighbors, now becoming more numerous, advanced in general prosperity. A church was formed in 1800; the town was incorporated by the name of East Andover in 1804."

The second of these brothers, Dr. Silvanus Poor married Mary, the daughter of Ezekiel Merrill. She was a woman of uncommon beauty; of an active, cheerful temperament, full of sensitiveness and sweetness; and had been educated at Fryburg, the well-known school. Dr. Poor was a man of good education; a strong and independent thinker; Arminian in theology; a Jefferson democrat in politics; a stern man, with a certain grim humor and immense powers of sarcasm. He was a member of the convention which framed the constitution of Maine; his mental power was recognized by all who came in contact with him, but an indolent temperament prevented his making the full use of his abilities. He was, at the same time, physician and farmer; for many years postmaster, the books of the Social Library were kept at his house; the relatives and friends who came and went, kept up connection with the outside world.

John Alfred Poor, their second son, was born January 8, 1808. He passed his childhood at home; when he was twelve years of age, the family received a visit from his aunt who had married Hon. Jacob McGaw, a graduate of Dartmouth College, and a lifelong friend and correspondent of Daniel Webster. Mrs. McGaw was a person of great beauty, vivacity, and social talent, the "Miss Poor" who is alluded to in Mr. Webster's published correspondence.

Mr. Webster came to East Andover to see her, and his visit is still remembered. As darkness came on, he found himself far from his destination, and rode up to the nearest farmhouse to ask a lodging for the night; but the good woman of the house took him for a highway robber, and shut the door in his face; and he was obliged to drive three miles farther until he reached Dr. Poor's house.

The boy Alfred was so beautiful and intelligent that his uncle invited him to go to Bangor, Maine. Upon his way he stopped at Belfast, Maine, to visit his uncle, a clever physician, and there for the first time, he saw the ocean; it was an epoch in his life. He often alluded to it, and nearly fifty years afterwards spoke of it, in an oration delivered at Belfast. "I was brought up among the grandest mountain scenery of New England; but my heart panted for a sight of the ocean, whose sublimer aspects and mysterious revels had been pictured to my youthful mind by stories of travellers and descriptions in the impassioned language of poetry; and when, a boy of twelve, I first beheld, in the clear sunlight of a winter morning, the outstretching waters of Belfast Bay embosomed by its surrounding hills and distant islands, I experienced all those sublime emotions of delight that Wordsworth has recorded in the finest of his poems. 'The Wanderer,' as enjoyed by the young herdsman, when on the top of the high mountain

"'He beheld the sun
Rise up, and bathe the world in light! He looked—
Ocean and earth, the solid frame of earth

And ocean's liquid mass, beneath him lay
In gladness and deep joy. The clouds were touched
And in their silent faces did he read
Unutterable love. Sound needed none,
Nor any voice of joy ; his spirit drank
The spectacle ; sensation, soul, and form
All melted into him ; they swallowed up
His animal being ; in them did he live
And by them did he live ; they were his life.
In such access of mind, in such high hour
Of visitation from the living God,
Thought was not ; in enjoyment it expired.'

"This first visit to the seaside influenced, no doubt, my whole life, made me fond of adventure on the ocean, eager for geographical knowledge, and studious of those agencies that stimulate commercial progress. I love the ocean with almost filial devotion, and without a daily sight of it I am never fully satisfied and contented."

Mr. Poor paid another visit, which impressed him permanently, to Dr. Vaughan, of Hallowell, a friend of Dr. Silvanus Poor. This learned man was born in Jamaica, educated at Cambridge, and studied medicine in Edinburgh. His political opinions were so radical that he was forced to leave England at the time of the French Revolution, went first to France, thence to Maine. Here Mr. Poor saw for the first time a noble private library.

After two years at the Academy, he returned to Andover, where his work upon the farm was varied by occasional terms of school and steady study with his brother-in-law, Rev. Thomas T. Stone, of Andover, pastor of the Congregational church ; he taught school for one winter at Bethel, Maine. Whenever the farmer's team went to Portland for supplies, it was driven by him. Mr. Poor distinctly recollected the first time he tasted liquor: on his way home, one cold winter's night, a grown man gave him "something to keep him warm." Mr. Poor never touched tobacco in any form in his whole life; although he might drink ale or wine on occasions, he did not even take wine regularly at dinner. Undoubtedly he owed to those Andover years the splendid physical vigor which stood him in such good stead throughout his laborious life. During these Andover years the appointment of cadet at West Point was offered to him, but declined at his mother's urgent request.

Finally, Mr. Poor decided upon his plan of life. On the 5th of September, 1827, he left Andover, returned to Bangor to study law, and entered the office of his uncle, Mr. McGaw, who was at that time the president of the Penobscot bar. Mr. Poor's earliest writings date from this period. They are: an account of Andover, furnished for Mr. Williamson's "History of Maine," which was so full and accurate that he received the thanks of the historian; a Report of the Committee of the Young Men's Lyceum against Nullification; a lecture delivered before the Bangor Lyceum upon the Advantages of Debating Societies; a lecture on Temperance; and, strangely enough, an elaborate paper delivered before the Lyceum upon the Theory of the British Government, and the Constitution of the British Colonies, showing how early he was impressed with the subject he afterwards developed—English colonization.

On his twenty-fourth birthday, Mr. Poor was admitted to the bar. Mr. McGaw proposed a partnership on equal terms with himself, but Mr. Poor preferred to begin his professional life alone. He removed to Oldtown, twelve miles above Bangor, entered at once upon a lucrative practice, though his active mind took hold of the needs about him.

The remnant of the tribe of the Penobscot Indians was living upon an island near Oldtown, and one of them, named Pol Susof (Paul Joseph), had shown some talent for art. Mr. Poor became interested in him. In connection with some young men of Bangor, he sent the young Indian to Bangor to study painting with a professional artist. Mr. Poor wrote an account of him which was made the basis of a flowery article by Mrs. Child, the editor of the *Juvenile Miscellany*. But civilization had no real hold upon Pol Susof; he soon returned to his Indian friends, leaving one or two paintings behind him, and could never be induced to leave Oldtown again. For some time the Indians had been without a priest at Oldtown Island, and as they expressed a great desire for the services of the Roman Catholic Church, Mr. Poor wrote on their behalf to the Roman Catholic Bishop of Boston. Accordingly Bishop Fenwick of Boston sent a priest to the Indians, and a letter of thanks to Mr. Poor.

But, in eight months, Mr. Poor returned to Bangor, where he married, in 1833, Elizabeth Adams Hill, eldest daughter of Hon. Thomas Adams Hill, a prominent lawyer, candidate for Governor of the anti-masonic party, and a nephew of the celebrated Hannah Adams. Mr. Poor formed a law partnership with his uncle, Mr. McGaw, continued till that gentleman retired from practice. He then formed a partnership with his youngest brother, Henry Varnum Poor, Esq., a graduate of Bowdoin College.

A short but admirable biography of Mr. Poor was written by Charles W. Tuttle, Esq., of Boston, and published in the *Historical and Genealogical Register* of October, 1872, and of this memorial we shall make as much use as possible. Mr. Tuttle says: "During the fourteen years he was at the bar in Bangor he earned the reputation of being a sound lawyer and a public-spirited citizen. His practice was large, and extended to all branches of the law. Among the notable causes in which he was retained was the suit of Veazie *vs.* Wadleigh, involving title to valuable lands and water-power on the Penobscot. This suit attracted a good deal of public attention at the time, not only on account of the parties interested, and the matter in issue, but of the great eminence of the counsel engaged. Daniel Webster was opposed by Jeremiah Mason, the then acknowledged heads of the bar in New England. Mr. Poor, who was associated with Mr. Webster as junior counsel, prepared the history of the legal title to the disputed territory with so much completeness that Mr. Webster personally complimented him for the work. This was in 1835, only three years after his admission to practice." Mr. Poor felt the enthusiastic admiration which Mr. Webster knew so well how to inspire, and often spoke, in later years, of the profound impression made upon him by Mr. Webster. "I was awed," he said, "and felt myself in the presence of a great man." Mr. Poor wrote an enthusiastic account of Mr. Webster's visit to Bangor, which was published; and supported Mr. Webster for the Presidency in 1852, for Mr. Poor loved his friends.

Bangor was at that time a new and flourishing town, full of commercial and also of literary activity. A theological seminary supplied the scholarly element which is usually wanting in such towns. Mr. Poor shared in all the movements of an American town; he was a member of the city government; he gave both time and money towards church building at Bangor, Oldtown, and Hampden; he took a very prominent part in forming the Bangor Lyceum, a literary and debating society, and the Bangor Social Library. In one of his first letters from Montreal, dated February 17, 1845, he says: "Tell —— that I have catalogues from the Pencinian and Athenæum societies at Brunswick, the Athenæum at Portland, the great library in Canada, and some others, and I think I can do good service here in preparing for the new library." Many years later Mr. Poor made great efforts to establish a free public library in Portland; but he was entirely in advance of the sentiment of the town. Libraries had always an irresistible fascination for him. Amid all his business occupations in New York and Washington he always spent some time in the Astor Library or among General Force's books. How great was his delight when he discovered the beautiful L'Escarbot in New York.

But his attention was not confined to Bangor. He took an active part in politics, and was a member of the Whig State Committee. In 1839 he sent to the *Portland Advertiser* three letters, for which he received the thanks of the publishers, giving an account of the Northeastern boundary difficulties, those troubles on the borders of Maine and New Brunswick, which threatened to assume serious proportions; the militia of Maine was called out, the streets of Bangor were full of men arming for the "Aroostook War," when the matter was settled by the Ashburton treaty. A Canadian remarked: "As it displeased both parties, it was probably equitable." An article in the *Quarterly*, January, 1887, speaks of "that unfortunate Ashburton Treaty." The following communication explains itself:

"PORTLAND, Nov. 16, 1869.
"To HIS EXCELLENCY,
"THE GOVERNOR OF MAINE.
"SIR:
"I deem it proper to lay before your Excellency, a copy of the Executive Document, number 132, House of Representatives, 37th Congress, 1st Session, containing the Message of the President of the United States, under date of June 14, 1866, in reply to a resolution of the House of the 28th of May, requesting information as to the maps of the Boundary Survey under the Treaty of Washington, for the purpose of explaining fully to your Excellency the object I have in view in addressing you this note.

"While in Washington in the autumn of 1861, as Commissioner on the Coast Defences of Maine, I thought it advisable to look at the maps of the Boundary Survey, which might be of great importance in case of a war with England, by affording us valuable information as to the routes of approach and means of defence, etc.

"In the performance of these duties, I called the attention of the Secretary of State to the incompleteness of the maps in question; and, at my suggestion, George E. Baker, Esq., disbursing agent of the Department of State, addressed a letter to Lieut.-Col. I. D. Graham, under date of November 25, 1861, in reference to the maps in question, whose reply, in due course of mail, dated Chicago, November 30, 1861, is on pages 13, 14, and 15 of the Document 132 enclosed. His letter will put you in possession of information necessary to a full understanding of the object of this note.

"The maps of the line and adjacent territory, from the Monument at the source of the St. Croix to the St. Lawrence at St. Regis, a distance of 675 miles, were drawn upon a scale of four inches to one mile in separate sheets numbered from 1 to 63. Nineteen other maps made by the American engineers were also prepared of the several tributaries of the St. John, on our side of the Boundary.

"These maps were destroyed by fire, on the night of April 19, 1848, and afterwards reproduced under an appropriation of Congress under the direction of Col. Graham, on a reduced scale of two inches to one mile, one fourth only of the superficial size of the originals. These maps or drawings I found in 84 sheets in the State Department at Washington, but no index, maps, or any notes or other papers connected with the Boundary Survey.

"In accordance with the advice of Col. Graham's letter of November 30, 1861, under an appropriation of Congress, requiring copies to be furnished to the Executive of every State bordering on foreign territory, the maps in sheets were engraved or lithographed; a labor that required some years' time, but efficiently done under charge of George E. Baker, Esq., and copies furnished, as required by law, to the Executives of the different States.

"In the spring and summer of 1866, being in Washington engaged in prosecuting the payment of the claims of Maine and Massachusetts, in behalf of the European and North American Railway, to whose benefit they had been assigned, I applied to the State Department for the use of the maps in question, being mainly anxious to examine the index map and other papers connected with the boundary survey. But nothing had been done beyond the engraving of the maps. At my request the Hon. John H. Rice, representing the fourth district of Maine in the 37th Congress, introduced a resolution of inquiry, which was adopted on the 28th of May, 1866, in answer to which the Message of the President of June the 14th with the accompanying documents was returned; and the letter addressed by the Secretary of State to Gen. Delafield, Chief of Bureau of Engineers, under date of June 2, 1865, was drawn forth, and submitted as a part of the correspondence.

"I deem it proper to say, that the Hon. Wm. H. Seward, Secretary of State, took the liveliest interest and expressed the highest gratification at the effort I had made to cause the plans of the Boundary Survey to be perfected and preserved; and, at his request, I examined all the correspondence and other papers in the State Department bearing on the question, and prepared the abstract, or rather selected from the mass of papers on file such items of correspondence as I thought necessary to have reported to Congress, and as they now appear in Document 132.

"But the call of the Secretary of State upon the Bureau of Engineers brought at the time nothing in reply. At the request of the Secretary of State, I applied personally to Gen. Delafield and his subordinates, who took every means possible to get information as to the missing maps and official papers in the hands of Col. Graham at his death.

"I also opened correspondence with different officers upon the subject without any show of success, until I applied to Gen. George Thom, of the U. S. Army, in charge of the public works in Portland. He succeeded in recovering the index map in an incompleted condition, as also the astronomical observations of Major Graham, the tabulation of the angles and measured distances, and the tabulation of the monuments upon the line, and other papers referred to in Col. Graham's note to Mr. Clayton of May, 1849, given on pages 8 and 9, Document 132.

"The index map and other papers were obtained and forwarded by Gen. Thom to the War Department at Washington, as stated in his letter to me.

"On visiting Washington, in 1869, I called at the State Department on the matter, but found that nothing was known in reference to the index maps or other papers in question. I then visited the War Office, and after one or two unsuccessful attempts, found the index map in the office of Col. Woodruff, which had been returned to that office as completed on the 3d of March, 1869.

"Knowing that the index map was to be published by the State Department, by calling on Mr. Baker I ascertained from him that the balance of the appropriation on hand was adequate to pay for the engraving of the index map, and that the State Department would cause it to be done as soon as may be after receiving it. At his request I called on Gen. Humphrey, Chief of Bureau of Engineers, and laid before him the copy of Document 132, calling his attention to the note of the Secretary of State of June 2, 1866, requesting the deposit of the index maps and other papers in question in the State Department, which Gen. Humphrey assured me should be done.

"Since then I have received letters from Mr. Baker, the latest of which informed me that no index map or other papers connected therewith had been received at the Department of State.

"The large sums of money expended by the government in making the Boundary Surveys, the importance of the information thus obtained to the whole country, and to the State of Maine more especially, and the deep historic interest connected with the northeastern boundary question, leads me to hope that measures will be taken by you to secure the publication of the index map in question, and the other information which has been fortunately preserved."

The closing paragraph of this communication has been unfortunately lost, but it was signed John A. Poor, a citizen of Maine. One of the very last letters written by Mr. Poor, in the summer of 1871, was in reference to this matter. Up to that time the index map had not been completed; it is to be hoped that some other citizen of Maine will urge on the work where Mr. Poor's hand dropped powerless in death, and carry it to a successful termination.

But while thus active in whatever duty came to his hand, the real inspiration of his life had not yet arisen. We resume our quotations from Mr. Tuttle's memoir: "Many years before moving to Portland he became profoundly interested in the subject, then fresh, of locomotive railways. The introduction of railways into New England was an event that made a deep impression on his mind, and gave direction to his future life. He seems to have comprehended, at once, the full magnitude and importance of this new method of transportation, which he tersely characterized as 'the great achievement of man, the most extraordinary instrument for good the world has yet reached.' The year 1834 is memorable in the history of locomotive railways in New England. On the 16th of April of that year the first locomotive engine, with passenger cars attached, ran over a railway freshly laid between Boston and Newton, and afterwards extended to Worcester and beyond. A large number of persons were present in Boston to witness this novel experiment of travel by railway. Among the spectators who waited with breathless anxiety the first movement of the train was Mr. Poor, then only twenty-six years of age, who had come from Bangor to witness the introduction of this new wonder of the age. Many years after the event, he described this scene and the impression it made on him. 'Placed,' he says, 'upon the track, its driver, who came with it from England, stepped upon the platform with almost the airs of a juggler or a professor of chemistry, placed his hand upon the lever, and with a slight move of it, the engine started at a speed worthy of the companion of the "Rocket," amid the shouts and cheers of the multitude. It gave me such a shock that my hair seemed to start from the roots rather than to stand on end; and as I reflected in after years, the locomotive engine grew into a greatness in mind that left all other created things far behind it as marvels and wonders.' This kindled in him an enthusiasm on the subject of locomotive railways which continued to the end of life. He returned to Maine to meditate and reflect on what he had seen with his own eyes, little dreaming of the fame he was to achieve for himself in railway enterprises within the next forty years.

"In 1836 the first locomotive railway was built in Maine, singularly enough, between Bangor and Oldtown. The practical working of this road was under his own observation; and from it he probably learned his first lessons in railway economy. This new mode of travelling soon commended itself to the public. The Legislature adopted measures which led to the survey of several routes, for a railroad, between the seaboard in Maine and the St. Lawrence in Canada. That which connected Belfast and Quebec was regarded the shortest and most practicable route. This enterprise died in its birth, and nothing, but the report of the engineer ever came of it. A railway from the seaboard to the St. Lawrence was more and more desired in Maine, as well as in Canada. In 1839 a survey was made for a railway between Portland and Lake Champlain; but this enterprise also died. It was obvious now that a hand to execute, as well as a head to plan, was needed in such an undertaking; that vast energy, rare executive powers, and great persistency were required to carry out so great an enterprise.

"While Mr. Poor was busily engaged in his profession in Bangor, he was not unmindful of what had been going on. He was studying the whole subject of future railways in Maine from the highest point of view, and aiming to construct a system. Thoroughly acquainted with the physical geography, the commercial, agricultural, and manufacturing capacities of the state, he had a grasp of the entire subject superior to any other person; and in 1843 he made public his plan for two great railways, both coming from without the state, traversing it nearly its entire length, and converging on Portland. The eastern terminus of one road was Halifax, and the western terminus of the other, Montreal. This stupendous project of connecting two empires by a common interest, besides the inestimable commercial advantages designed for Maine, looked to the shortening of the time of passage between New York and Liverpool, about two days, and to a direct railway route from

Portland to Montreal, thence to the great lakes and prairies in the west. This magnificent scheme, which must have seemed impossible of execution to most persons when he projected it, in the infancy of railways in Maine, he lived to see accomplished, through his own agency and indomitable perseverance, in less than thirty years."

These may fairly be called the first international railways in the United States; they were also based upon the idea, then new, that railways should serve to develop the country, build up business; not, according to the Massachusetts theory, act as local lines in an already settled community. When it is remembered that there was not, in 1844, a railway east of Portland, the *Boston Journal* is correct in saying : " Mr. Poor is the father of the railroad system of Maine, especially in its relations to British North America."

Thus early he made practical application of the idea he expressed in writing in 1852 : " The true principles upon which all public improvements should rest are the simplest laws of physical geography and commercial advantage."

Of the origin of his railway plan, Mr. Poor wrote in 1860 : "The plan of the railway from Portland to Montreal was the work of my own mind exclusively. I never received a hint or suggestion that ever aided me from any quarter." Of the train of thought which led to this conclusion, we find a description in the speech delivered at Bangor in 1869. "From 1830, onward, I watched with eager curiosity the development of the railway, its mysterious workings and marvellous power; and I sighed and longed for the introduction of railroads into Maine. I saw how the railroad, wherever introduced, attracted capital and industry. As early as 1835, I perceived that the tide of immigration into Maine, from other parts of New England gradually diminished, and finally was checked completely by the growth of manufactures. I could not help seeing that a tide of emigration from Maine was rolling on; for in 1843, on a visit to my native town with less than seven hundred people, eighty young persons had been drawn from it to the workshops and factories of Massachusetts. I felt irresistibly impelled to an effort to resist if possible this state of things. I tried in 1843, as a citizen of Bangor, to move in a plan for a railway east, toward St. John and Halifax, but the time had not come, and I threw my energies into the project of a line from Portland to Montreal, as the great section to begin upon. I saw then, as now, that the travel and traffic between Montreal and Halifax must pass across Maine."

Another wrote: " While the first section of the Atlantic and St. Lawrence Railroad was in construction, we met at Norway village and took the mail stage to Portland. I asked him what suggested to his mind an enterprise of such vast magnitude as uniting Montreal and Portland by a railroad. He answered that it was a matter he felt disinclined to make public, but as I was a Swedenborgian, he could tell me without prejudice, as perhaps I might understand the philosophy of it. Said he: 'It was a vision, in which I saw the whole line pass before me like a grand panorama, and in continuation a vast system of railroads permeating the whole country, from the Bay of Chaleur to the Gulf of Mexico; with new cities with a dense population; with every facility for ocean steamships from every country; and the coast of Maine lined with cities rivalling the cities on the coast of the Baltic." His vision is fast becoming a reality, for seaside cottages now line every shore of Maine, and a summer city bears witness to the unique beauty of Bar Harbor.

In the winter of 1843-4 he wrote petitions which were presented to the Legislature of Maine, and referred to suitable committees. In January, 1837, Mr. Poor had lost the wife of his youth when they had been married three years and six months. Some years after, he married Elizabeth, daughter of Hon. Benjamin Orr, of Brunswick, a member of Congress, and one of the most brilliant lawyers who have ever practised in Maine; she died suddenly; three daughters had previously died in their infancy, but one child, a daughter, was left. He was a man of the strongest domestic affections; he had found his happiness in his charming home; but henceforward he threw himself into carrying out that idea which seemed to absorb his whole being. August the fifth, 1844, he wrote in his private journal as follows: "Man has a duty to perform, and a destiny to fulfil. I have been more than most men stimulated to action by the allurements of life and the incitements of the imagination. Real sorrow calms and moderates the expectations of youth."

Mr. Poor was at this time thirty-six years of age; although not a rich man, he was not a poor man;

and there was no reason that he should leave a well established business to work where he had no property to be benefited, and without suitable pay; no reason except that the inward voice had called him; and he obeyed. Mr. Tuttle says: "In the autumn of 1844, having matured his plans, he bravely entered upon the execution of his great design to connect Portland and Montreal by an international railway, the first ever projected on this continent. The undertaking then might well seem appalling: more than two hundred and fifty miles of railway, at an estimated cost of $10,000,000. He traversed the valley of the St. Lawrence, from Lake Erie downwards, to gain information for his purpose. From Montreal he crossed over his projected route to Portland, part of the way on foot, examining the country and making known his railway project."

He caused public meetings to be held at Sherbrooke, Canada; Canaan, Vermont; and Colebrooke, New Hampshire: at which he spoke. He wrote a communication to the *Sherbrooke Gazette*, September the fifth, 1844, a date memorable as the beginning of a new era in Maine—the commercial and historical era.

For Maine proper it began in the homestead of Silvanus Poor. From that farm-house Mr. Poor wrote a communication to the *Portland Advertiser*, September tenth, 1844. The citizens of Andover, Maine assembled there to listen to Mr. Poor, and made up a purse to pay the expenses of Deacon Samuel Poor, who accompanied Mr. John Alfred Poor to Portland.

Portland was at this time known throughout the State as "the deserted village." Mr. Tuttle says:

"His letter created a profound sensation in Portland, which he compared to 'an alarm-bell in the night struck by the hand of a stranger.' He went to Portland with a deputation from the country, and urged the citizens to embark in the undertaking. The principal citizens, appreciating the force of his arguments, and seeing the advantages certainly to accrue to the city, immediately came forward, headed by Judge Preble, to assist the Bangor lawyer in his great enterprise. The favorable action of Portland was felt throughout the whole length of the proposed route, and the work of preliminary organization went rapidly forward. A provisional survey of the route was executed before December. He devoted his energies to the organizing of a company and to the procuring of a charter for the road. Just before the charter was obtained it was discovered that the wealth and enterprise of Boston were in Canada, urging the Canadians to unite with that city and build the road to Boston. This created great alarm among the friends of Mr. Poor's project. It was a critical moment for Portland and for Maine interests. Canada desired an outlet for her staple products and merchandise, and it mattered but little to her in which of the Atlantic ports she found it."

It may be well to give a more detailed account of the opposition; we will, therefore, copy what Mr. Poor wrote some years later: "Before the road to Montreal had been suggested in Portland, three great lines from Boston to Montreal had been entered upon, the necessary charters obtained, and the projects themselves, well endorsed by Boston capital, in full possession of the public ear of Canada. These lines were the Boston, Concord, and Montreal railroad charters in 1844, acting at that time in connection with the Passumpsic road, whose charter is of an earlier date; the Vermont Central Railroad, in connection with the Northern Railroad of New Hampshire; and the Rutland and Burlington Railroad, as an extension of the Fitchburg road. All these companies were in the field; all had their agents in Montreal in advance of Portland, and during the whole time that the railway policy of Canada was under discussion in the Provincial Parliament in 1845."

At the head of the opposition was the Hon. Erastus Fairbanks, afterwards Governor of Vermont, backed by that celebrated letter of advice to the merchants of Montreal, and Canadian Parliament, which was signed by the Hon. Harrison Gray Otis, Hon. Abbott Lawrence, and three hundred and fifty-seven others, certified by the Mayor of Boston to be "among the most wealthy capitalists and business men of the city," admonishing the citizens of Montreal and the Parliament of Canada not to listen to the emissaries from Portland who were advocating the Portland route. This celebrated document, among other statements, has the following, viz.: "If a communication is to be opened between Montreal and the Atlantic Ocean, it must be from Boston, etc. Any grant by the Provincial Parliament giving a preference to a different route would be calculated, we believe, to defer, if not ultimately defeat, the object so much desired by business men in Canada and the United States." A document quite worthy of the calm assumption of superiority characterizing the Massachusetts person.

By the very irony of fate, Boston merchants representing the Chamber of Commerce met a committee of the United States Senate in Boston, September, 1889, and declared before it that the "Grand Trunk Railway is to New England what the Erie Canal is to New York."

Mr. Poor hastened to Canada to prevent the Board of Trade of Montreal from committing itself to the Boston interests. He set out from Portland at midnight on the fifth of February, five days before the Legislature of Maine granted the charter for his road, in the face of the most terrific snow-storm of the winter, and drove through deep snows to Montreal, reaching that city on the morning of the fifth day of his journey, when the thermometer was standing twenty-nine degrees below zero. Some years later, Mr. Poor wrote an account of his journey, which we will give entire. His passage of Dixville Notch is sufficient to cause that mountain-gorge to be forever associated with his name:

"A snow-storm among the mountains is the most fearful thing in nature. The earthquake, the volcano, the hurricane are fearful exhibitions of the strife of the elements; but these, in the nature of things, are limited in extent and of short duration. But a snow-storm among the mountains or in the polar regions is a fearful type of vengeance, of terror, and of wrath. The dwellers in the city, or those who traverse the deep have no power to conceive of the sublimity or the grandeur of the snow-tempest among the hills. I made the trial once, and found it more than my fancy had painted it.

"On the morning of the fifth of February, 1845, at half-past twelve o'clock, the writer started for Montreal in a storm not unlike that of yesterday. Some people in Portland may remember the event. The recollection of it has haunted the writer of this as a lurid dream or a tormenting nightmare ever since. The storm of February sixth, 1845, was remarkable for its severity and its extent. At that time we had no telegraphic announcement of its approach. A few days of clear, bright weather gave promise of an easy ride through the woods to Canada. Delay was caused by the tediousness in preparing the necessary papers, and it was finally arranged that I should leave at midnight, between the fourth and fifth, on the arrival of the eastern mail. Some preparations had been made for relays of horses to Sherbrooke, and the roads for some days prior had been in good condition for that season of the year. A dark and portentous sky hung black over the east all the day of the fourth. . . . At ten o'clock in the evening the wind had increased almost to a gale, and slight specks of snow came dancing through the air. 'It is too cold to snow,' was the common remark, and the thermometer stood at thirty-five degrees below the freezing-point. Before twelve o'clock the snow fell fast, but it was like ice or hail; the wind, blowing with violence, seemed to sweep it almost entirely away. The fierce howl of the blast, and the clatter of the snow against the window-panes and awning-posts made every one anxious to keep within doors. Entreaties and remonstrances were showered upon me to desist from the effort. But it was felt to be a turning-point in the history of our railway to Montreal. The mission undertaken in fair weather must be performed in spite of the tempest. Subsequent events proved the necessity of its performance.

"Only one man could be found in Portland to encounter with me the first seven miles. At half-past twelve o'clock, we started for Gray. A gentleman volunteered his spirited horse, in a sleigh for that stage of the journey, and I took the reins for the start. The horse seemed more wise than his driver, and resolutely determined to turn back. He dodged the drifts, plunged over stone walls, upset us time after time, from his inability to face the pelting snow. The rising snow cut the face like a knife, and the only way in which we could protect our eyes was to allow the icicles to hang from our eyebrows, and then with the end of one finger to melt a small orifice through which to see.

"The snow came down so fast that the track was lost, where the snow was not thrown out of the road: and after six hours of incessant labor, we reached Teak's tavern in Falmouth, seven miles from Portland, frozen in hands and face. Before daylight, a foot of snow had fallen on a level, and before noon that day, it had reached a depth of eighteen inches. Starting again with the first streak of day, we reached Gray Corner before noon, and Waterhouse's hospitable house at Paris, by dark.

"The wind had come round to the northwest, and the drifts were higher than the tops of the fences everywhere. Nothing could induce the experienced and daring Waterhouse to move out on that night, but the first dawn found us on our way to Rumford and Andover; through fields, over fences, and everywhere that a track could be forced. The way in which the northwest wind sweeps down the valley of the Androscoggin, and through the valley of the Ellis River, and the size of the drifts that are piled across the road in that region, are the terror of the inexperienced traveller. But there is nothing so sweet to the young mountaineer, as storms and snowdrifts. The air is bracing; the nervous system wrought almost to a pitch of delirium; and to wrestle, to combat with cold and snow, is a pleasure.

" At Rumford, where I found acquaintances, I sent out videttes as horseback riders, who made a single horse track to Andover. The young men of the country, as many as six or eight in number, mounted on the best horses, broke the path. At Andover, I found friends in waiting to aid me; a few miles brought us into the roads, but those miles were the most trying we had met. The drifts, the terror of all travellers, disappeared after entering Andover Surplus and through to Umbagog Lake. That night, however, the thermometer stood at eighteen degrees below zero. There was not a track from Andover to Colebroke, over forty miles, and the level of the new snow in all that distance was two feet. From Andover, till we had passed Dixoille Notch, our speed with two horses in a single sleigh was but two miles an hour.

"The passage of the Dixoille Notch was the great feat in the expedition; for when this was accomplished, the northwest wind would abate its fury. The terrific howl with which it sweeps down those giant cliffs eight hundred feet high; the huge mountain bank of snow that is piled in the bottom of the gorge, at the summit line of the road, make one shudder at the recollection. The Rev. T. Starr King thus describes Dixoille Notch: 'The first view of it is very impressive. It opens like a titanic gateway to some region of vast and mysterious desolation. The pass is much narrower than either of the more famed ones in the White Mountains, and through its whole extent of a mile and a quarter has more the character of a notch. One cannot but feel that the mountain was rent apart by some volcanic convulsion of nature, and the two sides left to tell the story by the correspondence, and the naked dreariness of the pillars of rotting rock that face each other. There is little more than room for a road at the bottom, and the walls slope away from it so sharply, that considerable outlay is required from the state every year to clear it of the stones and earth which the frosts and rains roll into it every winter and spring. No description can impart an adequate conception of the mournful grandeur of the decaying cliffs of mica slate which overhang the way. They shoot up in most singular and fantastic shapes, and vary in height from four hundred to eight hundred feet. A few centuries ago the pass must have been very wild, but the pinnacles of rock which give the scenery such an Alpine character are crumbling away. Some have decayed to half their original height, and the side walls of the notch are strewn with the debris which the ice and storms have pried and gnawed from the decrepit cliffs. The whole aspect is one of ruin and wreck. The creative forces seem to have retreated from the spot, and abandoned it to the sport of the destructive elements. One might entertain the thought that some awful crime had been committed there, for which the region was blasted with an everlasting curse.' If such an impression was made upon the mind of a visitor in the quiet autumn, what language can adequately convey to others an idea of its fearfulness, its terrific grandeur in a winter's storm.

"The first thing that struck us on approaching the gorge was the fact—the road is lost! The road in summer leads far along a narrow steep of rock, winding its sinuous course along its eastern side. At this time, not only were all signs of a track gone, but we could see no way in which a man on foot could find room to pass; the sides presented perpendicular walls of snow. Our experienced guide, known as the "Notch-Tender," led the way with shovels, others soon made a foothold for the horse; the sleigh and baggage were carried over by hand, until we came to the principal barrier, a mountainous drift twenty feet high, rising directly across the gorge.

"Two young men of Erroll, N. H., by the name of Bragg, assisted by three others enlisted on the way, after two hours' labor, opened a cut, through which my horse was pushed. The fearful thing to the uninitiated is the danger of being smothered in the snow.

Every few steps we had to turn round to catch our breath. The wind blew through the Notch a fearful gale, so continuous as hardly to exhibit a lull or pause, and the air was dark with the drifting snow. The place is over two thousand feet above the level of the sea, and the biting sharpness of the cold can hardly be described. Slowly and toilsomely we made our way onward, shifting horses as we could find them, keeping an outrider ahead to engage relays. To break a track to Sherbrooke, in a depth of eighteen inches of snow, was no trifling task, though the northwest wind on the other side of the White Mountains made the depth of snow somewhat less. I reached Montreal at half-past five in the morning of February tenth, but on the opposite side of the St. Lawrence River. The river was full of broken and drifting ice, and for some time, I could find no one to carry me across. Finally, I prevailed upon a Frenchman; after struggling with the ice for an hour, we reached the Montreal shore. I arrived at the hotel at seven in the morning, and the thermometer stood at twenty-nine degrees below zero.

"In accomplishing the entire journey, I took off my clothes but twice, and slept but seven hours during the five days; a frame of less vital power might have yielded on the way. My appearance at Montreal bringing information, two days in advance of any other news from the Atlantic coast, was looked upon with surprise."

Speaking in another place of his dreadful journey, and his mission, many years later, he said: "Every fibre of my frame thrills with horror at the recollection of it. I accomplished my task. I met the Montreal Board of Trade at ten in the morning of that day, and prevented the adoption of a resolution, previously prepared, in favor of going to Boston with their line instead of Portland, which would have been carried unanimously but for my sudden appearance and the assurance given by me of the superior advantages of Portland over Boston. I was justly proud of the achievement. In return, I carry in my person the renewals of suffering, which fever and sciatica, following in the train of fatigue and exposure, have entailed upon an otherwise strong constitution. I could not go through such another exposure again, if I would, and I would not do it for all the wealth of the world. The terrors of a Canadian winter are too fearful to encounter in this way a second time. But my heart was in the enterprise, and my health, my life, and my future sufferings were not thought of. All the events of this early history are more fresh in my mind than those of the last session of the Legislature, for I trembled at every step with the timidity of a youthful adventurer over the perilous Alps, in view of the vast importance of the enterprise to the state."

Another adjunct to the success was described as follows: "After much discussion at Montreal by Mr. Poor and the Boston agents, it was decided to run an express team from Portland to Montreal on the arrival of a certain steamer from Liverpool, which was to touch at Portland and proceed at once to Boston. The express team was to start from Portland at the time of the steamer's arrival there, and the express to start from Boston at the time of its arrival there. The steamer was expected to arrive at Boston about the first of February, 1845.

"Much interest was manifested in both cities, and great efforts were made by the friends of both routes to be ready for the race, and both parties were anxious to secure the favor of Montreal. Teams were provided and stationed along the route from Portland at distances from five to fifteen miles apart, and the right road at different places was marked out by sticking up evergreen bushes on each side of it, that there should be no delay by taking the wrong road in the night-time; and all was in readiness several days before the arrival of the steamer.

"The steamer arrived at Portland about the tenth of February, 1845. Part of the mail from England for Montreal was obtained, and put into a small bag made for the occasion, and strapped to the shoulders of a Mr. Haskell, and the race began. Mr. Waterhouse drove at the farther end of the route, and reached Montreal, with his coach-and-six decorated for the occasion with the stars and stripes flying, more than twelve hours before the express reached there by way of Boston, and cheer after cheer was given by the people there for the route to Portland." Mr. Tuttle says: "But for his well-directed efforts in Montreal, the road would have been built to Boston instead of Portland. This struggle for the Atlantic terminus of the road was severe and protracted. He fought, single-handed, against every argument which wealth and commercial pres tige could devise, before the Committee on Rail ways of the Canadian Parliament, then in session. The arrival of Judge Preble at Montreal, a week later, with the charter granted by the Legislature of Maine, assisted him in giving a final blow to the opposition."

On his return Mr. Poor went to Boston, where he was seized with a frightful illness. For weeks, he suffered such pain as would have killed an ordinarily strong man; and raved in delirium, until two men could not hold him. In one of his intervals of pain he had a strange vision. He felt that he had died, and was in the other world. He saw the friends whom he had lost; was free from pain, and perfectly happy; when he heard a voice telling him, that his work on earth was not done, and that he must go back. He begged and implored to stay, but in vain, and he was conscious of unutterable anguish as he returned. The inflammation settled in the sciatic nerve of the left leg; and for several months he could walk only by the aid of two crutches. He apparently recovered perfect health, but was never again free from pain and sensitiveness in the left leg, at any change of weather.

Before Mr. Poor started for Montreal, several Portland men raised the sum of one hundred and fifty dollars for his expenses. Every generous heart will throb with indignation to know that the Atlantic and St. Lawrence Railway Company considered five dollars a day for six weeks' time sufficient pay for Mr. Poor's services in procuring the charter; and that for money spent in 1844 in acquiring information, for his frightful illness, and for his enforced idleness during six months Mr. Poor was never paid.

In 1846, Mr. Poor removed to Portland, to devote himself more fully to the interests of the railway. Rumors of war between England and America having alarmed the Canadians, discouraged subscriptions to the capital stock: a party of Canadian gentlemen visited Washington with Mr. Poor. There they heard Mr. Calhoun's speech on the Oregon question: listened with much interest to Hon. R. C. Winthrop's account of the dangers and difficulties of entering Boston harbor. In a letter, Mr. Poor says: "The Canadians left for home, satisfied that continued peace is in store for us, full of faith in our success. They will now take up the balance of the $1,200,000 and go to work." Portland, June 16, 1846: "The railroad is going on. Peace is secured for years to come by the Oregon Treaty." Mr. Tuttle says: "The work of organizing under the charter, and of procuring subscriptions to build the road, went rapidly forward. Judge Preble was chosen president, and Mr. Poor a director, of the Atlantic and St. Lawrence Railroad Company; this being the corporate name of the American part of the line." So important was the undertaking considered, that the Fourth of July, 1846, was selected to begin the construction of the Portland end of the line. In the presence of the assembled senators and representatives of Maine, and a vast concourse of citizens and strangers, and with great ceremony and applause, the work of building began on this memorable day, at Fish Point, at the entrance to Portland harbor. This must have been a proud day for him. The Canadian company having organized, the work of construction began also at Montreal.

At the time of their visit to Washington, the Canadian gentlemen and Mr. Poor also visited the engine shops and car manufactories in Boston, New York, and Philadelphia, and soon after Mr. Poor's return to Portland he organized a company, and procured for it a charter, for the manufacture of locomotives and cars. This was an entirely successful enterprise, and a great benefit to the city as well as to the state. For some years he was president of the company, and on resigning in 1851 he received the thanks of the officers for "originating and carrying forward the company."

The Atlantic and St. Lawrence Railroad went laboring on under many difficulties, but with rare magnanimity Mr. Poor never relaxed his watchful care over it. The question of gauge for the road arose at the very beginning, and threatened for a time to destroy all possibility of uniting the two lines at the border. Some of the Canadians wished to have the English broad gauge of six feet. A small minority, under the influence of Boston ideas, desired the gauge of four feet eight and one half inches. A. C. Morton, Esq., the chief engineer of the road, proposed the gauge of five feet six inches. This had just been fixed as the standard gauge for the railway system of British India, by a committee of the English Parliament, after a long and thorough investigation. There is no doubt that it is intrinsically the best gauge in the world, but the narrow gauge would nevertheless have been adopted, but for Mr. Poor's great exertions then and afterwards. The blow which had been dealt in 1845 by the capitalists and business men of Boston was repeated in 1847. On the last of July, on the suggestion of some Boston men, a law was passed in the Canadian Parliament fixing the gauge of the St. Lawrence and Atlantic road at four feet eight and one half inches, unless the Governor in Council shall by an order in Council, within six calendar months, determine upon any different gauge, etc., "and any different gauge so established shall be the one used in the said road," etc. His interference led to a long and full investigation of the question of gauge by the authorities of Canada, in concurrence with the public men of the Lower Provinces. In October, 1847, Mr. Poor and Judge Preble were despatched to Montreal by the Board of Directors of the Atlantic and St. Lawrence Railway.

Accompanied by a delegation from the Board of Directors of the St. Lawrence and Atlantic Railway of Montreal, they had an audience with Lord Elgin, the Governor-General of Canada, and in a week they returned to Portland, bringing with them the "Order in Council" establishing the gauge of five feet six inches. Again in 1851, when the question of gauge for the Great Western road of Canada was before the Canadian Parliament, Mr. Poor went to Toronto, and before the Parliamentary Committee urged the adoption of this gauge with success. The gauge of the Atlantic and St. Lawrence Railway was determined upon, therefore, after the fullest consideration, and Mr. Poor hoped, by the adoption of a third rail, ultimately to extend this gauge to Boston and New York. Although the railroads recently built have followed the four-feet-eight-and-one-half-inch gauge, simply because it was fixed upon the country by the first railroads built, it must be remembered that in 1845 the question of gauge was an open one. Nothing is easier than for amiable theorists to criticise the past by the light of the present; but the pioneer succeeds precisely because he does not cling to theories, but skilfully adapts himself to the emergency of the hour. All great institutions are founded upon compromises; but for this the road would not have been built at all! Undoubtedly, too, the road was aided by the sentiment of state pride in having a gauge of its own, which was known in Boston as "John A. Poor's gauge."

A public speaker long afterwards said: "John A. Poor was the bold man that struck out for a policy adverse to the policy of Massachusetts in railroad matters. He struck out for the English broad gauge, for the very purpose of not having such a connection as would enable Boston to control the railroads of Maine through her narrow-gauge system. He fought as the lion fights for her whelps, in this cause of gauges, and so far as the Provinces and Maine were concerned he triumphed for a season; and the triumph was a progressive one, and a glorious one. Your Grand Trunk Railway was built under that triumph in hostility to Massachusetts, and especially to Boston. Boston fought that, not so much because they cared for having a railroad, but they did not want a railroad that should break the gauge and throw an impediment in the current of business to their own centre. They fought it, but they failed; the Grand Trunk was laid."

Mr. Poor had not forgotten, however, his original

design to build a single-trunk line east, extending ultimately to St. John and Halifax, and throwing off branches to the other parts of the state, north and south. It was proposed to use the Atlantic and St. Lawrence Railway, as far east as Lewiston, then make an extension to Gardiner and Augusta, with a branch of Brunswick and Bath. But as soon as this was proposed, the people of the Kennebeck valley began a rival line to the east from Portland, on the narrow gauge in 1845. In 1846 a broad-gauge line, called the Androscoggin and Kennebeck, was started from Danville Junction east, by the aid, and under the auspices of the Atlantic and St. Lawrence Railway, but only after assurances from the latter company that they would make connection with the roads leading out of Portland on the western side. As early as 1846, the directors of the Atlantic and St. Lawrence Railway, by a committee (of which Mr. Poor was the leading member), agreed that such a connection should be formed, and that the Atlantic and St. Lawrence Railway Company would transfer all passengers and merchandise desirous of going west of Portland, to and from the railway station of the Boston roads, without unnecessary delay, and without additional cost or charge on account of such transfer. This agreement, made at Waterville, in 1846, was ratified by the Board of Directors of the Atlantic and St. Lawrence Railway Company. The idea itself originated with Mr. Poor, who thus early recognized the impolicy of placing any restriction upon railway transit. To carry it out, he suggested the building of a new street, extending across a part of the city from the station of the Atlantic and St. Lawrence Railway to that of the Boston roads, on which a railway track should be laid. Strange to say, this met with most violent opposition from some of the directors of the Atlantic and St. Lawrence Railway and from the owners of wharves and flats. But Mr. Poor persevered until the street was built; Mr. Poor was opposed, however, to granting to any one railway company the exclusive use of this street, saying, "that it should be left open for the use of all railways." Commercial Street has resulted in the Marginal Way, a street one hundred feet wide, which extends around the city for three miles.

This war of the gauges was closed by the consolidation into one line of the parallel and competing railroads from Portland to Waterville, by Boston capital, with the Boston gauge. By this the whole control of the business of Maine was transferred to Boston. Mr. Poor had maintained for many years that *pro rata* rates for passengers should be established upon the Maine railroads, to destroy the discrimination which had existed in favor of Boston as against Portland. But such a measure would be forever rendered impossible, if the railroads were controlled in Boston. In May, 1870, a series of meetings was held in the City Hall of Portland for five successive evenings. Mr. Poor spoke for four evenings; at Waterville, he made another speech. But consolidation was a foregone conclusion; the weakest must always go to the wall. The Boston newspapers consolingly remarked, "that it was no wonder Maine felt badly to lose the control of her railways; the only wonder was that she had kept it so long."

Fortunately Mr. Poor did not live to see the absolute reversal of the original system. Since his death every prediction which he made has been fulfilled. The consolidated railways now extend to the boundary of New Brunswick, run around Portland, and no stranger would imagine that a city lay behind the hill; the gauge has also been narrowed upon the Grand Trunk Railway. It was, of course, state pride which inspired Mr. Poor's opposition, natural and pardonable in him, though uncommercial. It must be distinctly understood that Mr. Poor did not oppose all railway consolidation of short lines as such,—he was too sagacious and practical a man for that,—but only this particular consolidation as injurious to Maine. He would not have objected to a consolidation supporting the railway system of Maine, and run in the interest of Maine. As early as 1848, he wrote: "The state of Maine, from its geographical position, has, naturally, less connection with the neighboring States than with the British Provinces. Her railway system, now partially developed, based upon the natural laws of trade, has but few relations to the other railways of New England, and has been projected upon a plan of complete independence to them all.

"Instead of following the lead of Boston—which city originally held all New England in commercial subjection, and now controls the railways of New Hampshire, Vermont, Massachusetts, Rhode Island

and a portion of Connecticut,—the state of Maine entered upon a railway system of her own in 1844, making the Portland and Montreal road the base line of her operations. *Portland is the natural seaport of the Canadas.* This one statement explains to the people of other lands, the motive of our exertions, and the cause of our success, and is the key to the whole movement toward building the railway to Montreal. But the line does not stop at Portland."

An important adjunct in the success of the Montreal railway was so well explained in an article written by Mr. Poor, February the seventh, 1848, that we copy part of it: "It is now three years and a little more, that the project of a railway to Montreal has occupied the attention of our people. The scepticism and incredulity at first excited by its suggestion soon gave way to a deliberate conviction of its importance; and the success which has attended the measures put forth by its friends have nearly, if not quite, demonstrated to the minds of the most sceptical the certainty of its ultimate completion.

"In Canada the project at the outset met with general indifference. A railway from Boston to the eastern townships had been somewhat talked of in Canada as a measure likely to take place at some future day, but among the merchants of Montreal it met with comparatively little favor. Canada was at that time prosecuting the great system of canals, with a view to diverting the trade from the Erie Canal through the St. Lawrence. The protection then extended to colonial produce by the British government gave to Canada a monopoly of the trade in bread-stuffs between this continent and Great Britain. Had there been no change in the commercial relations between Canada and the United States, it is difficult to believe that the railway could have been carried through—at any rate without great delay and embarrassment—with the means at the command of those first engaged in it.

"The Portland and Montreal Railway was first suggested by the Welland and St. Lawrence canals. The idea was purely commercial. New York by the Erie Canal had drawn to her own port the trade of Lake Erie and the regions of the lakes beyond it. Boston by the Western Railway had afterwards diverted a portion of this trade to her own doors. New York and Massachusetts on the one side, and Canada through the St. Lawrence on the other, were striving for the trade of the valley of the lakes, and the idea of a cheaper and more expeditious channel to the sea had not then been proposed. Hence at the outset the Montreal road had to encounter opposition from the shipping interests of Montreal on the one hand, the merchants of New York and Boston on the other, and the more formidable obstacle, the indifference of our own capitalists at home.

"Its success depended on a change of opinion and feeling in Canada. The merchants of Montreal had at that time no fear of the consequences of our proposed drawback law upon their trade, or even of its passage for years to come, and treated with perfect indifference the suggestion of her losing the trade of Upper Canada when that project should become a law. The passage of that law, and the loss of trade to Montreal immediately following it, was the great measure wanted to ensure the hearty support of her merchants to the railway.

"The supplies for Canada West at once sought their way through the Erie Canal instead of their former channel, the St. Lawrence, and numerous other projects sprung up at once, all aiming at the same object as ourselves, a more direct channel of the trade for the west than the Erie Canal or the St. Lawrence River. The railway from Ogdensburg to Boston was proposed; another from Cape Vincent or Sackett's Harbor to Rome was projected; and another from Oswego to Syracuse was got up and carried forward to completion; and the New York Erie Railroad, which had been suspended, was revived and put in progress. The Concord and Stanstead road, the Cheshire road, the two roads from the Connecticut River to Burlington were all pushed vigorously forward by the respective friends of each; some of them, as was remarked at the time by one of the Boston papers, 'for the purpose of heading off the Portland and Montreal Railway.'

"Among all the projects named there is not one that has gone forward with so much success, under all circumstances, as our own. Without attempting more than we could perform, the steady perseverance of its friends and the impregnable advantages of our position have given our enterprise a standing and a name beyond that of any railway project in the country.

Montreal is the natural depot of the business of the St. Lawrence valley. At the head of sea navigation, and at the foot of the great canals connecting her with the lakes, the policy of Canada must forever give her the command of the trade of the St. Lawrence. She could now draw the trade from the Erie Canal to her wharves, if her proposed outlets to the sea were open.

"But a question more important to Canada than our drawback law has since occurred—a change of the commercial system of Great Britain. If any measure were wanted to ensure the completion of our railway, the repeal of the corn-laws would only be required. To the consternation and surprise of the British colonies, this repeal came years before it was generally believed possible; and from and after February 1, 1849, all protection to colonial produce is to be withdrawn. The famine in Ireland last year led to a suspension of the corn-laws till March 1, 1848, and the trade in bread-stuffs between this country and Great Britain the first year has been free. This has given Canada a foretaste of her future position under a permanent system of free trade in bread-stuffs. It has revolutionized opinion throughout Canada. Unconditional free trade is now demanded, and a repeal of the navigation laws. The Portland Railway from an object of indifference has now become the favorite and paramount measure, not only of Montreal, but of Canada.

"The political opinion has been as much affected as the commercial ideas of Canada within the last four years. There is not time now to review her history, and I allude to it only in connection with its bearing upon the railway. The troubles of 1837 are still fresh in mind. In 1838 Lord Brougham urged the Whig ministry to adopt measures for 'uniting together the whole of our North American possessions, to form an independent and flourishing state which may balance the colossal empire of the west.'

"The advice of the greatest of British statesmen was unheeded, and Canada has been convulsed with political dissensions. The great struggle has been on the question of 'responsible government,' which principally caused the outbreak in 1837 in Upper Canada; Lord Durham, Lord Sydenham, and Sir Charles Bagot favoring the Liberal party, and Lord Metcalfe the Tory. The present Whig ministry have taken up the idea of Lord Brougham; and in a despatch from Earl Grey to Lord Elgin of December 31, 1846, his Lordship clearly indicated the union of all the British American colonies as an ultimate measure, and proposed a meeting of delegates or commissioners to agree upon such preliminary arrangements as would favor this plan. A meeting of these delegates took place in Montreal in September last, where, among other measures, the Portland Railway came up for discussion, and the gauge of five feet six inches was adopted in concurrence with the views of the commissioners from the Lower British Provinces.

"In 1844 the Liberal ministry of Canada, of Sir Charles Bagot, disagreed with Lord Metcalfe on the question of responsible government, and resigned their places on the ground of certain objectionable appointments. Parliament was dissolved, and a new election ordered. The Tory party came into power, and Sir Allan McNabb was elected Speaker of the Assembly by a majority of three votes over the Hon. Mr. Morin. But since the arrival of Lord Elgin the Metcalfe ministry have failed to command a working majority in the Assembly, and a new election was ordered some eight or ten months before the expiration of the former Parliament.

"In this new election, the commercial policy of Canada was a new element in the controversy, and the Liberal party came out strongly for unconditional free-trade. Many of the merchants of Montreal who had formerly voted with the Tory party united with the Liberals, and Messrs. La Fontaine and Holmes were proposed as candidates for Montreal, and triumphantly elected upon their pledges of support to the principles of free trade, and government aid to the Portland Railway.

"The meeting of Parliament is fixed for the fourth of March next, and Mr. Morin, who is to be president of the Portland Railway, will undoubtedly be one of the new ministry. In his annual report, as president of the railway, he gives notice that application will be made by the St. Lawrence and Atlantic Railway Company to the next Parliament for aid in such form as will be most acceptable to the government. The *Montreal Herald* of the 26th January, in its summary of news for the European mail, says: 'The Legislature, at its next meeting, will grant a guaranty for a dividend of six per cent. in favor of the shareholders in the St. Lawrence and Atlantic Railway.' It will be recollected that Lord Elgin, in his address to the people of the colonies, on assuming the reins of government, pledged himself to render all proper aid and encouragement to public improvements, and all those measures calculated to promote intercourse and develop the resources of the country.

"The commercial and political changes in Canada have been largely affected by the increasing intercourse with the United States, and the inquiry is openly made among themselves of the comparative advantages of colonial dependence,—of a separate government composed of all the British North American colonies, or of a union with the United States.

"It was distinctly asserted by the authorities of the British government, a few years since, that to yield to the demand of the Radicals of Canada for responsible government was a virtual separation of the colonies from the crown. These principles are now triumphant in Canada as well as in Nova Scotia, after the fullest and fairest trial, and the recent movement toward a colonial union was stated by one of the delegates to be an intimation to the colonies, in behalf of the home government, to take care of themselves. The time was when Great Britain would have perilled every thing for the purpose of retaining these colonies. The extent of her colonial possessions has satiated the love of dominion, and the prevalence of free-trade principles has laid the foundation for a complete change of colonial policy. Commercial and not political connectives are now the aim and object of British statesmen.

"*Maine is the natural sea-coast of the Canadas.* Every thing now betokens a speedy realization of the truth of this remark. Canada will soon be at the boundary with her railway, on her way to the sea. Shall we meet her there?"

In 1848 Mr. Poor went before the Legislative Committees of New Hampshire and Vermont to procure charters across these states. He met with much opposition from the Boston influence, all powerful there, but finally succeeded in his delicate mission. In 1849 the road threatened to be brought to a standstill for want of money. Mr. Poor, afterwards, wrote in relation to this: "The people of Portland and Canada embarked their means in the construction of the Atlantic and St. Lawrence Railway with confidence in its ultimate success, but without being able to see in what precise mode, or from what particular source, the looked-for assistance would come. This feeling of confidence forever flagged when they had expended a million dollars at each end of the line, and failed to see the expected assistance from England coming to its support. The report of the directors of the company in 1849, concurred in by a very large majority of the board, was regarded abroad as an admission of defeat; or, at any rate, of a prolonged suspension of the work,—a result equally fatal to the interests of Portland. Had the proposed suspension then taken place, the completion of the line would have been postponed to an indefinite period. The Montreal Company would in that event have confined its exertions, for a long time to come, to the completion of the line to Quebec, and the Boston roads would have secured the great prize for which we had contended. This was the critical period in the history of Portland and of the Montreal Railroad. But the plan by which the road was carried through in 1849, and 1850 — the contract with Black, Wood, & Co.—was the salvation of the line. It was a plan of my own creating. Morton and Galt aided, but the plan was my own; the results of our interview at Lebanon in 1849, in which Galt, Black, Wood, Morton, and myself took part, were clearly stated by me before the meeting. I lost my election as director in 1849 through the jealousy of some and the hostility of others to the plan itself; yet I had the pleasure of seeing the plan adopted in all its parts. I urged the payment of a large price for the work, as the only means of saving the contractors from failure, and this wise policy was violently assailed at the time, but the contract with Black, Wood, & Co. was the salvation of the line." The plan was to place the whole road under contract as one line.

Mr. Poor spent the winter and spring of 1849 at the Astor House, New York; and purchased the *American Railway Journal*, which afterwards was owned and edited by Mr. Henry Varnum Poor. He was urged to stay in New York, and after he was turned out of the directorship of the Atlantic and St. Lawrence Railway would have been perfectly justified in so doing; but, with rare magnanimity, remained in Portland. The Gas-Light Company having fallen into difficulties, the work had been suspended; Mr. Poor was chosen president of the company, held the office until the sale of half of the capital stock to the city placed the company on a firm basis, and resigned the presidency in 1852, receiving the thanks of the company.

In 1851 Mr. Poor was chosen president of the York and Cumberland, now the Portland and Rochester Railway. He carried the road successfully through a lawsuit with the contractors, reorganized the company, and secured the building of the line from Gorham to the Saco River. In connection with this road, a plan was suggested for a continuous track around Back Cove, to render that suburb more accessible to Portland. He resigned the presidency in 1852, receiving the thanks of the company.

On his return from Montreal, in 1847, he published two articles in the *Bangor Whig*, in relation to the railroad to St. John; and wrote as follows to his brother, Portland, December 1, 1847:

"I beg of you to put forward the petition for the St. John railroad. Do, I pray and beg, put that along. It is time and high time to do it. . . . You want a reconnaissance this fall. You can get one, if you start now; as soon as you move, we will square away at it here." Mr. Poor also wrote articles upon the subject of the road to St. John, which were forwarded to Montreal and incorporated into the annual reports of the directors of the St. Lawrence and Atlantic Railway for two successive years, a fact which has never before been made known to the public.

The following account of a rival scheme was written by Mr. Poor afterwards: "No sooner had the Portland and Montreal Railway been fairly entered upon, and the plan of the line east from Portland to Halifax suggested, than the rival project of a railway from Quebec to Halifax was started, and threw much embarrassment in the way of Portland. The more immediate dependence of the people of the Lower Provinces upon England, and the strong antipathy of the people of Nova Scotia to the Yankees, gave force and vigor to the effort. The Provinces paid for a survey, and offered £20,000 sterling annually each, and any amount of public lands on the route in case the home or imperial government would undertake the accomplishment of the scheme. For a time it diverted the attention of Canada (Mr. Poor and Judge Preble met the agents of the Quebec and Halifax road at Montreal in 1847), but the idea itself was destitute of commercial merit. After much diplomatic shuffling, the British ministry, by a despatch of Earl Grey, under date of June 19, 1850, gave a decided negative to the application of the British Provinces for assistance to the Quebec and Halifax line; and the people of the Lower Provinces at once gave support to the Portland route. Quebec proposed to connect with the Portland and Montreal road at Richmond, forming thereby her connection with the Atlantic coast at Portland instead of Halifax; and also connection with Montreal, and eventually with the Lower Provinces."

In 1850, therefore, the Quebec and Halifax scheme being disposed of, the extension of the railroad from Portland to Montreal being assured by the contract with Black, Wood, & Co., Commercial Street being provided for, the two rival lines to the east having reached Waterville, Mr. Poor's plan for the railway to St. John began to crystallize.

Mr. Tuttle says: "Early in the summer of 1850 he petitioned the Legislature to authorize a survey to discover the best and most practicable route between Bangor and the New Brunswick line for this road. In this petition he took occasion to present strong reasons why the state should favor the building of this railway. Very soon after, as chairman of a committee of citizens of Portland, he issued a circular-letter addressed to the Governor and Council and the Legislature of Maine, and also to railroad companies and to friends of public improvement, in the United States and in the British Provinces, inviting them to attend a convention at Portland, to consider the project by which it was claimed the transit between the two continents would be reduced to five days, and between London and New York to seven." The idea of the convention exposed Mr. Poor to merciless ridicule.

Mr. Poor wrote: "The earliest maps and charts of North America were projected upon the simplest laws of navigation, in view of the then existing commerce of the world. That portion of this continent which approaches nearest to Europe formed the baseline of their calculations, and the distance across the Atlantic was shown to be 1,700 miles, and not 3,000 miles, as commonly stated in modern geographies. These teach us that the passage of the Atlantic is 3,000 miles simply because the common route of travel is between points thus remote—New York and Liverpool. In our proposal to shorten the transit between New York and London, we are merely revising and bringing into practice the ideas clearly entertained by the great navigators of the fifteenth and sixteenth centuries. The idea of an Atlantic ferry, according to Lord Bacon, between those points 'where the ends did nearest meet,' has been a controlling sentiment ever since John and Sebastian Cabot discovered Newfoundland in 1497, months before Columbus came in sight of the mainland of the continent."

From a history of the European and North American Railway, published in the *Portland Advertiser* December 27, 1869, we take the following account of the convention: "The seal of the European and North American Railway Company represents what twenty years ago was familiarly known as the Atlantic Ferry. In the spring of 1850 the Britannia tubular bridge across the Menai Strait had been opened, and the trains from London on the Northwestern line swept past Liverpool, over the strait and out into the Irish Channel to Holyhead, whence in three hours and a half the steamers ran to Dublin. From Dublin the Midland Railway of Ireland was already half completed, aiming at Galway Bay on the Atlantic coast, and from Galway to Nova Scotia—the nearest portion of the American continent—the distance is hardly 2,000 miles, and the Collins line had just been subsidized for ten years by the United States to ply between New York and Glasgow. The route from Galway to Halifax, saving one third of the distance over seas, was happily named the Atlantic Ferry, and the Britannia bridge even suggested the possibility of still further shortening the sea-voyage by bridging the Gut of Canso, and sailing from Louisburg in Cape Breton.

"The convention assembled in the City Hall on the thirty-first of July, and was a great and indisputable success. The walls of the hall were hung with maps of New Brunswick, Nova Scotia, Canada, and the New England States, and the best English charts of the American coast and the Atlantic Ocean. Behind the president's chair a map of the proposed line was displayed, measuring eleven feet by eighteen, and on either side hung the Cross of St. George and the Stars and Stripes. From the roof of the building the flags of the two English-speaking nations floated side by side. Governor Hubbard presided with great dignity. The Executive Council, both branches of the Legislature, the judges of the State and United States Courts, the reverend clergy, and the leading business men of Maine, from Portland to Calais, mingled with the delegates from Canada, New Brunswick, and Nova Scotia. Leading members of the provincial parliaments and governments were in attendance as delegates. It was the first social reunion of American rebels and loyal colonists, after the angry separation seventy years before, and a fine glow of fraternal feeling pervaded the assembly. Dr. Chickering prayed for a divine blessing on the deliberations of the convention. Memorials were read from railroad meetings at Bangor, Calais, Bridgetown, Fredericton, St. Stephen, St. John, Annapolis, Amherst, Pugwash, Wallace, Truro, Pictou, Dorchester, Windsor, Kentsville, and Granville. Letters were received from President Fillmore, who said substantially nothing; Edward Everett, who thought the passage to Liverpool would be reduced to nine days; from our Maine Senators and Congressmen, who were watching the Fugitive Slave Bill in Washington, and could not get away; from M. F. Maury, who obligingly hinted that Congress ought to give some part of the public domain to the enterprise as a military road; from Charles Sumner, who quoted Tibullus:

> ' Quum bene Saturno vivebant rege ; priusquam
> Tellus in longas est patefacta vias,'

in order to say that, in his opinion, Tibullus was mistaken, and the Golden Age was still to come, after the long ways are opened. Latin was as free as water in the convention.

"'The only ripple of dispute was occasioned by the proposition of Mr. J. W. W. Johnston, of Halifax, to connect by steamer across the Bay of Fundy, and he was put down at once by Mr. Gray, of St. John, who favored an all-rail route, and said 'the Bay of Fundy was a statio malefida carinis.' For three days the enthusiasm kept mounting higher and higher, reaching the maximum when General Dearborn, of Roxbury, predicted that within five years he should ride over the road to Halifax, and there embark for Galway, Holyhead, and London.

After adopting rose-colored resolutions and choosing an executive committee, the convention at last adjourned with "three notable and astounding cheers." Mr. Poor, who had been repeatedly recognized as the moving spirit of the enterprise, though modestly disclaiming any credit, was made chairman of the committee.

The convention naturally excited great attention at home and abroad. Speaking of it, the *Boston Journal* said : " The convention was one of the most pleasing, interesting, and important which have been held in our country for many years. . . . Of the importance of the proposed work there can be but one opinion."

The *London Chronicle* (England) of October 31, 1850, said : " The great importance of this project to the United States is so evident that it does not require further notice ; but to the British Provinces, and, in connection with them, to Great Britain, the advantages are so vast, that it may not be out of place to point out where and in what way they may be best employed. The convention appears to have selected Galway, on the west of Ireland, and Whitehaven, Cape Canso, in Nova Scotia, for packet stations. . . . Of the advantages Ireland would derive from such an establishment, an estimate can hardly be formed ; but to make her the highway and place of embarkation to and from the New World, for the tens of thousands who annually cross the Atlantic, must bring advantages that will materially aid in rescuing her from the misery and degradation under which the people are suffering. It is to be hoped that the promoters of this project may find any appeal they may make in this country, either to the government for countenance or to the public for assistance, may receive the attention it deserves.

From all that is shown it promises well as an investment for capital; but that it is an undertaking of great importance, both politically and commercially, is beyond contradiction. It may interfere with the particular interests of companies now established, and may divert some portions of trade from the present channels; but the British Provinces, and consequently the mother country, will be great gainers if this enterprise is accomplished, and in this sense the public will value it."

The *New York Journal of Commerce* notices the convention and the scheme in the following manner: "This convention excited the most extraordinary interest, not only from its numbers, but for the display of business talent, and of the most exciting eloquence. We have looked over the account of the proceedings, and can but consider the convention as one of the most fortunate events of the times. . . . Much of interest that attaches to the scheme grows out of its international and intercolonial character."

The *Fredericton* (New Brunswick) *Head-Quarters* said : " This magnificent project was not provincial; it was not colonial; it was not national; it was cosmopolitan. It laid a massive hand upon the world's necessities; and finding us athwart the directest practicable route, proposed for its own great purposes to lay down a road which, while created for and controlled by those paramount interests, would yet, as a fortunate incident, bring us into communication with the other world."

The executive committee at once opened communications with the British and American governments concerning mail contracts, with the directors of the Midland Railway of Ireland, with the proprietors of the Cunard and Collins steamers, and with the various railway companies between New York and London. The Maine Legislature granted a charter forthwith, appropriated $5,000 to survey the route in this state, and instructed the Governor to apply to the United States for aid. In New Brunswick a charter was granted in March, 1851, with liberal land grants, and a cash subsidy equal to the private subscriptions which might from time to time be expended upon the line. In Nova Scotia the Hon. Joseph Howe, of the Executive Council, in a speech of remarkable brilliancy and force, had taken the ground that the railway should be a public highway, and as such should be built by the government, and he had accordingly been sent to England to secure an imperial guaranty to the Nova Scotia bonds to be issued for this purpose. The guaranty was granted in 1851, with some reluctance, on condition that, by the co-operation of New Brunswick and Canada, a connection should be secured through British territory, from Halifax to Quebec. The line of such a road had been surveyed by the imperial government when the Portland and Montreal road was begun, and the colonial line was a revival of the same project, thrice abandoned but never forgotten. The condition proved too onerous, and Mr. Howe's mission came to nothing.

In 1851 Mr. Howe visited Portland, and made an eloquent speech in favor of the Halifax and Quebec road, and he was answered by Mr. Poor, speaking for the European and North American road as international and commercial rather than intercolonial and political.

In 1851 Mr. Poor's committee applied to the Massachusetts Legislature for a grant of the public lands in Maine belonging to the former state, and came very near obtaining them. Very favorable reports were made by both branches of the Legislature, but were defeated by small majorities. In 1852, he applied again to the Massachusetts Legislature, and a joint committee from both branches, embracing their ablest men and including Hon. Caleb Cushing, and Hon. R. B. Curtis, afterwards Judge of the Supreme Court of the United States, after full hearing and investigation, unanimously agreed to report a bill loaning the credit of the state to the amount of $500,000. But the bill was defeated by the combined influence of the merchants of Boston, the attorneys of the Vermont railways, and the agent of the Cunard steamers. Failing in this, Mr. Poor persuaded the Legislature of Maine to purchase the lands from Massachusetts. In 1852, he was appointed one of two commissioners to conduct the sale, and Maine became the owner of all her public lands.

In 1852, Mr. Poor's committee applied to the Congress of the United States for aid. Mr. Poor wrote to the Maine members of Congress: "The great point to be aimed at, is the passage of the land bill now awaiting the action of the Senate, granting to Maine 1,350,000 acres of the public lands of the United States (known as Bennetts' land bill). If this land can be secured in aid of this great road, it will be built." And he drew a bill giving these lands and permanent mail contracts to the European and North American Railway Company. This was one of the railway bills which have since been adopted by companies asking land grants; but Bennetts' land bill did not pass. The road was presented as a means of shortening the mails, and supported by resolves from the Legislature of Maine.

In 1852, Hon. Francis Hincks, a leading statesman of Canada, went to England to seek assistance from the imperial government towards building a trunk line of railway for Canada. By means of the branch from Richmond on the line of the St. Lawrence and Atlantic Railway to Quebec it would extend from Quebec to Montreal, from thence to Toronto, and could be prolonged as far as desirable. Wearied out with the delays of the Colonial Office, he finally decided to adopt a commercial basis, and made arrangements for the building of the line with the principal firm of English railway contractors, Messrs. Jackson, Brassey, Peto, and Betts. One of the contractors personally explored the wilderness from Quebec to Fredericton, New Brunswick, and thence to Halifax with a view of extending the line from Quebec to Halifax. Mr. Poor met the contractor at Fredericton; he adopted Mr. Poor's suggestion of a connection between Canada and the Lower Provinces across Maine. To give the most direct and practicable route, the scheme included also a cut-off from Bethel to Bangor, by which Bangor would be only thirty miles farther than Portland from Montreal, and would receive its supplies directly from the west by way of Montreal, and the extension from Bangor to St. John by the way of Calais, along the shore. The English contractors proposed to build this line from Waterville, Maine, to Halifax, advancing 80 per per cent. of the money needed, intending to bring the scheme out in London as a grand whole. The charter was refused by the Legislature, through the jealousy of a few men in Bangor. The Grand Trunk scheme was delayed for the Bangor part until April, 1853, and then brought out alone in London. Such was the abundance of money at the time, that nine times the capital of the Grand Trunk was offered by responsible parties, which would have built the Bangor cut-off.

But though the European and North American Railway was thus slain in the house of its friends, Portland received from the agitation of the scheme, an incalculable benefit. In 1852, Mr. Poor had accompanied the English contractor from St. John to Halifax, and then learned the plan of the great trunk railway for Canada. "But what," said Mr. Poor, "will become of your western freight, when Montreal harbor is closed in the winter? You should lease the line of railway from Montreal to Portland, and thus secure yourself a winter harbor." Mr. Jackson was much impressed by the idea; he proposed it to his partners in England.

The Canadian idea had originally been of mere local traffic between Montreal and Toronto; but the contractors saw that a through business was necessary, and wished to provide for extension at both ends. The western extension has been carried out to Chicago; when a through train from Chicago rolled into Portland, Maine, in 1889, Mr. Poor's visions were magnificently fulfilled. The eastern extension was proposed to the Portland and Montreal road. The same spirit which had turned Mr. Poor out of the directorship in 1849, which had opposed the opening of Commercial Street, and scoffed at the project of the Portland convention, appeared again; and it was only after hesitation that the directors accepted a lease at six per cent. In August, 1853, the lease of the line, composed of two companies, to the Grand Trunk Railway of Canada was formally concluded. It was all the more timely, as the contractors afterwards had to spend a million and a half on the Portland end; another million from the boundary to Montreal to make it workable. For this inestimable service, Mr. Poor never received even a vote of thanks from the directorship, or the city of Portland; though by a most brilliant commercial victory the city retained both its road and its money.

However others may have aided in carrying out Mr. Poor's movements, we unhesitatingly claim for him the whole credit of this lease, which saved the stockholders and the contractors. Some time afterwards, Mr. Poor wrote: "The advantages of this lease are to be found in the extension of the line rather than in the transfer of the Portland and Montreal section at its cost." It has well been called "one of the most splendid triumphs of commercial warfare." The Grand Trunk Railway was opened to Montreal in 1853. In 1856, when it was opened to Toronto, a magnificent celebration was held at Montreal, in which Mr. Poor took part. The Canadian historians date the new era of prosperity in Montreal from 1853 and the Grand Trunk Railway: but the Grand Trunk Railway itself grew out of the Portland convention of 1850. "That first act of re-union, after a separation of seventy-four years, had all the freshness of novelty and the charm of intense earnestness." "The effect of that convention," said Mr. Jackson, "on the public mind of England was greater than any event since the war of 1812, if not since the Declaration of Independence, in the United States."

Nothing could be more quaint or interesting to an American than St. John, New Brunswick, before the Portland convention. To see its inner life was to turn back a hundred years; to be in the manners and customs which prevailed before the Revolution. It was settled by loyalists fleeing from New York and Boston in 1783; among its first councillors are names still borne in New York and Salem. In its graveyard lies the last Royal Attorney-General of Massachusetts; in a church the last Royal Coat-of-Arms in the revolted colonies. It was separated from Nova Scotia in 1785, became a distinct province with a charter government of its own. Then came a succession of royal governors from "Home," and regiments of soldiers. The Province Buildings at Fredericton, where the Parliament met, held an arm-chair where the Governor sat to represent royalty; above which was the British Coat-of-Arms. Large square wooden houses grew up, in the style which we acknowledge as "colonial," filled with old mahogany, silver, and china, with embroidered coats-of-arms, and portraits by Copley. All their ideals were English; "the States" were an unknown and dreaded world, seen for the first time at the Portland Convention.

Mr. Poor afterwards wrote: "The carrying out of our international railways brought in its train the reciprocity treaty. I foresaw this as early as 1843, when I saw the effect of the Treaty of Washington of 1842 on the public mind of New Brunswick and Maine." Of the Reciprocity Treaty Mr. Poor was one of the warmest advocates and earliest friends; at the request of the Board of Trade of Portland he wrote a petition in favor of its renewal, which was presented to Congress. Mr. Poor went even further than this: he suggested the establishment of an American Zollverein between the United States and the British North American Provinces; in other words, as free and unrestricted trade between us and them, as between the States of the American Union. For while Mr. Poor advocated the policy of protection for American interests towards foreign countries, he felt and maintained that commercial intercourse between the English-speaking people on this continent should be free. This idea is more fully developed in a letter to the Chicago Ship Canal Convention in 1863.

The first period of railway building had passed in Maine; the people were not ripe for another. Had Mr. Poor been merely a business man, he would at once have left Maine, gone where there were new railways to be built, and allowed Bangor to take the consequences of her inconceivable folly. Instead, finding that all hope of foreign aid was lost in 1853, Mr. Poor determined to seek assistance at home, undaunted at the prospect of years of toil; the European and North American Railway was not begun in Maine till 1867.

Mr. Tuttle says: " Finding that he was unable to reach the public mind and to give an exposition of his plans of rail-extension through the medium of a press guided and controlled by others, he resolved on finding means to give his views to the public, and to advocate his measures in his own way. To this end he established a newspaper in Portland, which he owned and edited from the time of its first issue in 1853 to 1859, when it became merged in the *Daily Advertiser*, a paper in which he had purchased an interest. It was called *The State of Maine*—a name purposely and felicitously chosen, since it was specially devoted to the advocacy of the development of the great interests of the state, and was issued daily, tri-weekly, and weekly. His foremost purpose in this enterprise was to educate the public to a full comprehension of the importance to the interests of Maine of building the European and North American Railway, and to secure for it favorable legislative action. To the carrying out of this great railway enterprise, projected by him many years before, he labored with his pen without ceasing. He made the columns of his paper a vehicle to carry far and near every argument which could be devised favorable to the execution of this great undertaking. He saw regretfully the wasting of the best energies in the state in party strifes, and he lamented that for a period of forty years struggles for personal success in politics had been paramount ideas, with a few intermittent exceptions, in Maine, while the great natural resources of the state excited no public interest and lay undeveloped." He always contended that if a state policy favorable to railways and to manufactures had been early adopted, Maine would have been, at this time, not inferior to Massachusetts as a manufacturing state.

The establishment of *The State of Maine* gave a new start to the newspaper press of the state. It was the first attempt to supply full telegraphic reports of news, in the manner and style of the newspapers of large cities, which were published in *The State of Maine* simultaneously with the Boston and New York newspapers. It was larger than any other of the Portland papers, and was the first newspaper in the state to furnish verbatim reports of speeches, phonographically reported. The next morning, after a dinner given to the officers of the *Sarah Sands*, the first ocean steamship from Liverpool which ever arrived in Portland harbor, *The State of Maine* gave a full report of the dinner and speeches, almost six closely set columns of matter. The plan of the dinner given to Lord Elgin, in Portland, also originated with Mr. Poor. An account of this reception, and Lord Elgin's speech, are given in the life of Lord Elgin, published in London.

Up to 1856, the newspaper had not been political; but the repeal of the Missouri Compromise startled the whole North. Mr. Poor at once pronounced this to be the "death-blow of the Democratic party," and felt that party politics had been raised to the dignity of great moral questions. In 1856 he was offered ten thousand dollars, and an office in addition, to support Mr. Buchanan for the Presidency, as in the breaking up of political parties the third or Whig party then held the balance of power, but he refused, and supported the Republicans; and in April, 1857, in the prospectus of his newspaper he wrote: "The wrongs of Kansas, the degradation of the Supreme Court to the uses of the slave power, the disenfranchisement of man on account of race or color, are wrongs that must be redressed."

In politics, as elsewhere, Mr. Poor proved himself a leader. His articles upon public affairs were a day in advance of those of the other Maine newspapers, which waited for the arrival of New York and Washington papers and letters, to express an opinion or advise a policy; but Mr. Poor's leaders were written as soon as the news arrived, and almost invariably coincided with those of the ablest newspapers in the large cities, when they afterwards reached Portland.

He had also the courage of his convictions, as to making Prohibition a political question; for the struggle which has extended over the whole country began in Maine. *The State of Maine* newspaper took the lead against it, as Mr. Poor considered it illegal and unphilosophical; and for this he was absolutely persecuted by the Prohibition portion of the Republican party. The newspaper was a total pecuniary loss, but was undoubtedly a necessary means to his life-work.

During these years he had never ceased to present to the public, on every possible opportunity, the claims of the European and North American Railway; articles in its favor were written for his newspaper; the charter was twice extended. A writer in the *Portland Advertiser* said: "The European and North American Railroad Company of Maine had been organized in 1853; Mr. Poor had been chosen president. For the next ten years the road was perpetually coming up before the Legislatures of Maine and Massachusetts and the Congress of the United States in the most ingenious and surprising disguises.

Mr. Poor had written and published in *The State of Maine* newspaper articles calling attention to the great value and fertility of the lands in Aroostook County, Maine. To everybody except the lumber merchants of Bangor, "the Aroostook" was as truly an unknown land as an island in the South Seas. In 1857 Mr. Poor wrote and presented to the Legislature of Maine a memorial signed by himself and a number of the most respectable citizens of the state, embodying the same idea. To develop these lands, Mr. Poor suggested opening them to settlement by means of a railroad, bringing settlers to them by immigration from foreign countries, and establishing manufactures in them by exempting manufactures from taxation for a term of years. It was called a New State Policy, and three thousand copies of the memorial were printed by order of the Legislature in spite of a protest by some newspaper against "Mr. Poor's plan for developing resources of Aroostook by exhausting those of the state." Mr. Poor drew up a bill, which was passed by the Legislature of the state, enabling aliens to hold real estate, this having been forbidden by the makers of the state constitution.

In 1858 he made another memorial, asking for a geological and water-power survey of the state, and general statistics of Maine: and the state lands to secure the construction of the European and North American Railway, with branch lines to Aroostook and Piscataquis counties. Three thousand copies of this memorial were also printed by order of the Legislature, in consequence of which, a large immigration of our own citizens, and especially of the young men of the state, took place into Aroostook County for several years afterwards.

The memorial of 1861 carried out his own suggestions, for it contained an historical sketch of the state; an elaborate statistical review of the various resources and industries of the state, with plans for developing them by means of settlements on the lands and by encouraging manufactures; statistics of manufactures, applied in support of this argument in the interesting manner which Mr. Poor knew how to use towards all statistics; an elaborate geological sketch of the state, furnished to Mr. Poor by Sir William Logan, the state geologist of Canada; finally, the recommendation that the State lands should be given to secure the building of the European and North American Railway and the branch lines. This also was printed and distributed by the Legislature.

In the winter of 1862, the European and North American Railway was carried to a larger audience. In the autumn of 1861, Mr. Seward called the attention of governors of states to their coast defences. Mr. Poor at once wrote a communication in relation to the defences of Maine, which was signed by the Governor and forwarded to the President; and accepted the position of " Joint Commissioner on the Coast Defences." The Commission proceeded to Washington, where they had audience with the President and the Secretary of War. They discovered an appropriation of $100,000 for a fort at the mouth of the Kennebec River, which had been overlooked by the Maine representatives for several years. They petitioned that work should be put in progress on this fort; also that it should receive the name it now bears, Fort Popham,—both of which petitions were successful. They had audience with the Secretary of the Treasury, and made arrangements that the money advanced by the state of Maine should be returned by the United States in twenty-year six-per-cent. bonds, which was regarded as highly patriotic on the part of Maine. The senior Commissioner, Mr. Williams, then left for home, and Mr. Poor remained in Washington. The President, the Secretary of War, the Chiefs of the Engineer and Ordnance Bureaus expressed much interest in the subject; but Mr. Poor met with vexatious delays, which are well understood by all persons familiar with business in Washington. In his report to the

Governor, he wrote: "The pressure of the routine of daily duties consequent on the Rebellion drew off attention from these 'extraordinary matters,' as they were pleased to call those set forth in your letter of October 23d; and I may venture to express the belief, that but for the presence of an agent in Washington in your service, following up in a constant round of visits the same officers then in charge, much greater delay would have occurred in the preparation of their reports on the defences of Maine. The frontier position of Maine, remote from the national government, the few people of the State visiting the Capitol for the purpose of influencing public action, compared with the numbers that throng all its avenues, and often absorb, if not monopolize, with their own projects the time of public officials; the habit of command thus acquired by men of the larger and more central states, lead one to expect, as a matter of course, that the claims of a distant state like Maine will be undervalued, if not overlooked and disregarded. Hence, the moment the public mind was moved by the unfortunate affair of the *Trent*, upon the first whisper of danger of hostilities with England, the overwhelming and paramount claims of the city of New York threw aside the admitted demands of Maine. . . . It was in vain urged, in the midst of the exciting pressure, that the great point of danger in a collision with England was Maine."

Mr. Poor forever persistently haunted the Engineer and Ordnance Bureaus until the proper armament was despatched to the forts of Maine, and reports were published on the subject. These reports suggested fuller appropriations for the existing forts, and a sum of $550,000 for temporary fortifications of towns unfortified. These recommendations passed Congress and became a law in February, 1862. It will be seen, therefore, that the commission accomplished important work, viz.: putting in progress the fort at the mouth of the Kennebec, hastening the work of the Engineer and Ordnance Bureaus, larger appropriations for existing forts, and the sum of $550,000 to be expended at the discretion of the President. President Lincoln offered to Mr. Poor the expenditure of this sum of money as "Commissioner in Charge of the Northeastern Defences." But Mr. Poor declined this, because he felt that it was unnecessary to create such an office, and Mr. Lincoln said: "I will not call you Mr. Poor, but Mr. Strong."

It was a time of the greatest excitement in Washington as regarded financial matters. Mr. Poor's versatile mind was turned in that direction, and he wrote a letter on the national finance which procured for him the offer of a position in the Treasury Department, to which we have alluded, but which he declined. Mr. Poor was not to be turned from his original purpose. At the War Office he had met with the most cordial support from Secretary Stanton in his plans for coast defence. He received a card admitting him at all hours at a time when the general public were limited to a single day a week, and when Congressmen often besieged the door in vain. Instead of sending a memorial to Congress on a further plan for coast defence, Mr. Poor addressed a letter to the War Office; in addition to the other means for defending the coast of Maine, he suggested the building of the European and North American Railway as a military railroad. Accompanying this letter was a bill to carry out these measures by making a small annual grant to the European and North American Railway for carrying mails, troops, munitions of war, etc., per mile. Afterward this proposition was supported by a letter addressed to Secretary Stanton by a distinguished engineer. These documents were forwarded to the Senate by Mr. Stanton, who expressed great interest in them all, but gave no opinion upon their merit officially. The bill, with accompanying documents, was introduced into the Senate, and into the House also, but it did not pass. Congress could not be made to realize that any thing was due to Maine. In the autumn of 1863 Mr. Poor made an application to Congress, but in vain.

A newspaper said: "The people of Bangor had gone astray after Oldtown and Lincoln road, the Penobscot road, the Aroostook road. In 1863 Mr. Poor had the pleasure of uniting all these enterprises under the name of the European and North American Railway." This route as finally adopted was much longer than the original plan under the English contractor. In 1864 the annual application to the Legislature of Maine was crowned with success; after being encumbered by branch lines to Piscataquis County, the European and North American Railway received from the Legislature a grant of about 800,000 acres of public lands lying on the

Penobscot and St. John waters, subject to a claim of Massachusetts for $250,000 for payment for the lands bought in 1852, and also of all the claims of Maine against the general government prior to 1860, held jointly with Massachusetts. The Legislature also passed resolves recommending the road to the Legislature of Massachusetts and the Congress of the United States.

To Washington, therefore, hastened Mr. Poor, alone and unaided. He prepared a report giving a history of the northeastern boundary question, and suggesting that Maine should be repaid for her sacrifices to preserve peace at that time, by aid to the European and North American Railway. As Texas had received a gratuity of ten million dollars for surrendering doubtful claims to a much less valuable territory, the claim of Maine had a good foundation in precedent, as well as in justice. By most unusual success, he succeeded in forming a special committee of the House of Representatives who adopted his report; the road was also indorsed as a military road by General Dix, major in command of the Department of the East, in January, 1864. In the summer, Mr. Poor organized a visit to Maine of the Congressional Committee on Defences of the Northeastern Frontier, with a number of invited guests from abroad, and from home. The committee visited the coasts of Maine, Bangor, and St. John, New Brunswick, in the United States Revenue steamer *Mahoning*. The visitors from abroad were delighted with the scenery and commercial advantages of Maine, and convinced of the importance of the European and North American Railway. In 1865 Mr. Poor, as president of the European and North American Railway, made an application to the Massachusetts Legislature, asking an assignment of its claims against the United States, held jointly with Maine, a discharge of the debt due from Maine on account of the purchase of the public lands, and a loan of state credit—all in favor of the European and North American Railway; also a memorial to the Governor, suggesting an exchange of state of Maine bonds. We quote Mr. Tuttle: "On application to Massachusetts for aid, it was refused, on the ground of a statute of Maine, passed in 1860, forbidding the change of gauge on any railroad in Maine, which was regarded as unfriendly legislation. Without the aid of Massachusetts, the grant by Maine to aid the building of the road was not available. Mr. Poor regarded the statute of no advantage to the interest of Maine, but otherwise, and he applied at once to the Legislature of Maine, then sitting, for a repeal of it, and for leave to lay a third rail on the Portland, Saco, and Portsmouth Railroad, with a view of extending the broad-gauge line from Halifax to Boston and New York. He appeared before the Committee on Railways on the fourteenth of February 1865, and made a long argument in favor of repeal, reviewing at length, and with great ability, the railway interests of Maine and the history of the various roads, which is printed. He claimed that there should be no restriction on railway transit. The Legislature of Maine, not without much opposition from interested parties, and from those of narrow views in these matters, repealed the act, and then he prevailed on Massachusetts to release its claim on these lands granted by Maine, and also to allow the road the part of her joint claim with Maine against the general government in May, 1865."

As the general government had repudiated these claims for more than thirty years, the gift cannot be called munificent; whatever the European and North American Railway got from Congress for them may be, therefore, considered as absolutely created.

It would be interesting to follow the political changes of New Brunswick, so far as they affect railway matters, as we have those of Canada. But we may briefly say, that the Halifax and Quebec, that is, the Intercolonial plan, was offered incessantly to New Brunswick instead of the European and North American Railway, the International and Commercial plan. New Brunswick had steadily opposed the confederation of all British North America, year after year, and had steadily clung to the Commercial Railway. Mr. Poor had kept up communication with the New Brunswick politicians ever since the Portland Convention. In February, 1865, a strong anti-confederation government had been formed; as soon as the business was settled with the Massachusetts Legislature, Mr. Poor hastened to St. John, in June, 1865. Fortunately, for the anti-confederation party was turned out of power in 1866, a strong confederation party came in, who would have opposed the European and North American Railway.

In 1865 Mr. Poor, in behalf of his company, proposed to complete the lines in New Brunswick and Nova Scotia for an annual subsidy of $80,000, from the two provinces, guaranteed until the lines should pay six per cent. of the cost. The New Brunswick government declined to enter into this arrangement, but voted $10,000 a mile to complete the line from St. John westward to the boundary. Mr. Poor, as president of the Maine Company, made a contract with the European and North American Railway Company of New Brunswick; he then made a contract for building the entire line through the state and the province as one line. The city of Bangor loaned its credit to the amount of $1,000,000, and work began at St. John in November, 1865, contractors being induced to take hold by this plan of a long line. But for this timely contract, the golden opportunity would have slipped by. The glittering bait of the Intercolonial Railway, built by the imperial government, proved too tempting to New Brunswick and Nova Scotia; both accepted the confederation in 1867.

Both Mr. Poor and the contractors made great exertions to induce Boston capitalists to share in the enterprise, but they refused. However, in 1866 Mr. Poor applied again to the Massachusetts Legislature. In April he left the negotiation in charge of the late Governor Andrew, who entirely failed to get any thing from the Legislature. Mr. Poor went alone to Washington, where, instead of a separate committee, his bill was assigned to the important Committee on Foreign Relations. Mr. Poor appeared before them, made a speech, and the committee reported in favor of his bill. On the very last night of the session, at midnight, Mr. Sumner, chairman of the committee, rose twice to present the bill to the Senate; but more eager men pushed in to catch the Speaker's eye, till the time for closing came. In leaning upon Massachusetts Mr. Poor had leaned upon a reed. He was thrown out of the presidency; Pennsylvania capitalists came in and obtained the grant from Congress.

Ground was broken at Bangor in January, 1867. The road was completed some years before the Intercolonial, and was opened to the public by a grand celebration at Bangor, and another at the boundary line, in both of which the President of the United States and the Governor-General of Canada took part, in October, 1871. Mr. Poor had died six weeks before.

One writer has said : " Its construction in this generation is due absolutely and entirely to the perseverance and unyielding courage of its projector and first president." " His name," says another well acquainted with the history of the road, " will be forever associated with the European and North American Railway, as inseparably as the name of De Witt Clinton with the Erie Canal. With no funds to build the road except a small land grant and an assignment of the claims of Maine and Massachusetts upon the general government, claims which that government had repudiated for more than thirty years, he went to work alone, and by ceaseless industry, and by using influences which no one else knew how to wield, by persistent and unanswerable arguments everywhere applied by both pen and tongue, he enlisted legislators in Congress and public men in the states in his favor, secured the confidence of capitalists, overcame all difficulty, bore down all opposition, wearied out delay itself, and achieved a final and complete success."

If annexation ever take place, the railways will be the most powerful instruments in bringing it about. The recent protests from Boston and Portland against refusing bonding privileges to the Canadian Pacific Railway, show how intimate is the connection between New England and Canada. If Bangor has not received all she hoped, she need only remember that she might have had the railway years before. The consolidated lines now extend to the boundary by the same terms of lease which Bangor refused in 1853; the name of the European and North American Railway is gone. The location of the Piscataquis Railway was not what Mr. Poor desired, but he was obliged to accept it because the Legislature would not give the state lands to the European and North American Railway until the members from Piscataquis County were satisfied.

In 1869, Mr. Poor made the following remarks at the Bangor Centenary, which were omitted from the published volume, and they show his foresight: "Radiating from Bangor as a necessary centre of trade, lines of trade must strike in all directions, and before many years, Bangor, with a line direct to Montreal by way of the St. Francis valley, will shorten to its lowest limit the time of railway transit from Montreal to St. John, Halifax, and Newfoundland. By completing your line to St. John with a branch to Woodstock and Little Falls, bringing the basin of the St. John to your market, you will double the population of your city; you will construct another line to Bucksport, Ellsworth, and along the coast line to Calais; you will extend your Piscataquis branch to Moosehead Lake, and it will erelong cross the border and follow the Chaudière to Quebec."

While he was in Washington, the Portland fire of 1866 took place. In spite of the heat of the weather, Mr. Poor exerted himself to get up a public meeting, and subscription for the sufferers by fire. The Mayor of Washington publicly thanked Mr. Poor for the plan of organization which was suggested by him, and led to so large a subscription for Portland from Washington. Mr. Poor's exertions for this object, during the heat of a Washington summer, brought on a sunstroke and a partial paralysis of the optic nerve of one eye. He eventually recovered his sight perfectly, but for the remaining years of his life he was obliged to dictate all he wrote. The great amount of work he accomplished under this drawback is amazing.

His physician ordered entire rest of body and brain, but in the winter of 1867, in reply to a request from the governor of Maine, he wrote a report upon the confederation of the British North American possessions, which was adopted by the committee of the Maine Legislature, and passed both branches. It was dictated at one sitting.

The spring of 1867 brought forth the realization of a long-cherished idea of Mr. Poor's—the hydrographic survey of the state. Mr. Tuttle says: "The history of this is but another illustration of Mr. Poor's devotion to the development and utilization of the natural advantage of his native state." The original idea of the survey is found in the following letter:

"PORTLAND [1845 or 1846].
"MY DEAR BROTHER,—

"I send you some memo. touching the distances and elevations on the railway line. You see that Umbagog Lake is twelve hundred and fifty-six feet above the water, falls one hundred and forty-one feet from the lake to the head of Berlin Falls; the river then falls three hundred and thirty-four feet in sixteen miles. Here is unquestionably the greatest water-power in the country. The upper lakes are unquestionably many hundred feet above Lake Umbagog. Richardson's Lake is, at least, three hundred feet higher than Umbagog. From Lake Umbagog to Berlin Falls is some twenty to twenty-five miles. You will see, therefore, that a vast and inexhaustible water-power is here."

And he gives in the same letter tables of elevation above tide-water of other points on the line of the Atlantic and St. Lawrence Railway. In one of the memorials in favor of the European and North American Railway: "Maine," he says "with its extended and deeply indented sea-coast, on the line of favoring winds; its mountainous regions that distil in profusion the clear waters that swell its rivers, descending from high elevations, by circuitous courses, in a succession of cascades to the ocean, amid rich forests, and through a productive soil, may in time rival any region of the globe in the extent of its manufactures and commerce. Its great and distinguishing natural feature is its water-power, surpassing that of any section of the globe of equal extent." In a memorial to the Legislature, prepared by him for the Agricultural Society of Maine, in 1858, he strongly urged a public survey of the water-power of the state. This appeal was renewed and supported with a great variety of illustrations, in a memorial to the Legislature in 1861, prepared by him in behalf of the European and North American Railway Company.

In September, 1866, Mr. Poor wrote to the governor, in spite of his own ill health, upon the material development of the state, and especially upon the advantages of a hydrographic survey, and the governor recommended it. Mr. Tuttle says: "The expediency and necessity of such a survey were at length recognized by the Legislature; in the spring of 1867 it authorized such a survey to be made, under the direction of three commissioners, to be appointed by the governor and council. He was appointed one of the commissioners and chairman of the board. In December, 1867, the commissioners made their report to the governor. This report, filling thirty closely printed octavo pages, was written by Mr. Poor, and it bears all the marks of his vast knowledge and full appreciation of the geographical and physical characteristics of Maine. The result of the survey is two printed volumes, making over eight hundred pages, containing a full description of the water-power of the state, prepared by Walter Wells."

In connection with the hydrographic survey, he endeavored to form a statistical society, and sent out the following circular-letter, which met with no adequate response: "The undersigned citizens of Maine, believing that an association for the collection and publication of facts and statistics, showing the history and profits of industrial and manufacturing enterprises now in operation in this state, and the advantages and resources of the state for all branches of manufacturing and productive industry, respectfully invite a meeting of all persons interested in the prosperity of Maine, at Portland, on Tuesday, August 27, 1867, at ten o'clock in the morning, for the purpose of taking into consideration the best method of accomplishing the objects aforesaid; and, if found expedient, of forming a Statistical and Industrial Society, or Union, within the state."

In 1868 the commissioner of the general land office in Washington applied to Governor Chamberlain for an account of the progress in population, manufactures, agriculture, and commerce, in Maine, since the last national census. The Governor immediately requested Mr. Poor to furnish this important information, recognizing in him the best qualified person in the state for this undertaking. He accepted the commission, and executed it with his usual ability and to the entire satisfaction of the government. His elaborate statistical report fills fourteen closely printed pages.

In 1867 Mr. Poor was invited by the citizens of Belfast, Maine, to address them on the subject of railways. On the Fourth of July, 1867, he delivered an address, with interesting and carefully compiled statistics, it is true, but full also of poetry and eloquence. Tied down to no one railway project, his imagination had full play in describing what he had been so early to recognize—the wonder and beauty of the locomotive railway, the triumph of man over nature. The same idea is rendered with perfect skill in one of Turner's greatest pictures, "Rain, Steam, and Speed," where an advancing train crosses a lofty viaduct, and the light from the locomotive gleams luridly through the streets of pouring rain. Unfortunately, the Belfast and Moosehead Lake Railway Company did not follow Mr. Poor's advice in the location of their railway; he insisted upon Newport as its point of contact with the Maine Central Railway. Mr. Poor suggested a complimentary dinner, from the citizens of Portland, to Messrs. Potter and Brydges, the president and vice-president of the Grand Trunk Railway of Canada, but Mr. Potter's unexpected return to England prevented their acceptance in 1869.

Mr. Poor received letters requesting assistance and advice in distributing copies of reports of commissioners to revise the United States Statutes, and sent names of persons who should receive such reports.

Mr. Poor also lived to see successfully carried out a measure which he had suggested many years before; though the working details were all performed by others. We use Mr. Tuttle's account of the Swedish immigration into the state: "One of his favorite plans for developing the material resources of the state and adding to the public wealth was legislative encouragement of settlements on the unoccupied public lands. His grand idea of the capacities of the state, and his plans of improvement, looked to an almost indefinite enlargement of the wealth and population of the state in this direction. The state of Maine," he says, "from the extent of its territory, its geographical position, its physical geography, and its geological structure, has all the elements essential to an independent empire. By a development of its resources, it can sustain a population at a rate per square mile equal to that of the most densely populated countries in Europe." In several memorials written by him, and presented to the Legislature between 1849 and 1862, he fully set forth his views on this subject, and urged the Legislature to adopt a state policy favorable to settlements on these lands.

As early as June, 1850, he wrote: "We have failed so far as to attract to the state the most valuable class of immigrants that seek for a climate and soil similar to that of Germany and Switzerland, which resemble our own. If proper encouragement were held out to them we might expect the immigrants from the north of Europe to prefer the soil and climate of Maine to those of the Mississippi valley."

He aimed at arresting emigration from the state, as well as inviting immigration to it. A comparative view of the population at various epochs showed that emigration from the state was constantly going on. "This," he says, "is a great drawback to her prosperity. No finer people are born on the face of the globe, and those who leave her distinguish themselves all over the country. Our duty is to keep those men at home, to develop our own state; to rear villages at all the waterfalls; to cultivate the rich soils of the Penobscot, the Kennebec, the Aroostook, and St. John valleys; to own, as well as build and sail, our own commercial marine." Persuaded that some immediate legislative action favorable to immigration and settlement in the great forests of the state was required, he delivered a public address, in 1864, in the hall of the House of Representatives, giving his views on the subject, and urging public action in the matter. Gradually the importance of his suggestions began to be favorably received. In 1870 the Legislature of Maine established a board of immigration to carry out this plan of settling a Scandinavian population in the northeastern part of the state; and in July of that year the first colony from Sweden arrived and settled in the valley of the Aroostook. This colony has since been much increased, and is in a flourishing condition, promising to be as great a public benefit as he anticipated twenty years before."

Mr. Poor was requested by the American Social Science Association, of which he was an original member, to furnish them some information for the hand-book of immigration which the society was then preparing for publication. He sent them an elaborate paper upon "Maine: its Climate, Resources, and Adaptation for Immigrants," for which he received the thanks of the association.

Cut down in the midst of his labors, he left behind him enterprises begun, or suggested, greater than those he had accomplished. As an incidental thing, Mr. Poor sent to the Legislature a petition that a new county should be formed of the towns now lying in the valley of the Sebasticook River, to be called Sebasticook. He was much pleased with the idea of making a naval and military station of Mount Desert, Maine; wrote a communication to the governor upon the subject, with statistics, and procured the passage through the Legislature of a resolve requesting the governor to apply to Congress to carry out this idea, which originated with General Totten, Engineer Corps. It was also through his persistent efforts that the water between Cape Sable and Cape Cod was named the "Gulf of Maine." It was first so called on the map of the United States Coast Survey, at his personal application. Mr. Poor received no pay for his reports on the Hydrographic Survey, on Confederation, to the General Land Office at Washington, to the American Social Science Association, for his address at Belfast,—all dictated after his illness in August, 1866; nor for his historical labors.

These things, however, were but the secondary suggestions of a mind which neglected nothing that could conduce to the prosperity of Maine. The great work of the closing years of Mr. Poor's life was his third great railway project. This was in fact the complement of the other two, for he felt that the commercial position of Maine and of Portland would not be complete till this should be carried out. Through Mr. Poor's whole life, no one had been more keenly alive to the demands of the hour than he. The great problem of "cheap transportation" impressed itself very early upon his mind, and the third great railway which he projected rose beyond the limits of a local line and was an attempt to solve this problem. We have but imperfectly described Mr. Poor, if the reader has not recognized in him, an enthusiasm which was capable of inspiring others to action, a pertinacity which never relinquished an object of which he had once really taken hold, a versatility which enabled him to seize new phases of a cause, and thus to turn the most overwhelming defeats into final victory. To carry out this third railway scheme would, therefore, have been entirely within the limit of his powers.

That the problem of "cheap transportation" had suggested itself to his mind, before it became universally recognized as the great question of the hour, in the United States, is proved by Mr. Poor's letter to the Chicago Ship Canal Convention in 1863, where he says: "Your call . . . may fairly open the entire question of the internal commerce of the country, and the means of transit between the grain-growing regions of the interior of the continent, the great Northwest, and their place of market. Questions of this character are of interest to all, and must for years, if not for generations to come, become the most engrossing topic of public concern. . . . With the aid of all existing canals and railroads, a bushel of wheat in the Northwest is only worth one half its value in Liverpool, so enormous is the cost of present transportation. The question is, How shall this difficulty be overcome? . . . What is wanted are cheap and expeditious means of transit from the Upper Lakes to the open sea." And the same idea is the key-note of all the speeches, memorials, and documents written by Mr. Poor from 1868, onward, in relation to this railway.

Mr. Tuttle says: "Always aiming to achieve great commercial results, and to make great public improvements, regardless of political boundaries and prejudices, he directed the whole force of his energies, early in 1868, to the carrying out of his long-meditated plan of making an eastern outlet, for the great staple commodities of the West, superior to any in existence or hitherto projected. His plan was to connect, by railway, Chicago, and other great commercial centres in that direction, with the capacious harbor of Portland, the ocean terminus of his other great railways. But this did not embrace his ultimate design, for he grasped the commercial relations of the whole continent, leaving no room for another railroad projector between the Atlantic and Pacific Ocean in these latitudes. He looked upon this line, designed to afford cheap and ready transportation of bread-stuffs to the Atlantic States, and to Europe, as 'a chief link in that golden belt which is to span the continent of North America at its widest part, under the name of "The Transcontinental Railway."' This stupendous design had for its object the connecting, so far as possible by railway, of the great commercial centres of Europe, North America, and Asia."

Indeed, in 1869, Mr. Poor wrote in a private letter: "For more than thirty years I have contemplated as a certainty the completion of a line of railway across the continent of North America, at its widest part, as the means of securing the shortest possible transit of passengers, mails, and valuable merchandise between the centres of Europe and Asia. As early as 1845 I had correspondence with Asa Whitney on the subject."

Mr. Poor procured from the Legislature a charter from Portland to Rutland, Vermont, by way of the Ossipee Valley, White River Junction, and Woodstock. The line then went to Whitehall, at the head of Lake Erie, thence to Oswego, near the lower end of Lake Ontario, from Oswego to Buffalo, at the foot of Lake Erie, thence to Detroit and Chicago. In 1868 Mr. Poor wrote from Portland: "A line running due west, striking White River Junction, Woodstock, Rutland, and Whitehall, at the head of Lake Champlain, will enable the traveller by way of Schenectady, the Suspension Bridge, and Detroit, to reach Chicago in a distance of 1,045 miles from Portland, or 83 miles shorter than by any other route from Europe." In a prospectus Mr. Poor invited attention to the road as "the channel of a vast trade between the seaboard and the interior. Its line will be a great immigrant route to the West, as it occupies the most important section of the Transcontinental Railway, and must command a large through travel. Its construction will add largely to the trade and business of Portland *as the natural shipping port of the Northwest."*

It was also to make Portland the distributing point of western produce to Boston and New England, as the Grand Trunk Railway had done before it. In his speech at Bangor, in 1869, Mr. Poor said: "The greatness of Maine cannot be fully comprehended till the Transcontinental Railway is understood, and we realize in practical effect our commanding geographical position. If Portland is not so near the West as New York City, she is practically and geographically vastly nearer to Europe. The products of the great West come to the seaboard for a market. Chicago, the great centre of western trade, sends her surplus produce to New York. This is now the beaten track. New York capital takes from the western farmer, or his Chicago merchant, his crop by advancing money on its delivery to the railway. But the market for the western farmer is not New York City, but New England and Europe, and the practical question of the day is, how shall the western farmer reach the manufacturing towns of New England and the larger markets of Old England and other European countries. Nearly all the states outside New England raise their own bread in the field. New England raises hers in the workshop and exchanges with the western farmer. Now what we of Portland are considering is this question: Can we offer the cheapest rates of transit, or, in other words, the highest price for western produce? A direct line of railway from Chicago to Portland, with favorable grades and cheaper cost, will allow all the manufacturing towns on the Merrimac and Saco to get their supply by this route without handling or transshipment by means of intersecting lines of railway, and we can at Portland bring the railroad alongside the ocean steamer, affording cheaper transit from Chicago to Liverpool or Bremen than can be found at New York."

Had the citizens of Portland supported Mr. Poor's plan, the road might have been in operation long ago, as a railway-building period continued until the panic of 1873; but they preferred to follow their own devices, and opposed him violently. It would be amusing, if it were not pathetic, to see how constantly men are opposed when they are sincerely endeavoring to benefit their fellow-men by something new. Mr. Poor offered to Bangor, in 1853, the railroad she most needed; Mr. Chester W. Chapin offered to Boston the road which Commodore Vanderbilt purchased, and which became afterward the New York Central; the Iron Mountain Railroad, which is "the beginning of the greatness of modern St. Louis and the first dawn of the new era of thrift in Missouri," could not borrow $100,000 in St. Louis, and was obliged to go to New York for it. Professor Agassiz said that as soon as he announced a discovery in science people laughed at him; next they said it was not true. When he succeeded in proving it, they declared that they had always thought so. Mr. Poor's experience was precisely similar. Portland had already the Portland and Rochester road running westerly, and Mr. Poor, as an experienced railway man, proposed to utilize this by making it a trunk line for at least eighteen miles, then tapping it at proper distances for the Oswego road, and the new line which Portland favored, to Ogdensburg, N. Y. He made his proposition to the two railways, and it was distinctly refused, though it would have given one paying road to the city. Mr. Poor's railway plan ran through the level valley of the Ossipee, over a thickly settled country to a trade centre; the Ogdensburg through the White Mountains. The Ogdensburg plan was well known to Mr. Poor; he had killed it once. While in Canada in 1847, the Portland delegation were approached by Boston gentlemen interested in other lines. A road from Boston to Ogdensburg had been proposed simultaneously with the line from Portland to Montreal, as a rival to that project; and the friends of the Ogdensburg road proposed that Portland should abandon the Montreal connection, turn west at Island Pond to Ogdensburg, before reaching Montreal. But the Portland gentlemen thought differently, and declined the proposition; the growth of Montreal and the decay of Ogdensburg have proved their wisdom. The Portland and Ogdensburg Railroad, after taking nearly two millions of dollars from Portland, has passed under the control of Boston.

But in the true pioneer is a sacred fire, which sneers and frowns fan rather than extinguish. As the *Boston Journal* said: "Mr. Poor never faltered before ridicule, nor succumbed to indifference. A volume might be written of his efforts—a volume worthy to stand on the same shelf with the life of Stephenson and other great pioneers of railroading on both sides of the water." Instead of allowing Portland to take the consequences of her folly, Mr. Poor formed a plan for building the Oswego road.

Mr. Poor's favorite method for impressing an idea in the strongest manner upon the largest number of minds, was by a public convention. His immense acquaintance among men prominent in political, historical, as well as commercial circles, made him peculiarly fitted to call together these conventions. Mr. Tuttle says: "He conceived the idea of advancing the interests of his projected road by an international commercial convention to be held at Portland, for the purpose of concentrating public attention upon the splendid harbor there, as the cheapest port of exportation of western produce, as well as upon his great plan of a direct railway across the continent from the Atlantic to the Pacific shore. He prepared a call for the convention, in which he set forth, with a masterly hand, his railway plans and designs." The convention met in Portland on the fourth of August, 1868, and was presided over by Governor Merrill, of Iowa. More than three hundred persons responded, and were present, many of them distinguished in public life, from all parts of the United States and the British Provinces. In spite of active opposition from many citizens of Portland, the convention was a brilliant success, and Mr. Poor's plan was heartily endorsed.

He said: "Two facts are necessarily to be established to secure assent to the doings of this convention. First, the superiority in speed of railway transit over water transportation; and second, that the widest part of the continent of North America lies in the direct line from Hong Kong to London. These two propositions admitted, no one can doubt that the laws of commercial gravitation will force the construction of such lines of railway as will reduce the transit between the Orient and the Occident to its lowest possible limit of time and expense." Mr. Poor's rallying cry, "From Hong Kong to London," has now been adopted by the Canadian Pacific!

Mr. Tuttle says: "In the last of June, 1869, he delivered before a railroad convention, at Rutland, an address on the subject of his plan for a continental railway, but more especially in favor of building, at once, the road from Portland to Rutland and Oswego. This address fills seventy-five octavo pages, and bears the mark of a mature judgment, profound and various knowledge on the subject of the economy of railroads, and of their relations to the commerce of the country."

Mr. Poor drew up a bill which was presented in Congress, in January, 1871, and which was to be applied in aid of the Portland, Rutland, Oswego, and Chicago Railway. Mr. Hamlin, January nineteenth, asked and obtained by unanimous consent leave of the United States Senate to bring in a bill to secure cheap transportation of breadstuffs and provisions from the West to the seaboard at uniform rates throughout the year. He explained it thus: "It secures direct and rapid communication between the West and Europe by finding an ocean outlet two hundred and sixty miles nearer Europe than any other in the United States that has commercial advantages; and prevents the extortions of combinations by placing a regulating power in the hands of the government. It does not take a dollar from the public treasury, or ask a foot of land. It asks the government to become a guarantor, by the issue of its bonds, and receive as security the first mortgage bonds of a first-class corporation, on such terms as will protect the nation from loss in any contingency." It will be found among the printed writings.

The *Boston Journal* said: "His bill does not ask a cent of money nor an acre of land from government; it is the first of the kind introduced to the attention of Congress—a novelty in its way. It provides for a contract by the Postmaster-General with the Portland, Rutland, Oswego, and Chicago Railway Company to construct and maintain a double-track line of railway, with an adequate equipment, and with steel rails and iron bridges. Upon the completion and equipment of forty miles of the road, the Secretary of the Treasury is to issue to the company United States bonds, payable in thirty years, to the amount of fifty thousand dollars per mile, which issue shall constitute *ipso facto* a first mortgage on the whole line of the road and property of the company, and so on for every forty miles completed; the interest and bonds as they fall due to be paid by the company; the location to be approved by an engineer appointed by the President of the United States; and the railway is declared to be a 'national highway and a post-road'; Congress to pass all needful laws for protection of the same; and it is made the duty of each state through which it passes to cede jurisdiction over the territory occupied by the road. In case of failure to pay the interest on bonds, it is made the duty of the Postmaster-General to take possession of the line and run the road to the expense of the company, and Congress shall dispose of it 'as to justice and equity may appertain.' The rate of fares and freight to be established by the company shall be subject to revision and alteration by Congress, and to be uniform throughout the year. Government may at any time take possession of the road, franchise, and property of the company, paying such compensation therefor as may be awarded by commissioners."

In July, 1871, occurred the annual meeting of the Portland, Rutland, Oswego, and Chicago Railway Company. It was made the occasion for another convention, in which prominent men took part from all sections of the line. The Governor of Maine presided. Senator Hamlin made a speech explaining the bill before Congress. Mr. Poor, as president of the company, presented their annual report at the meeting. His versatile and comprehensive mind had prepared a plan for building the road. Six railway companies along the projected route had agreed to unite and act as one company. The representatives of five companies were present, ready to sign the contract of union; owing to the delay of one company, the joint agreement could not be carried into effect at that meeting, and it was adjourned till the twenty-ninth day of September. On the fifth of September, the great head of the enterprise died suddenly without a moment's warning, forty-four years from the day of leaving home, twenty-seven years from his communication to the *Sherbrooke Gazette*.

The *Christian Mirror* said: "The deceased wrought to the very last in his life's mission. The same morning Mr. Poor died, the *Argus* contained an article on 'Railroad Improvements,' with the well-known initials J. A. P.

"As Mr. Poor left his office Monday night, for the last time, and handed some manuscript copy to his clerk, he playfully said: 'What will the railroad people do after I am gone?' This may have been the involuntary suggestion of overwrought nature, made all unconsciously by one who forgot himself in his work; but the first thought in many a mind on hearing of Mr. Poor's death, Tuesday morning, was in substance the last official expression of his lips the night previous: What will become of our railroad interests now that Mr. Poor is gone? Who like him will make the public weal his mission, so that it may be said of his life, its flower and fruitage was the public good?"

Mr. Tuttle said: "His death made a profound sensation, for he had been publicly and widely known for a quarter of a century. All classes of the community expressed the sincerest sorrow. In the Superior Court appropriate notice of his decease was taken by the Bar. The City Government and the Board of Trade of Portland passed resolutions expressing their sense of his merits and the public loss. The Maine Historical Society held a special meeting, and passed a series of resolutions, expressing a sense of deep obligation to Mr. Poor for his great services in the department of history, as well as in behalf of the material interests of the state, and declaring that he is entitled to be considered a public benefactor, and to be held in grateful remembrance by his fellow-citizens." The newspapers of Rutland, Woodstock, Glenn's Falls, Oswego, Jackson Michigan, and Boston contained notices of him; a despatch from a prominent railroad man said: "It is no less a public calamity than a personal sorrow." The Michigan newspaper said: "His loss at this time is national rather than local. Twenty millions of people, including those of the entire Northwest, are interested in the new outlet proposed to the ocean; and it will be difficult, if not impossible, we fear, to find the man or men to fill the place he has left vacant." No one has been found; the road was never begun; and the Canadian Pacific Railway has carried out Mr. Poor's idea with a terminus in Canada.

The technical cause of his death was the breaking down of the walls of the heart; but it is doubly true that he died of a broken heart. The loss of his suit against the European and North American Railway; the accusation that he was working in the interest of Boston; the triumph of consolidation; the delays in the Oswego road, actually brought him to his death. "Then burst his mighty heart," —in the fulness of his intellectual powers, in the splendor of his undimmed beauty, he passed to his reward in a better world.

The early history of Maine is as picturesque as its scenery. Not more do its pine-clad, wave-washed cliffs differ from the flat, sandy shores of Massachusetts, than do the grim and colorless lives of the Puritan settlers from the conflicts and vicissitudes of the Maine colonists. French Protestant and French Romanist, gentleman, fisherman, priest; English Cavalier, English Puritan; Scotch, Scotch-Irish, German, Dutch, assisted immigrant, have in turn owned and occupied its territory, each contesting the land title of its predecessor. Undoubtedly the vigor and originality of the Maine character is due to the admixture of races. Barbarous Indians could easily swoop down from Canada upon its exposed frontiers whenever the interests of France demanded it.

It is hard to realize that before the Pilgrims set foot on Plymouth there were English fishing stations, and even settlements, on its coast; that Robert Jordan, a Church-of-England clergyman, in 1640, by his intelligence and firmness suppressed the first attempt of "the villainy of witchcraft in Maine"; that Maine eastward from the Kennebec was first Acadia, then Nova Scotia until 1759, when Massachusetts formally set up its jurisdiction on the Penobscot; that French settlements existed at Norridgewock holding the Kennebec until 1724, at Castine until 1745, at Lubeck in 1758; that France claimed the territory until after the Revolution; that patriots fled from Nova Scotia to Machias, Maine, and by their bravery and wisdom caused the St. Croix instead of the Penobscot to become the boundary line of the United States; that tories fled from Boston to Castine "to seek an asylum from the tyranny of Congress," and endeavored to found the royal province of New Ireland, to extend from the Penobscot to the St. Croix; that the final evacuation of the United States was not at New York in 1783, but at Castine in January, 1784; that in the war of 1812 the inhabitants of Machias and Eastport were required to take the oath of allegiance to the British Crown, as occupying British territory.

Mr. Tuttle says: "Mr. Poor's historical investigations, which form no inconsiderable part of his title to public consideration and remembrance, occupied much of his attention during the best years of his life. However widely different this interest may seem from the leading pursuit of his life, it is embraced in his early design to place his native state, in all respects, where the motto on its official seal assigns her. 'If there is any thing,' he says, 'which I desire above all things else, it is to do what in me lies for the honor, the welfare, and the glory and renown of Maine. It is my native state, and I inherit, perhaps to a fault of weakness, a love for her as my native land and home. I have seen something of other states and other lands, and until I had gone abroad, I never knew the true beauty, the inherent greatness, the wonderful resources of Maine; so rich in its natural scenery, so full of all the elements of wealth and power, and so capable of the highest results of the most refined civilization.'

"His interest in local history must have begun early, for he furnished Williamson for the history of

Maine, a sketch of his native town, while a student of law. Some acquaintance with the provincial and ante-provincial history of Maine he must have made while tracing the title to lands in the Veazie suit. His interest in the history of Maine was much stimulated by his experience in Canada, in 1845, when the commercial position of Maine was matched with Massachusetts in the contest for the Atlantic terminus of his projected railway. His opponents did not spare his native state, nor forget how recently she was substantially a province of Massachusetts. Neither commercially, nor politically, nor historically, was she allowed the standing he claimed for her, by those opposed to Portland as the terminus of the railway. His indignation was thoroughly aroused, and he resolved to examine more thoroughly, not only the merits of his own state, but the foundation of the pretences of her assailants.

"The next year, 1846, he was chosen a member of the Maine Historical Society, and was a most useful and active member to the end of his days. It was at this time that Gorges' 'Briefe Narration' appeared in the second volume of the collections of the Maine Historical Society, and fixed his attention upon this great author whom he never after ceased to praise and to honor. He devoted his leisure time to the study of the early history of New England, seeking for the facts in documents and publications of that period, rather than in later writers.

"His interest in the subject grew stronger as he advanced, and when he traced English navigators and English settlers to the shores of Maine prior to

1620, the assumed beginning of New England history, the subject became a passion with him, and never abated while he lived.

"Among the memorable historical occurrences, connected with early English colonization in America, those which transpired within the limits of Maine prior to any consecrated in our popular history, made a deep impression on his mind. Not less impressive was the fact that prominent among the noble men concerned in that great achievement which secured for England a portion of the vast domain of the New World, was Sir Ferdinando Gorges, the illustrious founder of Maine. As soon as he had mastered the history of English colonization on this continent, he resolved to give to Maine and to her great founder their true historic position in New England history.

"The first fruit of his historical studies and investigation, was an elaborate paper on 'English Colonization in America,' which he read before the Maine Historical Society, in June, 1859, and also before the New York Historical Society, in October following, receiving the thanks of both societies. In this paper, which attracted a good deal of attention among historical students, he declared his intention to be " to trace the earliest practical efforts to plant the English race in America, and to vindicate the claims of Sir Ferdinando Gorges, the proprietor of my native state, to the proud title of *Father of English Colonization in America.*"

"The title by which England held possessions in North America, and the services of those actively concerned in securing this title, and maintaining it by acts of jurisdiction and possession, to the exclusion of other European nations, were the points which he aimed to make conspicuous, to which to invite public attention. He fixed upon the royal charter granted by King James of England to a company of his subjects, April 10, 1606, authorizing the 'planting of colonies or plantations in North America,' between the thirty-fourth and forty-fifth degrees of latitude, as the initial step in the establishment of English title to New England. The taking of formal possession under this charter, at the mouth of the Sagadahoc, now Kennebec River, August 19, 1607, by a band of English colonists, he regarded as the consummation of the English title, and as the great event in American history.

"To the enterprising Sir Ferdinando Gorges, whom he so much resembled in energy of character, persistency, and public spirit, he awards the merit of saving the territory of New England from the grasp of the French, and of introducing and settling it with English colonists. 'But for Gorges,' he says, 'the western continent must have fallen under the dominion of Roman Catholic France, and Celtic civilization would have changed its destiny; for all New England was in possession of the French prior to 1606.'

"He expresses his indignation in strong terms at the treatment which Gorges and his associates received at the hands of their Puritan contemporaries, and of our historians on account of their religious and political attachments in that age, and rejoices that the time has come when a more liberal spirit prevails, and when the merits of these men can be recognized. 'But Gorges' fame,' he adds, 'shall yet eclipse that of any other name in our American annals. My native state has been remiss in the discharge of this duty, and supinely allowed the history of New England to cluster around the rock of Plymouth instead of standing clearly out in the earlier deeds of the great minds that saved New England and the continent from the grasp of the French.'

"Designing to procure some honorable recognition in Maine, for the name of Gorges, he drew up, in 1860, a petition addressed to the secretary of war, and procured signers to it, asking that the new fort in Portland harbor may be named Fort Gorges, and it was ordered to take this name. He had a design to form an association for the purpose of erecting a monument to the memory of Gorges, within the limits of the ancient 'Province of Mayne.'

"The position he had taken with regard to the historical and political significance of the royal charter of 1606, and the settlement at Sagadahoc the following year, awakened a new interest, especially in Maine, in the subject of English colonization in New England. The transfer of the point of the initial movement of English colonization from the shores of Massachusetts to the shores of Maine, and the placing of Gorges at the head of it, *created a new era in historical investigation.*

"Believing the settlement at Sagadahoc to have all the significance which he claimed for it, he aimed to direct public attention to the event, and to revive the memory of the actors in the great enterprise. In the autumn of 1861, he persuaded Mr. Williams, his associate commissioner on the coast defences of Maine, to join with him in an application to the Secretary of War, requesting that the new fort about to be erected at the mouth of the Kennebec River, on the site of the first settlement, may be named *Fort Popham*, in honor of the venerable George Popham, who led the first British colony into New England in 1607. This name was approved by the national government, and the work of construction begun.

"His associates of the Maine Historical Society, approving his design of attaching these historic names of Popham and Gorges to great national works of defence within the state, joined readily with him in a design to place a memorial stone, with appropriate inscriptions, in the walls of Fort Popham. Leave to do this being obtained of the government, it was agreed by all interested to make the act of placing the stone in position one of solemn commemoration; and August 29, 1862, being the anniversary of the settlement, was selected for the commemoration service. A large executive committee, of which Mr. Poor was one, consisting of leading citizens in all parts of the state, carried out the design on a scale commensurate with the magnitude and importance of the occasion. He was selected to deliver the historical address, while several of his distinguished associates of the Historical Society performed conspicuous parts in the commemoration services. He delivered the address at Fort Popham on the two hundred and fifty-fifth anniversary of the event, in the presence of the principal officers of state, and of many distinguished persons from other New England states. It is estimated that six thousand persons were present on the occasion. It was a day never forgotten by him; for this act and this ceremonial were the result of his own efforts to secure for Maine her true place in history. His address was appropriate, full of historical research, and contained a complete narrative of English colonization on these shores. He enforced his views of the importance of the event with vigorous reasoning and with full historical illustration. This address, and the one on English colonization, with many historical papers procured by him from European archives, are printed in the memorial volume of the Popham celebration.

"About this time he drew up a memorial asking for an appropriation to defray the expense of procuring copies of documents bearing on the early history of Maine, from the British State-Paper Office; and was joined in this by the Rev. Dr. Woods and the Rev. Dr. Ballard, both eminent historical scholars, and deeply interested in Mr. Poor's historical investigations. This memorial was presented to the Legislature and an appropriation made." A similar memorial was presented to Congress in 1889 signed by college professors and officers of historical societies throughout the country.

"Commemorative services have been held annually ever since at Fort Popham. On nearly every occasion he has been present and taken part in the proceedings. In 1868 he prepared and read there an elaborate address, in which he restated his position on the 'Popham question,' as it is called, added some freshly discovered evidence in support of his views, chiefly from De Carayon, and reviewed the various attacks made on the position he had taken with regard to the historical and political importance of the settlement under Popham. He was present there, for the last time, on the two hundred and sixty-second anniversary of the event, and made a brief speech.

"At the field meeting of the Historical Society held in the ancient town of York on the twenty-ninth of August, 1870, he was present and read a carefully prepared paper, reviewing the events leading to colonization on these shores, and introducing important documentary evidence, recently obtained from European archives through the agency of the Rev. Dr. Woods, bearing on the title which England asserted to the territory of New England in 1613, when Argall destroyed the French settlement at Mount Desert. It appears that the English government justified the act of Argall on the ground that the French were then within the limits of territory granted to English subjects, 1606, who were in possession of the same; and that France acquiesced in the claim. A few days later, at a joint meeting of the Maine and New Hampshire Historical Societies, held at Portsmouth, he was present, and made a brief characteristic speech, reviewing the early history of the two states, which closed his public historical addresses.

"It is quite impossible to give an adequate idea, in this brief sketch, of Mr. Poor's historical labors, covering a period of more than fifteen years. The results are known and appreciated by historical students. Besides awakening a general interest in our early history, he gave an immense impulse to the work of the Maine Historical Society; resulting in sending the Rev. Dr. Woods to Europe to make historical researches, bearing on the early discovery and settlement of Maine, and in the publication of a valuable volume on discovery, soon to be followed by others on colonization. Long before his death he had no superior in knowledge, and in appreciation of our early history. He was member of the New England Historic, Geneological Society, and corresponding member of the Historical Societies of New Hampshire, Vermont, New York, and Pennsylvania."

Mr. Poor's main proposition is incontrovertible, though it has been misunderstood and therefore misrepresented.

It is well explained in the following newspaper article written by Mr. Poor himself answering attacks:

"The value of the Popham settlement, as it seems to me, depends upon its influence in establishing the title of *Old* England, to the territory of *New* England. To determine this, we must resort to the cotemporary history of the times. We need not claim for it anything more, as a settlement, than a writer declares it to have been, 'an abortive settlement on the sand spit at the mouth of the Kennbec,' if it accomplished the purpose of making good the title of England to the country. That is the question involved in the celebration, and those who have examined it, in the light of modern discovery, find the proof satisfactory to their own minds.

"The discovery of the continent of America changed the commercial if not the political ideas of Europe. The Pope promptly donated the new world to Spain and Portugal. But in the reign of Elizabeth, the people of England, having become enfranchised from Catholic rule, asserted a new doctrine in regard to the rights of nations, repudiating the claim of the Pope, and held that *possession* of a newly discovered country was essential to the establishment of title. France agreed to the same doctrine, and in all the early charters of both France and England for the peopling of North America, there was a reservation that no right of occupation was granted where the country '*was actually possessed by any Christian Prince or people.*' This language was used in the first Virginia charter of King James, April 10, 1606, granting the country between the 38 and 45th deg. north latitude. The French charter to De Monts, of Nov. 8, 1603, granted the territory between 40 and 46 deg. of north latitude, under which the country was possessed, from Cape Breton to Cape Cod. This charter was revoked in 1607, and before Champlain had obtained foothold in Canada. This Act in the English grant took precedence of the French title to Canada, and in this way, the *forty-fifth* parallel of latitude became the boundary line, from Lake Champlain to the Connecticut, between the French and English. But for the revocation of De Monts' charter, in 1607, the French, as all now admit, would have held the country from the 40th parallel north. If your readers will examine the letter of the French historian, L'Escarbot, to Louis XIII, written in 1618, a translation of which will be found in the Popham memorial volume, they will be able to comprehend the importance of the settlement of Sabino.

"Formal possession of the country was there taken, Aug. 29, 1607, claiming it from the 34th to the 45th deg. north latitude, and this claim was always and pertinaciously maintained. The question was a novel one and information limited, and there was great difficulty in getting parties to remain in the country. Gorges actually hired men for this purpose. The title of Sagadahoc was fully established by continuous occupation. The French Jesuits say, that the English were there in 1608 and 1609. When Samuel Argall made a voyage from Jamestown to Bermuda, in 1610,— according to Pinchon (vol. IV, p. 1758,) 'missing the same on account of the fog, he put over *to Sagadahoc.*' Edward Harlow and Nicholas Hobson made voyages there in 1611. Richard Vines who came over in 1609 remained continuously in the country and wintered at Saco in 1616. They all claimed to hold the country under the charter of 1606, and the Frenchmen occupied West Sagadahoc after 1607. So anxious was Gorges to hold the country, against the French, Spanish, and Dutch claimants, that he invited the Leyden flock hither in 1617, and they came over in 1620, under the protection of Gorges. Capt. John Smith in 1614 gave the country the name of New England, and made a map of it from actual surveys from the 45th parallel South, which map was published in England in 1616. The title rested on the charter of 1606, which was publicly read at Sabino, Aug. 29, 1607, with the constitution and code of laws establishing their government. I might multiply proof on this head, but these are sufficient for my purpose; not to undervalue the Plymouth settlement of 1620, but to show that the English title to North America dates back to Sabino.

"In the New England charter of 1620, granted before the Plymouth settlement on the Petition of Sir Ferdinando Gorges, it is stated, that he '*had actual possession* of the country,' and '*had already settled some of our people therein.*' In the letter of Gov. Bradford to Gorges, dated at Plymouth June 9, 1628, he says, 'you have ever been, not only a favorer, but a most special beginner and furtherer of the good of this country, to your great cost, and no less honor.' In the commission of Sir Ferdinando Gorges as Governor of New England, the King says, you made '*the first discovery of these coasts and the first seizure thereof.*'"

It is another proof of Mr. Poor's deductive habit of mind, and also of the correctness of his intuitions, that these documents, procured from the British State-Paper Office, fully justified the positions which Mr. Poor assumed in his Gorges' address as early as 1859.

It was always his design to go to Europe, and there study the history of the period of discovery and colonization of New England, in the archives of maritime nations, and he eagerly looked forward to the time when he could devote himself to his historical studies. In one of the last letters written by him, in 1871, he says: "I am too much engaged in railroad labors to give much attention to historical matters, which I hope will be the solace and employment of my later days. If I now had the leisure I would devote my time to the investigation of American history, which is more the history of ideas in their active workings, than of outward events." Mr. Henry Stevens, to whom this letter was written, was so strong a friend to Maine and her documentary history that the following notice of him should be preserved, written by the London correspondent of the *New York Tribune:*

"Henry Stevens came to London in 1845, and soon, as he has often said, 'drifted' into the British Museum. He retained his connection there as agent for the buying of books till the last; none of his financial misfortunes terminated it. Panizza, who then ruled the museum in a sense far other than that in which Mr. Bond now does, was his staunch friend. He understood Stevens' value, and he made use of his services in a way for which an American can never quite forgive either of the pair. Mr. Bond writes the notice of Stevens in the *Athenæum*, and says with a touch of pardonable exultation that as the result of Stevens' efforts the British Museum now contains a more extensive library of American books than any single library in the United States. No doubt it does, and the fact is a reproach, not to Stevens, but to Americans in general, and to the Congress of the United States in particular.

"Henry Stevens, an American to the backbone, would have rejoiced to do for his own country what he did for England. But England employed him to do it and America did not, and it is too late to repair the blunder. No collection of American books equal to that in the British Museum can ever again be got together. The time is past. Stevens' catalogue of this, completed in 1857, is a volume of six hundred octavo pages, and includes twenty thousand volumes. When he began collecting for the museum, in 1845, the whole number did not exceed four thousand volumes. The other sixteen thousand are due to him. One of his reasons for printing the catalogue was to show, side by side, as he says, both the richness and the poverty of the collection. He effected his object, and between 1857 and 1862 the number doubled. That is to say, in 1862 the American department in the British Museum possessed forty thousand volumes, counting only books printed in America, and not counting books, maps, etc., in all languages relating to America, in which the museum is very rich, nor counting American books reprinted in this country.

"And I suppose for much of what we actually have in America concerning our own country we have to thank Henry Stevens. He was the agent of many American collectors, often with authority to buy on his own judgment. His best known general client was perhaps Mr. James Lenox, whose library, now one of the chief treasures and ornaments of New York, was formed by Henry Stevens. No man knew so much about early editions of the Bible; no one perhaps so much about early voyages and travels. These, with the Americana, were the subjects to which Stevens devoted himself, and on which he will ever remain an authority. Caxton was another topic which interested him, and he did much for the Caxton Exhibition at South Kensington in 1877, cataloguing the Bibles then shown. He had a wide and always an exact knowledge, not merely of books, but of subjects. Some of this he has put into print or read before literary societies, but the mass of it dies with him. He is a real loss to letters as well as to bibliography. The English papers abound in eulogies on him. I hope the American papers do as much, for he was a man who held high abroad the American name. 'Esteemed,' says the *Times*, 'for his knowledge, ability, and shrewd common-sense, he was even more beloved for his frank manliness, his kindly nature, and rich, genial humor.' The tribute is not too strong."

Mr. Poor showed his usual breadth of view by his strong desire to popularize historical knowledge, and his labors to that end. As early as 1867 he suggested that a course of lectures upon the history of Maine should be delivered by competent persons under the auspices of the Maine Historical Society. The idea was adopted and carried out by the Massachusetts Historical Society; such a course was actually delivered in Boston, and resulted in the publication of a large volume containing the lectures. Mr. Poor also proposed that the fiftieth anniversary of the incorporation and organization of the society should be celebrated. It was to occur in April,

1872; the plan was eagerly welcomed by the society, but no such celebration took place after his death. During the last two months of his life in 1871, this desire to extend the knowledge of the history of Maine was still more strongly expressed. Although the preparations for the annual meeting and convention of the railroad to Oswego demanded incessant labor, Mr. Poor, nevertheless, found time to write an elaborate report. As chairman of a committee of the society "for increasing the society's usefulness," he read this report before them at their annual meeting, July, 1871. It urged that all limitations as to the number of members, which is now confined to one hundred, should be removed; and that the number of members should be indefinitely increased; that special meetings should be called as often as desirable; that a public oration should be delivered annually. With this effort to benefit the many rather than the few, closed Mr. Poor's historical labors.

From his earliest youth Mr. Poor longed to become a good speaker as well as writer. His writings and his actions have been described; his speech must perish with him. But if we may judge by the effects it produced, the concessions it wrung from unwilling Legislatures, it must have been with power. He spoke with extraordinary rapidity, uttering three times as many words in one minute as ordinary speakers, and with much animation. His victories were won by appealing to the highest motives—to patriotism, or to international brotherhood, and by putting subjects on their broadest foundation. He cannot be called a lobbyist, because he spoke only from conviction, and upon his own railways; although he met in debate leading men of Canada, the Lower Provinces, and the West; and spoke before committees of the Legislature in Maine, Massachusetts, New Hampshire, Vermont; of the Parliament of Canada, of the Congress of the United States; and the Historical Societies of Maine, New Hampshire, Vermont, and New York.

He left behind him a mass of letters, many of them from prominent men in the United States and the Dominion of Canada. A very influential man of Boston, at the close of a long letter, wrote to him as follows: " I have read with great interest and instruction your argument before the Committee of the Maine Legislature upon ' Restrictions on Railway Transit.' Apart from the simple purpose of the argument in that case, which is so ably and adroitly put, the comprehensive and philosophical views of the capabilities, resources, and growth of the New England States, and the statistics bearing upon the relative advantages of different localities, are most valuable. . . . I only wish we had in Boston some gentleman of your intelligence, experience, tact, and energy, who would devote himself to the interests of the city and state as you do to like interests in Maine. With the amount of business and capital here to back up his efforts, I think he might do two things: make this one of the greatest cities on the continent; and make for himself a fortune while living, and secure a statue among its benefactors after he is gone."

But Mr. Poor died a poor man, and Maine has erected no statue to her benefactor. When he was once reproached that he did not make money his first object, he answered: "I thought if the work were good the money would come."

It is not too strong to say that he had a contempt for office. His political, being as keen as his other instincts, he was the first man in Maine to support General Taylor for the Presidency in 1848, and the office of Postmaster of Portland was within his reach. The following letter was written in November, 1848: "I thank you for the frank manner in which you have expressed yourself. I have very little ambition for any place myself; and if I could be gratified by any thing, it would be to be in a position of greater independence, where I could pursue with greater zeal certain ideas which have occupied my thoughts for some years." He declined the office of Consul-General to Canada in 1861, and an important position in the Treasury Department at Washington in 1863; and the only offices he ever held were those created expressly for him, which lapsed when he gave them up. He also refused what was to him a greater temptation—a share in railway enterprises in the West.

Mr. Poor married in 1860 Mrs. Margaret Gwynne, of Cincinnati, daughter of Mr. William Barr, a pioneer, and a man of great force of character. Mrs. Poor, who had a fortune, would have been glad that Mr. Poor should live in Cincinnati, or at least that he should spend his time in Europe. But neither ease nor pleasure could draw him from his work, and

Mrs. Poor cheerfully accommodated herself to his plans. In the success of that work he found his happiness; and in spite of a sensitive and melancholy temperament, he was an exceptionally happy man,—happy also in his domestic life, and in the scenery and climate of Maine. He declared that the daily sight of the White Mountains was a "perpetual inspiration" to him. But had it been otherwise, he would still have been cheerful, for he considered cheerfulness in and for itself, to be an absolute duty.

It was sometimes a regret to him that he did not live among libraries, pictures, operas, noble buildings, for he keenly loved all these, understood and appreciated them. He enjoyed large, high rooms, and beautiful, becoming dress for women; and not through ostentation, but pure love of beauty in every form. But a man who is trying to help his fellowmen by great industrial undertakings that bring prosperity to thousands, can be happy without the embroideries of life.

Mr. Poor was a man of splendid beauty, six feet two inches in height, weighing at last two hundred and fifty pounds; of noble and commanding presence, with clear-cut Grecian features, and a sensitive yet resolute mouth; Horace Greeley said that he had a mouth like Henry Clay's. In the winter of 1849, when Mr. Poor was forty-one years of age, he was living at the Astor House, New York. While standing one day in the office, he saw that he was closely watched by a man, who walked around him several times, and finally spoke to him thus: "I beg your pardon, sir, but have you ever been in the ring?" "Never," said Mr. Poor. "Then you should go in at once; with such a figure you would make your fortune." The man proved to be the most celebrated prize-fighter of the day.

His genial manner, his hearty laugh, his suggestive talk, made him fascinating in society; one of the Canadian public men said: "We really loved Mr. Poor"; his playfulness and tenderness made him passionately beloved at home.

His anger was terrible; yet it would be a great mistake to suppose that Mr. Poor was naturally belligerent. His opinions were so advanced and original, his nature so earnest, that he could not fail to differ; yet it is strictly true to say that he never attacked others until they attacked him; but when stung to anger by misrepresentations, treachery, or ingratitude, his blows fell fast and hard. One of his contemporaries wrote: "His services to his native state we are confident will be recognized and honored. We desire now only to add our tribute to his character as a man and a friend; to record our admiration of his large-heartedness, his generous impulses, his ready recognition and encouragement of the merit of others, his freedom from all narrowness, his genial social qualities, his exhaustless fund of information ever at the service of his friends."

The growth of Mr. Poor's mind can best be traced from the books he bought and read. They were in early life, books of poetry and theology. Isaac Taylor, author of the "Natural History of Enthusiasm," Coleridge, and Robert Hall were then his favorite authors, read and re-read. Indeed, it was owing to a letter from him to a publisher that the works of Robert Hall were collected and published in this country; Mr. Poor having met them in a small English book of his selections. His love of poetry he retained to the very last of his life, and the evening but one before his death, he read through his favorite poem, "Comus." He was very fond of Byron's letters, but not of his poetry; he extravagantly loved Webster's speeches and Gray's "Ode on the Progress of Poesy"; he cared very much for beautiful style in music also,—Weber's were his favorite operas. In the last few years of his life he would read and re-read Gerald Griffin's poem, "The Sister of Charity," and Robertson's sermon upon the Queen Dowager Adelaide,—"The stranger not born in the land, but who came in to do good to it."

When *Cosmos* appeared, Mr. Poor studied with eagerness its successive volumes; he then read Lyell's books on Geology; for the last years of his life, early American history absorbed him more and more. The study of Humboldt and Lyell undoubtedly educated that instinctive eye for the topographical features of a country, which he seemed to possess. When the survey was suggested for the railway from Glenn's Falls to Oswego, New York, people talked of the impenetrable wilderness of Northern New York. No instrument had ever been put upon Pisceo Lake, but Mr. Poor knew the elevation of the land, the grade to the mile, the height of the mountains, and persuaded the people to make the survey. A most favorable route for a railway was found, unexpectedly to them, but not to Mr. Poor.

The height of the mountains was even less than he had predicted, the grade to the mile being thirty-five feet, where he had foretold forty feet.

It was said of Mr. Poor that he assimilated and digested into one harmonious whole, ready for use, every fact which he took into his mind. Yet he used these facts to justify himself in the conclusions at which he had already arrived, rather than to aid him in forming these conclusions, his habit of mind being eminently deductive, and his predictions justified by after discoveries; and this is still more clearly shown in his historical writings. Indeed, he was by nature an idealist; in his childhood he dreamed much, and walked in his sleep; in later years he would go to bed with all the perplexities of his business complications unsettled, and in the morning he would awaken with a definite plan of action formed, he knew not how,—a power uncommon and peculiar to some minds, but which Leibnitz recognizes when he says: "There are mental processes of which we are unconscious at the time, but which we recognize as having taken place, by finding certain results in our mind."

It must not be thought, however, that Mr. Poor spared himself the labor of study. He left behind him carefully prepared memoranda on all subjects which interested him,—memoranda historical, commercial, statistical. These were put into envelopes, which were marked on the outside, and arranged at his right hand, ready for use. Yet Mr. Poor was not in the least dependent upon a certain place, or certain surroundings, for ability to express himself in writing. Such was his power of concentration that no conversation in the room interrupted him. His memoir of Mr. Williams was written at his room in the hotel at Washington, in the intervals of business, and even his address at Fort Popham in precisely the same way, while subjected to a thousand interruptions. He never wrote with such ease to himself as during the last four years of his life, which were peculiarly busy ones, yet every thing was dictated.

No memoir is complete until we have gone behind its facts to seek what was their real inspiration, and what should be, therefore, their true interpretation. We have seen that books of theology interested Mr. Poor deeply. While a student of law in Bangor, he wished to become a member of the Trinitarian Congregational Church, but was withheld solely by doubts upon their points of belief, as defined in their own creed and formularies. Although holding opinions of his own which were Congregational as to church government, and Unitarian as to doctrine, he attended the services of the Presbyterian or Episcopal church with his wife or daughter. He had, however, a rich and full personal communion with God, and on one occasion he said, with the simplicity and force which can only come from experience: "You can never be happy until you give up your own will wholly. It is so simple. Then you will be perfectly satisfied and at peace." And in this spirit of absolute self-surrender to the divine will, he took up and carried to the end the peculiar work to which God had called him.

That the work opened gradually before him, and

led him on from step to step, he hardly knew how, is evident from expressions of his own at different periods of his life. The following, which were found in his private journal after his death, had never been seen before.

In 1860 he wrote: "The great purpose of my life is in a great measure accomplished. In sixteen years Maine has been raised greatly in commercial importance, and in the next sixteen years will take relatively a much higher position than now, though the growth of every thing in Maine is slow. What toils, what anxieties have I not suffered these sixteen years!"

In the year of his death, he wrote: "Portland, January 8, 1871. This is my sixty-third birthday. I have always looked forward to this day with a singular feeling of hope and dread, for I am sure that it is a turning-point in my life. A man of robust frame, with freedom from dissipation, reaches his maturity, or manhood, at forty-nine; and culminates, as a physical being, at sixty-three. So I have been taught by philosophers and naturalists. From this day forward, I run on in my career on the descending grade, or the downhill of life. . . . I am quite ready to take my leave of worldly objects, or, in other words, to give up my life, whenever it may please the Father of mercies to take it, but I intend to work with more diligence and labor with more system than ever, in the vocation to which I have been called. No one can conceive of the self-denial, the labor, and the waste of strength to which I have been subjected. . . . I have had an unquenchable desire for knowledge in certain departments of human thought, and an ambition for glory and fame as a friend of my race. I honor the men who have acquired success in the useful arts, as the great benefactors of their age. I have honored Watt, Arkwright, Stephenson, Fulton, and Whitney more than any of the heroes of war; and I had a desire from my first recollection to do something in this line. I resorted to the profession of the law, as a means of livelihood, and of honorable renown, but before I had been ten years in the profession, I had enjoyed all in it that I was capable of, and my career since in influencing the History, the Geography, and the Physical Resources of Maine has brought me an exceeding great reward—for I have enjoyed it.

"I thought the projecting and carrying out of the railway to Montreal from 1844 to 1853 was enough for any one man, and yet I had to carry forward the line of the European and North American Railway, and have yet to finish the Transcontinental line,—or the section from Portland to Chicago."

Such are the men who sink broad and deep the foundations of the Republic.

LIST OF PUBLISHED WRITINGS.

No. 1. Memorial to the Legislature of Maine asking for the opening of direct communication between the principal towns of Maine and the St. Lawrence River. January, 1844.

No. 2. Project of a railway from Montreal to the Atlantic coast at Portland, Maine. *Sherbrooke Gazette*, September 5, 1844.

No. 3. Plan for a line of railway from Portland to Montreal, through the northern extremities of New Hampshire and Vermont. *Portland Advertiser*, September 17, 1844.

No. 4. Railroad to Montreal. *Portland Argus*, September 25, 1844.

No. 5. Railroad from Portland to Montreal. *Portland Bulletin*, September 25, 1844.

No. 6. Extracts from the Report of the Directors of the St. Lawrence and Atlantic Railway Company advising a line of railway from Lewiston, Maine, to Bangor, and St. John, New Brunswick, in connection with the line from Portland to Montreal; written by John A. Poor, and adopted by the Directors in Montreal. January 19, 1847.

No. 7. Montreal and St. John Railroad. *Bangor Whig*, November 23, 1847.

No. 8. Extracts from Report of Directors of St. Lawrence and Atlantic Railroad Company in favor of a line to the east from Danville Junction to Bangor, and St. John, New Brunswick; written by John A. Poor. January 19, 1848.

No. 9. Portland and Montreal Railroad. *Portland Argus*, February 7, 1848.

No. 10. Portland and Montreal Railroad. *Portland Argus*, February 16, 1848.

No. 11. Railroads in Maine. *New York Railroad Journal*, November 18, 1848.

No. 12. Railway Economy; cost of running at high speed. *New York Railroad Journal*, April 20, 1850.

No. 13. PLAN FOR SHORTENING THE TIME OF PASSAGE BETWEEN NEW YORK AND LONDON, with map: petition to the Legislature of Maine in aid of the European and North American Railway. Octavo, pp. 24. 1850.

No. 14. Proceedings of Portland Convention, etc., European and North American Railway. Octavo, pp. 156. 1850.

No. 15. Prospectus of the European and North American Railway Company. Octavo, pp. 32. 1851.

No. 16. Petition to Legislature of Massachusetts for aid to European and North American Railway. Octavo, pp. 8. 1851.

No. 17. Remarks of John A. Poor upon the European and North American Railway at the City Hall, Portland, at a general meeting July 22, 1851, in opposition to Hon. Joseph Howe, of Nova Scotia. Octavo, pp. 8. 1851.

No. 18. Memorial to Thirty-first Legislature of Maine in relation to the European and North American Railway for shortening the transit of mails between New York and London. Octavo, pp. 16. 1852.

No. 19. Memorial to Congress of the United States for aid to the European and North American Railway. Octavo, pp. 16. January 20, 1852.

No. 20. Proceedings of Legislature of Massachusetts on petition in aid of the European and North American Railway. Octavo, pp. 8. 1852.

No. 21. Report of Directors of the York and Cumberland Railway Company. Octavo, pp. 8. 1852.

No. 22. Railroad Convention to unite the various railroad interests in Maine to better aid the building of the European and North American Railway. Octavo, pp. 16. October 14, 1852.

No. 23. Documents in relation to the disposition of the public lands of Maine. Octavo, pp. 30. 1853.

No. 24. Memorial of the Executive Committee of the European and North American Railway Company to the Legislature of Maine, for amendment of its charter and for state aid; containing an historical sketch of the state, and suggesting immigration. Octavo, pp. 24. 1853.

No. 25. Plan for building the European and North American Railway in Maine. Octavo, pp. 4. 1853.

No. 26. Memorial to the Thirty-third Legislature of Maine: a petition of the President and Directors of the European and North American Railway Company. Octavo, pp. 8. 1854.

No. 27. The Paris Exhibition. Octavo, pp. 8. 1854.

No. 28. Petition to the Parliament of Canada praying for a charter for the Northern Pacific Railway Company, Quebec. Octavo, pp. 8. Lovell & Lamoureux: reprinted by Ira Berry, Portland. 1854.

No. 29. Commercial importance of Portland, with map. Octavo, pp. 50. 1855.

No. 30. Memorial to the Legislature of Maine concerning the public lands of Maine, for a STATE POLICY, and for measures to promote the settlement and sale of the public lands, and to encourage manufactures. Octavo, pp. 12. 1857.

No. 31. Memorial to the Legislature of Maine of the Maine State Agricultural Society, for the adoption of measures to promote the settlement and sale of the public lands of Maine, and to encourage immigration and manufactures. Octavo, pp. 26. 1858.

No. 32. Memorial to the Congress of the United States of the Board of Trade of Portland, Maine, for the extension of the Reciprocity Treaty. Senate Doc., pp. 4. 1859.

No. 33. A VINDICATION OF THE CLAIMS OF SIR FERDINANDO GORGES, AS THE FATHER OF ENGLISH COLONIZATION IN AMERICA, with map and documents. Octavo, pp. 144. 1859.

No. 34. Report to the Legislature of Maine, of minority of Committee on Railways, in favor of a trunk line of railway across the state; and the granting of the public lands of Maine to aid its construction from Bangor to the eastern boundary of the state. Octavo, pp. 22. 1860.

No. 35. Memorial to the Legislature of Maine in aid of the European and North American Railway Company and for a STATE POLICY favorable to immigration and the encouragement of manufactures; containing a geological and historical sketch of the state of Maine. Octavo, pp. 52. 1861.

No. 36. Report to the Legislature of Maine of Commissioners on the Coast Defences of Maine, and documents relating thereto, in favor of building the European and North American Railway as a military railroad. Octavo, pp. 16. 1862.

No. 37. Letter to Hon. E. M. Stanton, Secretary of War, proposing to build the European and North American Railway as a military railroad. Octavo, pp. 26. 1862.

No. 38. THE NATIONAL FINANCES: Letter to Congress with statistics. Octavo, pp. 8. 1862.

No. 39. DOCUMENTARY HISTORY OF MAINE: Memorial to the Legislature of Maine for procuring papers from the British State-Paper Office in regard to the early history of Maine. Octavo, pp. 4. 1862.

No. 40. THE FIRST COLONIZATION OF NEW ENGLAND: An address delivered at the erection of a monumental stone in the walls of Fort Popham, August 29, 1862, commemorative of the planting of the Popham Colony on the peninsula of Sabino, August 19, 1607, with documents. Octavo, pp. 58. 1862.

No. 41. Proceedings of the Legislature of Maine, in favor of procuring documents from the British State-Paper Office, as to the early history of Maine. Octavo, pp. 4. 1863.

No. 42. Report to the Legislature of Maine on the Coast Defences, with documents, in favor of building the European and North American Railway as a military railroad. Octavo, pp. 32. 1863.

No. 43. Memoir of Mrs. Mary Barr. Octavo, pp. 10.

No. 44. Memoir of Hon. Reuel Williams. Octavo, pp. 66. 1863.

No. 45. THE FUTURE OF NORTH AMERICA: A letter to the Chicago Ship-Canal Convention suggesting a ZOLL-VEREIN WITH CANADA. Octavo, pp. 4. 1863.

No. 46. Memorial to the Legislature of Maine asking aid to the European and North American Railway by a grant of the public lands lying on the Penobscot and St. John waters; and of the claims of Maine against the U. S. Government held jointly with Massachusetts. Octavo, pp. 4. 1864.

No. 47. Report to the Legislature of Maine, of the Joint Standing Committee on Frontier and Coast Defences, with bills and resolves in aid of European and North American Railway. Octavo, pp. 24. 1864.

No. 48. Resolutions of the Legislature of Maine, in relation to the defences of the northern frontier of the state. Octavo, pp. 4. 1864.

No. 49. Report of Special Committee of House of Representatives at Washington on Northeastern Defences, with documents: in favor of building the European and North American Railway as a compensation to Maine for her territory sacrificed in running the line of the NORTHEASTERN BOUNDARY. Octavo, pp. 82. 1864.

No. 50. Prospectus of the European and North American Railway. Octavo, pp. 68. 1864.

No. 51. Memorial to the Legislature of Massachusetts asking an assignment of its claims against the United States held jointly with Maine; a discharge of the debt due from Maine on account of the purchase of the public lands, and a loan of state credit. Octavo, pp. 4. 1865.

No. 52. Memorial to the Governor of Massachusetts asking an exchange of State of Maine bonds: statement of facts. 1865.

No. 53. "NO RESTRICTIONS ON RAILWAY TRANSIT": Argument of John A. Poor before the Joint Standing Committee on Railroads, Ways, and Bridges, for authority to extend a broad-gauge track on the railway from Portland to Boston: delivered in the Senate-chamber of Maine, with documents. Octavo, pp. 75. 1865.

No. 54. Memorial of the European and North American Railway Company of Maine to Congress of the United States, praying aid in constructing a military road from Bangor to the St. John River, with map and documents. Octavo, pp. 38. 1865.

No. 55. Memorial of the European and North American Railway to the Legislature of Massachusetts for State aid, with documents. Octavo, pp. 42. 1866.

No. 56. Report and Resolves in relation to the Confederation of the British North American Provinces, Maine Legislature. Senate Doc. No. 87, pp. 8. Adopted by the Legislature. 1867.

No. 57. THE RAILWAY: Remarks at Belfast, Maine. Octavo, pp. 62. 1867.

No. 58. Report of the Commissioners of the Hydrographic Survey. Octavo, pp. 30. 1867.

No. 59. ACROSS THE CONTINENT: Atlantic and Pacific Railway; Portland and Rutland Railroad. Official record of the corporators. Octavo, pp. 59. 1868.

No. 60. Proceedings of the International Commercial Convention held in Portland, Maine, August 4, 5, and 6. Octavo, pp. 160. 1868.

No. 61. Prospectus Portland and Rutland Railway. Octavo, pp. 4. 1868.

No. 62. Report for the Social Science Society of general statistics in regard to Maine. Octavo, pp. 8. 1869.

No. 63. THE TRANSCONTINENTAL RAILWAY: Remarks at Rutland, Vermont, June 24. Octavo, pp. 78. 1869.

No. 64. Remarks at Waterville, Maine, at a special meeting of the stockholders of the Maine Central Railway Company. May 31. Octavo, pp. 50. 1870.

No. 66. Memorial to the Congress of the United States, for aid to the Portland, Rutland, Oswego, and Chicago Railway; with A BILL to secure cheap transportation of breadstuffs and provisions from the West to the seaboard, at uniform rates throughout the year, accompanying the same, January 19, 1871.

No. 66. First Annual Report of the Directors of the Portland, Rutland, Oswego, and Chicago Railway Company. July 26. Octavo, pp. 58. 1871.

FIRST ARTICLE ON THE ST. LAWRENCE AND ATLANTIC RAILWAY.

FOR THE SHERBROOKE GAZETTE.

THE recent movements, having in view the extension of a railroad from Montreal to the Atlantic coast, have attracted the attention of the business community throughout the Canadas and the Northern States of the Federal Union. That the accomplishment of the object desired will be eventually realized there can be no reasonable doubt, but as to the mode and manner, the time when, and the place where, there is still much room for discussion. Having recently traversed much of the territory in the neighborhood, and made myself acquainted with the proposed routes and the plans entertained by the respective friends of each, I felt inclined to state some facts, and make some suggestions that might perhaps be of interest to this portion of the country.

The great object in view is a railroad from Montreal to Boston. Two or three routes are proposed, but if we take into view the natural advantage of the country, the course of trade, and the circumstances favoring its accomplishment, the chances and the arguments are vastly in favor of the route by the way of Sherbrooke. Its central position as to Montreal and Quebec; its lying, too, directly in the line of the most easy and practicable route from both those cities to the Atlantic coast, or to any good port thereon, will, if the matter is understood, settle the point in favor of the Sherbrooke route.

There has been so little intercourse with Maine heretofore, that the people of this region are very generally unmindful of the fact that Portland in Maine, with one of the best, if not the very best, harbor of the United States, is one hundred miles nearer to Montreal than Boston; and taking into view the facilities for a railroad, there cannot be a doubt that the best way of reaching Boston from Montreal is by the way of Portland.

The route most talked of here is by the way of Concord, New Hampshire. The distances are as follows, viz.:

Montreal to Sherbrooke	91 miles
Sherbrooke to Stanstead	34 miles
Stanstead to Haverhill	80 miles
Haverhill to Concord	70 miles
	275 miles
Railroad, Concord to Boston	76 miles
Total	351 miles

The distances by way of Portland are as follows, viz.:

Montreal to Sherbrooke	91 miles
Sherbrooke to Canaan, Vermont	31 miles
Canaan to Colebrooke, New Hampshire	10 miles
Colebrooke to Letter B, Maine	30 miles
Andover to Portland	70 miles
	246 miles

Railroad, Portland to Boston............................	105 miles
Total............................	351 miles
The distance to make by Concord is..............	275 miles
The distance by Portland........................	246 miles

making an advantage of twenty-nine miles in favor of the Portland route.

If the railroad ran from Montreal to Portland, the British mail steamers might land at that place, which has a far better winter harbor than Boston, and is about half a day's sail short of Boston.

Boston has a vast amount of capital, and would at once construct a railroad to Montreal, if her business could be thereby proportionally increased. But it is the opinion of many men there that Montreal would gain more by the railroad than their city.

The people of Maine have, if possible, less information in regard to the business and importance of the Canadas than your people have of her resources. The intercourse between the two countries has been trifling. But now the settlements, having been pushed back toward each other, are beginning to meet, and their people to understand respectively their position to each other, and the importance of opening means of communication. They are beginning to awake to your movements and will, I have no doubt, meet you with corresponding efforts. There is much more reason to expect success by the people of this region pushing for Portland than for Concord. A railroad from Montreal to Portland is sure to go by way of Sherbrooke: there are competitors for the Concord route. Again, too, Quebec is as much interested in the route as the citizens of this region. The St. Lawrence River may be reached seventy-three miles from Sherbrooke; Quebec in one hundred and eighteen. Quebec will then be but two hundred and seventy-four miles from Portland, and the distance by the Kennebec route is three hundred miles.

But whether a railroad can be speedily expected or not from Sherbrooke to Portland, a good stage road can easily be made; thereby connecting the St. Lawrence River, at its different points, with Portland, the principal seaport, and Augusta, the capital of Maine, and that, too, in the most direct route to the Atlantic coast. The latter place is only fifty miles from Andover, making the distance from Sherbrooke to Augusta one hundred and thirty-five miles, and from Montreal to Augusta two hundred and twenty-six miles.

From Portland to Andover is one of the most level routes in the country, and a fine stage coach now runs three times a week each way, in twelve hours' time.

From Andover to the line of New Hampshire a good road would at once be finished, if exertions should be made here to extend the road from Sherbrooke to the Canada line. The enterprising people of Colebrooke are exerting themselves, and will cause the road to be opened across New Hampshire, as soon as the residue of the way is completed; so that the people of Montreal can, by the way of Portland and Sherbrooke, get European news one day sooner than by any other route.

The eighty-five miles of road between Andover to Sherbrooke are all passable with wagons, though some parts are rough and unfinished. If it all lay in one of the States, so important a line of communication would not be neglected a single day. Situated as it is, the citizens of Canada, New Hampshire, and Maine along this road need only see how important it is to their interests, to ensure its speedy and thorough completion.

The immense trade between Canada and the States is far from being generally understood; and it would rapidly increase, if facilities of communication existed. The recent census shows a population of about fifteen hundred thousand in Canada, and Montreal is the great depôt of its business.

For nearly six months of the year all communication by water with the home government is cut off. Her immense products want a passage to a place of shipment on the Atlantic coast. Let her have this, and there is no country under heaven that has equal advantages.

Her splendid canals will next year give her a line of inland communication of more than fifteen hundred miles, through one of the most fertile districts in the world; and with her magnificent water-power and great capacities for production, she need not fear comparison with any portion of the globe.

A Citizen of Maine.

SHERBROOKE, *September* 5, 1844.

FIRST ARTICLE ON THE ATLANTIC AND ST. LAWRENCE RAILWAY.

FOR THE PORTLAND ADVERTISER.

So much has been said, heretofore, in reference to a railroad from Portland, running north or west,—at one time proposing to connect with Lake Champlain, and at others with Quebec and the Canadas,—without producing any results favorable to the objects proposed, that any remarks upon the subject may seem idle and superfluous. But a recent visit to the territory naturally connected with Portland, and a knowledge of the measures now in progress in the Canadas to secure railroad communication with the Atlantic coast, lead me to make some suggestions for the consideration of the citizens of Maine, and particularly those of the city of Portland.

There was a plan entertained a few years since of running a railroad from some point on the Atlantic coast in Maine to Quebec. The movement, I think, proceeded upon an erroneous view of the Canadas. Quebec is a place of very little importance, except as a military station, and a port for the shipment of lumber, and its lumber trade is less than that of Bangor in our own state. Its high northern latitude and frontier position have caused its former trade to pass gradually into the hands of its more prosperous rival, Montreal. The city of Montreal is now the political as well as the commercial capital of the Canadas, and from its position and natural advantages is destined to be one of the three great cities of the continent. It is the natural depôt of the business of the valley of the St. Lawrence, the extent and value of which are very inadequately understood by the people of the United States; while the magnificent chain of its inland seas and the surpassing attraction of its variegated scenery are celebrated throughout the world.

The progress of the Canadas in business, population, and wealth is equal to that of the most favored states of the Union. A recent census, just completed, shows a population of about fifteen hundred thousand, which shows that it has nearly doubled in twenty years—a growth more rapid than that of the state of New York. Her business has increased in a still greater ratio, owing to her facilities of trade with the home government and means of supplying British goods along the two thousand miles of our frontier. These facilities are being rapidly increased. Her public works are of an equal cost with those of the state of New York, and are accomplished with greater assurances of success as to business advantages.

The *Rideau Canal*, one hundred and thirty-five miles long, connecting the Ottawa with Lake Ontario at Kingston, though undertaken as a military work, and paid for from the military chest, at an expense of seven million dollars, is a work of great importance in a business point of view, it being the upward route of the large steamers which pass down the Long Sault Rapids.

The *Welland Canal*, forty-two miles long, connecting Lakes Erie and Ontario for sloop navigation, passing Niagara Falls, originally cost two million dollars. This canal is now in the process of enlargement, to correspond with the great canals on the St. Lawrence River; and when completed will be furnished with fifty-five feet locks, and ten feet depth of water, so as to allow the passage of steamers of one hundred and eighty feet in length and four hundred or five hundred tons burthen. This is a link in the great line of canals commencing at Montreal.

Of these the first is the *Lachine Canal*, from Montreal to the village of Lachine (eight miles), which distance is now passed by stage in descending the river.

The next is the *Beauharnois Canal*, which extends sixteen miles, passing the Cedar Rapids, so celebrated for their disasters.

The third is the *St. Lawrence Canal*, now finished and extending twelve miles, and passing the Long Sault Rapids.

These three last-named works will cost over seven million dollars, and be completed, as will also the enlargement of the Welland Canal, during the coming year, 1845; so that, during the coming year, steamboats of a large size and other vessels will have a continuous line of communication from the Gulf of Newfoundland up the whole length of the St. Lawrence River through the Great Lakes to the head of

Lake Superior, if not to the Lake of the Woods, a distance of over two thousand miles.

The trade and traffic of the vast region drained by the St. Lawrence River on the Canada side, and much on the American, centres at, or radiates from, Montreal. Already containing a population of over fifty thousand, it is now increasing both in population and business, relatively faster than any city on the continent. There is only one drawback to the growth and prosperity of this city, and that is the interruption of the communication with the ocean for the long period of winter.

The climate of all British North America below the forty-seventh degree of latitude, except in the neighborhood of the Atlantic coast, is exceedingly mild, and the soil one of great fertility. Fruits of all kinds are abundantly raised at Montreal, and the climate is much softer than that farther south in the highland regions of Maine, New Hampshire, and Vermont.

The St. Lawrence River enters the ocean between the forty-ninth and fifty-first degree of latitude, and for six months in the year its navigation is dangerous or entirely obstructed. This is a serious check to the business of Montreal. One great staple of the Canadas—*flour*—can with difficulty be got to the market in season for fall navigation; and the fluctuations in price frequently lead to great losses, which a ready shipment would avert. Last winter almost the whole stock of flour lay over till spring; and, before it could be shipped, had fallen something like one dollar and fifty cents per barrel.

No one can fail for a moment to see that the city of Montreal must have an outlet to the Atlantic coast. This subject is now occupying the attention of the people of Canada, and her movements are attracting the attention of the people of the United States, on some of the proposed routes.

No little diversity of opinion exists as to the best route to be selected, but no one doubts the early accomplishment of this object. Meetings have been held in various places and moneys raised to explore and survey the best routes. I was at Sherbrooke a few days since, and was surprised to find so much interest and enthusiasm on the subject. This is a thriving Yankee-looking village, and the headquarters of the British-American Land Company, who own large quantities of land in the eastern townships. These townships embrace a territory equal in size to the state of Vermont, with a soil far superior in quality. This region is rapidly filling up, and improvements of all sorts are in progress. A cotton factory, eighty feet by forty, is now being erected at Sherbrooke.

Situated in the central position as to Montreal and Quebec and in the line of the most direct and practicable route to the Atlantic coast, the people of Sherbrooke confidently expect the proposed railroad to pass through their town. It is ninety-one miles from there to Montreal, seventy-three to the St. Lawrence River, and one hundred and eighteen to Quebec. A survey for a railroad is already in progress from Montreal to Sherbrooke, and the people of that region are seeking the best outlet to the ocean.

The distance to Portland is as follows:

Montreal to Sherbrooke	91 miles
Sherbrooke to Canaan	30 miles
Canaan to Colebrooke (New Hampshire)	10 miles
Colebrooke to Andover	43 miles
Andover to Portland	72 miles
Total	246 miles

Another route spoken of is by way of Concord, New Hampshire, to Boston; the distances are as follows. viz:

Montreal to Sherbrooke	91 miles
Sherbrook to Stanstead	34 miles
Stanstead to Haverhill	80 miles
Haverhill to Concord	70 miles
Concord to Boston	76 miles
Total	351 miles

Another route still talked of, by the way of Brattleborough, and thence to Sherbrooke or Burlington. But more difficulties are to be anticipated in finding a route there than by way of Concord.

Boston may be reached by the way of Portland as easily as by Concord; and by twenty-nine miles less of road to be built.

One strong reason requiring the opening of a railroad from Montreal to the Atlantic is the necessity of more rapid transmission of the great British mail. The difficulties of the navigation of the Newfoundland seas and the St. Lawrence are such that after this year the Halifax and Quebec line is to be given up, and the Cunard steamers will not touch at Halifax. It is exceedingly important that the shortest route should be preferred. Every citizen of Portland is aware that his city is more than one hundred miles nearer Montreal than Boston is; but the people of the Canadas are not generally aware of the fact. It is known, too, to almost every one in Maine, that the easiest and most practicable route for a railroad is by the way of Sherbrooke to Portland; and yet the people of Portland are far from being alive to the importance of this railroad to her prosperity. The vast products of Canada only want a road to make their transit to Portland, thence to be forwarded to England, or our goods taken in return. The sale of American goods in Canada is far more than is commonly supposed. American goods to over three million dollars in value paid duty at the city of St. Johns at the foot of Lake Champlain, in the year 1843; and this is believed by good judges to be less than one fifth of the whole amount which annually passes into Canada. An important portion of this trade would go by a railroad.

The citizens of Portland may rest assured that within a short time a railroad will be extended to some point on the Atlantic coast from Montreal. So much is certain, when and where is for them to say. It would require volumes to point out the advantages of it to your city, and I cannot believe they will remain indifferent while these advantages are within their reach.

P.

ANDOVER, *September* 10, 1844.

PLAN FOR SHORTENING THE TIME OF PASSAGE BETWEEN NEW YORK AND LONDON.

THE plan of extending a line of railway across the State of Maine and the Provinces of New Brunswick and Nova Scotia to the nearest available point of North America to Ireland has been frequently suggested to very many minds of both continents—looking at the question from various and distinct points of observation. No one familiar with the commonest principles of commercial economy can for a moment doubt the truth of the assertion, that at some time or other the necessities of trade will require the adoption of the shortest possible sea voyage between the continents of Europe and America. The discerning minds of both continents, have seen the rapid approach of this event in the various measures by which the lines of railway have been pushed out from the great commercial centres of England and the United States toward each other, in the general direction of the shortest line between them; and in the employment of steamships of the most approved models for speed and safety, in preference to the ordinary sailing vessels of former times.

To have attempted to carry out the idea of reducing the time of passage between New York and London to its lowest possible limit at the time the line of the Cunard steamers was established, would have been premature. The plan can never be properly successful till the business along the railway lines from London to the west coast of Ireland, and from New York to Canso, including through and way business united, will justify the investment of the capital necessary for its completion. Whether or not that time has arrived is a question which has been fairly propounded, and which the business men of both countries are now preparing to solve. The movement on this continent toward accomplishing this result has been made, in consequence of the grant of money made by the British government toward the completion of the Midland Great Western Railway of Ireland, to extend from Dublin to Galway; and in aid of the Britannia Tubular Bridge.

Under the impression that the completion of the line of railway across the Menai Strait and across the breadth of Ireland must change the course of travel, and the point of its embarkation to this continent from the British Islands and the continent of Europe, an effort was made to arouse the public mind of Maine in favor of a corresponding movement on this side of the Atlantic, at a railroad meeting held at Bangor in February, 1850. The interest awakened by the discussion on that occasion led to the presentation of the matter to the Legislature of Maine, in the following petition, which was laid before that body:

PETITION.

To the Honorable, the Senate and House of Representatives of the State of Maine, in session at Augusta, A.D. 1850:—The undersigned, citizens of Maine, respectfully request your honorable body to cause to be surveyed and ascertained, the most practicable route for a railway from the city of Bangor to the eastern boundary of the state, in the general direction of the city of St. John, New Brunswick; and to take such further action in the premises as will tend to favor the construction of a railroad from the city of Bangor to some good harbor on the eastern shore of Nova Scotia, or Cape Breton, best fitted to become the entrepôt and terminus for the most direct line of Transatlantic navigation.

From the easternmost point of Nova Scotia, Cape Canso, in latitude 45 deg. 17 min. N. and in longitude 61 deg. 3 min. W., to Galway Bay, in Ireland, in latitude 53 deg. 13 min. N. and in longitude 9 deg. 13 min. W., the distance is about 2,000 miles. Assuming a speed of seventeen miles an hour in steam vessels, the Atlantic Ocean can be crossed between these points in FIVE DAYS' time.

The nearest accessible harbor to Cape Canso—Whitehaven, in latitude 45 deg. 10 min. N., longitude 61 deg. 10 min. W., according to the authority of Admiral Owen, in a report on the subject made to Sir John Harvey, September, 1846—"is a most splendid and commodious port, at the nearest available point of North America to Ireland; its natural facilities greatly exceeding those of Halifax, or any other point upon the coast." Galway Harbor is one of the finest in the world, having great advantages over Bristol or Liverpool as a steamship terminus.

The Gut of Canso could possibly be passed by a bridge; but upon this point there is at present no satisfactory information. By means of a ferry across the Gut of Canso, the line could be extended to Louisburg Harbor in Cape Breton, still farther east, to a point less than two thousand miles distant from Galway Bay, as will appear by map or plan.

From Galway to Dublin a line of railway is nearly completed across Ireland, and is in actual operation from Dublin to Mullingar, a distance of fifty miles. From Dublin, the distance of sixty-three miles across the Irish Channel to Holyhead, is passed with steam packets, at the rate of eighteen miles an hour, to which place the Chester and Holyhead Railway is already finished, connecting with Liverpool and London—crossing the Menai Strait by the Britannia Tubular Bridge, which was opened for traffic on the 18th of March, 1850.

The route of the steamship from Liverpool to New York passes near to Cape Race in Newfoundland, Cape Breton, and Cape Canso, and thence along the coast of Nova Scotia by Cape Sable, and parallel with the general line of the coast of New Brunswick and Maine. From Cape Canso to New York the distance can be passed in about the length of line by land as by water, and in one third the time. From New York to Waterville the railway is already finished, a distance of four hundred and ten miles. From Waterville to the city of St. John the distance would probably be about two hundred miles; and from St. John to Whitehaven less than two hundred and fifty miles farther; making the entire distance from New York to Whitehaven from eight hundred to nine hundred miles in all.

From Whitehaven to the head of the Bay of Fundy, at Sackville, a feasible route for a railway has been ascertained, passing near to Pictou, through the valuable coal districts along the shore of the Gulf of St. Lawrence; and it is believed that the Legislature of Nova Scotia would cheerfully engage to construct that part of the line whenever the other portions are secured.

A line of railway from Halifax, passing in the vicinity of Truro, could be easily connected at some feasible point with the main trunk; and it cannot be doubted that the enterprising citizens of Halifax would engage in its construction at once. At the present time they are urging the completion of a line from Halifax to Windsor, and a survey of the route has been accomplished.

From the city of St. John to Shediac Bay, on the Gulf of St. Lawrence, a line has been surveyed for a railway on the general line of the route to Sackville, and Provincial aid to a large amount proposed. The Province of New Brunswick has recently appropriated £60,000 currency—$240,000, to construct that portion of the distance between Shediac Bay and the bend of the Petecodiac River—the head of navigation on the Bay of Fundy. No doubt can be entertained that the Province would extend this line from a point of connection with the Nova Scotia line to the city of St. John; and it is believed that the local business of the country between the city of St. John and the head of the Bay of Fundy would at the present time pay a tolerable remuneration to the stockholders.

From the city of St. John to Bangor it is supposed that a route tolerably direct can be found without encountering serious obstacles. The necessary information upon this point has never been ascertained; and it is for the purpose of asking that this service may be speedily accomplished, that we approach your honorable body. From Bangor to Waterville private enterprise has already demonstrated the fact that either of several cheap and practicable routes can be adopted.

The only grant asked of the Legislature, or that will be necessary to obtain, is an appropriation sufficient to secure the completion of the remaining link in the line of surveys, and at a suitable time, the necessary grant of a charter to carry forward this work, which, from the progress of events, must soon claim the public attention.

The citizens of Maine are generally aware of the importance of the question to the best interests of the state; but the work is too great for individuals to undertake with their present means. The proper surveys once being completed would place before the country the great advantage of the position of our state for a leading part in the commercial movements of the age. Private enterprise ought not to be so largely taxed as it must necessarily be without the grant of aid to the proposed survey in whole or in part by the state, for the purpose of procuring valuable information, equally desired by, or at any rate of equal importance to, all. Maine ought not, either, to remain indifferent to the great advantages which may now be brought within her reach by a proper attention to the great movements in ocean steam navigation and commercial affairs.

The most strenuous efforts are now made to revive the plan of the Quebec and Halifax line; and various projects are now engaging the attention of the British Provinces, with a view to secure in some form the aid of the home government. The movement is gaining favor in Great Britain. From Halifax to Quebec the distance, according to the survey for a railroad by Major Robinson, is six hundred and thirty-five miles; and this road is urged upon public attention with a view to draw over it a portion of the Western trade, and place the Lower Provinces in the great line of communication between the grain-growing regions of this continent and Europe. Without going into an extended examination of the merits of this project, it seems to us that it must strike every intelligent mind that the most natural—the cheapest and best—mode of obtaining a communication by railway between the Lower Provinces and Montreal and the West will be found by extending a line of railway in the direction of Bangor and Waterville, Maine. From Waterville to Montreal, a distance of three hundred miles, the entire line is finished or under contract for completion in 1852, and a branch to Quebec may be regarded as secured within three years from the present time.

The highest importance therefore attaches to every movement having reference to the extension of railways east of Bangor, or from the Lower Provinces in the direction of the St. Lawrence River. One great central line for the whole state, and for European communication, once laid down, into which the various branch lines could enter, on either side as required—connected with a line extending to Montreal and Quebec,—a system of railways would be secured surpassing in value and importance any that has yet been proposed.

It is not proposed to urge any one to embark hastily in the construction of the projected line; but to so far present the advantages of this route for the great ends in view, over any other possible line, as to secure for it such aid as in the progress of events its advantages may call forth. If the practicability of the line were properly demonstrated, it is believed that it would command support from the great commercial interests of Great Britain and the United States. If already built, no one can doubt the value of the undertaking as a mode of profitable investment. Those who may incline to hesitate, in yielding assent to the truth of this assertion, are invited to very carefully review the present condition of affairs.

The United States now embrace a territory of 2,187,490 square miles not organized into states, including Texas. If this whole territory was as densely populated as the state of Massachusetts, it would contain a population of over two hundred millions of people. The same extent of territory in

Europe, under similar climate, and with fewer natural advantages, contains a still greater population, while the United Kingdom of Great Britain and Ireland has a ratio of population to the square mile more than twice as great as Massachusetts. The twenty-nine remaining states, exclusive of Texas, comprise an extent of 1,065,158 square miles more. The increase of population in the United states from 1790 to 1800, was at the rate of 35.01 per cent.; from 1800 to 1810, 36.45 per cent.; from 1810 to 1820, 33.35 per cent.; from 1820 to 1830, 33.26 per cent.; from 1830 to 1840, 32.67 per cent. It is believed that the census of 1850 will show that from 1840 to 1850, the increase has been as great as at any other period of ten years. Causes now at work tend rather to increase than diminish the ratio of increase; and many now alive will see this nation numbering one hundred and fifty millions of people.

Commercial intercourse between the United States and Europe has gone on increasing more rapidly than the population of the country. In the year 1820, the attempt was first made to establish a line of packet ships to Liverpool, to sail on certain stated days. Almost every one prophesied their failure, though embracing only two in number, and of 450 tons burthen. At this time there are lines of regular sailing packets from all our large cities, embracing vessels of over 2,000 tons burthen, and reaching hundreds of ships in number.

About fifteen years ago, the scientific world listened with attention to the assertion of the learned Dr. Lardner, that it was impossible to navigate the

Atlantic Ocean by steam. This theory was disproved by the arrival of two steamers, the *Sirius* and the *Great Western*, in New York Harbor, one from Bristol, the other from Liverpool, on the 23d day of April, 1838, both on the same day. More than twenty steamships during the present year will run as regular packets between this country and Europe, while the number of sailing vessels is greater than at any former period.

The number of immigrants which arrived in New York in 1838 was 25,581. In 1849, the number reached 231,779. The number which left the United Kingdom of Great Britain and Ireland for the United States in 1848, was 188,223; and the whole immigration into this country in that year exceeded 250,000. In the year 1849, the number of immigrant arrivals reached 325,000; and it is estimated that the number will exceed 400,000 the present year.

Every year gives fresh impulses to the cause of immigration to the United States, and the disturbed condition of all commercial affairs on the continent of Europe is operating to invite a better class of immigrants than heretofore, embracing much of the skill and mechanical industry of Switzerland, France, and Germany.

The most indifferent observer will admit that the increase of facilities for travel with Europe, must increase far more rapidly for the next ten years, than at any former period. The trade between the United States and Great Britain is constantly increasing and at the present moment beyond any former example. The exports to England in 1840, were $24,599,666, in 1848 $71,752,315. The imports from England in 1830, were $22,755,040, in 1848 $59,763,522. Both exports and imports in 1847 exceeded those of 1848, but the extraordinary demand for food occasioned by the famine in Ireland, gave an unusual impulse to trade in that year.

A route which would enable the traveller to see an attractive portion of this continent, the best portion of Ireland, and the most extraordinary work of human skill, the Britannia Tubular Bridge, would of itself invite the pleasure tourist to take this route, if no saving of time or expense were secured. But it is confidently asserted that while to the man of business the same attractions would be offered by the plan proposed, the expense of a trip to Europe can be largely reduced, while it shall save him much if not all uncertainty as to the time of his arrival, and some days' time for purposes of business.

From New York to Liverpool, in the shortest line, is 3,000 miles, the route usually traversed is over 3,300 miles. By taking the railway from New York to Halifax or Canso, employing the swiftest steam packet from thence to Galway, crossing the Great Midland Railway from Galway to Dublin, a distance of about 120 miles, and from thence to Holyhead Harbor, a distance of 63 miles, and from thence to London, by the Chester and Holyhead and London and Northwestern Railways, a distance of 263 miles—employing about 1,200 miles of railway, and 2,000 miles of steam navigation,—the passage from New York to London may be reduced to seven days' time at all events, and possibly to six days within a few years at farthest.

This can only be achieved by shortening the sea voyage, and dispensing with the vast weight of coal and other superfluous load now carried. Vessels designed for crossing the ocean with speed, should be relieved of all load not requisite for steadiness and good carriage. Ordinary merchandise will always go more cheaply in sailing vessels. Valuable goods could be transferred to boats of still greater speed, from the ocean terminus, running if necessary to the various Atlantic cities, if too bulky to go by railway. In this way, the safest and swiftest passage would be secured. In a few years, instead of a semi-weekly, a daily arrival of steamships may be expected.

One hundred through passengers a day each way by the railway, would give a most profitable business to the road, in addition to its local business ; and the highest price would readily be paid for the carrying of the mails. The British and the American governments would willingly enter into a perpetual or permanent contract for this service, at rates of compensation representing a capital equal to one third the entire cost of the line. If the proper surveys were now completed, and the necessary charters granted, for a continuous line from Bangor to Whitehaven or Halifax, the scheme would offer inducements for the employment of capital, unsurpassed by any enterprise of the age.

Looking forward but twenty-five years only, we shall see this government containing fifty millions of people. Its great rivers and inland seas—its mineral wealth and inexhaustible soil—within a latitude favorable to health of body and vigor of mind,—all conspire to give the fullest development to the spirit of progress, requisite to supply means for the fullest gratification of every want known to the highest civilization.

Under any form of government known to civilized man, the progress of the race would be, under such influences, rapid and vigorous. When, therefore, an enterprising race, in the possession of such physical advantages as this country possesses, are stimulated to exertion by the action of a free government upon the energies of the whole people, we may confidently expect a higher development in the ideas and institutions of society, and a more practical application of knowledge to the wants and necessities of life.

Maine, from her frontier position and severe climate, has been heretofore regarded as the least favored of all the states in the Union; while it has the power to become the great manufacturing and great ship-owning state of the Confederacy, if not the first in point of commercial importance. Our climate and our geographical position, generally spoken of as our misfortunes, are in fact the great elements of our strength. The increased necessities which our climate imposes upon us, beyond those of a warmer latitude, are far more than compensated by our superior capacity for labor, our greater power of endurance, and our extraordinary fondness for exertion. With a more extended line of sea-coast than any other state in the Union, and more good harbors than all the other states together, Maine will present at some future day, along her bays and rivers, a line of cities surpassing those which are now found upon the shores of the English Channel, or the Baltic Sea.

This result will be hastened by attracting into our own state the great stream of European business and travel, where it shall divide into two great channels —one flowing northward to the St. Lawrence valley and the West, the other flowing southward to the great commercial cities of the continent.

Without the fertile soil of the West, or the rich deposits of coal and iron of Pennsylvania, Maine for twenty years past has not kept pace with the ratio of increase of the whole country. From 1820 to 1830, the ratio of her increase was 33.9 per cent., or about the same as that of the whole Union. From 1830 to 1840 the rate of increase was only 26.2 per cent. Notwithstanding the healthiness of our climate, the extent of our public lands, with all the facilities inviting emigration from the more densely populated districts of New England, immigration into the state had become nearly stationary, and the tendency of our people to emigrate west, remained unchecked, till the movement was made to construct a railroad from Portland to Montreal. The effect of that movement is already apparent upon the character, the enterprise, and the business of the state. A small portion only of the energy which has been applied to that undertaking, will speedily accomplish the end now proposed;—favorably affecting that great enterprise, and all the leading interests of Maine.

The time is not regarded by most persons as particularly favorable for entering upon new enterprises. The great interests of Maine, ship-building and lumbering, for some three years past have been severely depressed, furnishing less returns even than investments in railways. These, in common with all other business interests, are destined at times to suffer. Railway property will, however, advance in value with the growth and increase of business in the state; while it will also tend to foster industry and stimulate production in every department of labor, beyond any other species of investment.

It is in vain to expect to retain the natural increase of our population without holding out inducements for labor beyond what are offered by the pursuits of agriculture and lumbering; and we have failed so far to attract to this state the most valuable class of immigrants, that seek for a climate and soil similar to those of Germany and Switzerland, which resembles our own. If proper encouragement was held out to them, we might expect emigrants from the north of Europe to prefer the soil and climate of Maine to those of the Mississippi Valley. Instead of this, for a series of years we have been compelled to witness the gradual withdrawal of much of our capital into enterprises of other states, and a departure from among us of many of the most enterprising of the young men of Maine. Real estate has advanced but moderately in value for the last fifteen years, while the new states have grown up within that brief period into wealth and importance. Our frontier position, and the want of a proper state pride and a state policy, have been pointed out as the principal hindrances to the growth of Maine. The opening of the great avenues already in progress and proposed, placing Maine in the direct line of the great commercial intercourse of the globe, will create new relations in every department of business, and call into exercise such agencies as will soon give to Maine a strength and a position equal to that of any portion of the Union.

The present period seems to us favorable for the proposed movement. An experiment is now making to run steamships from Galway to Halifax, aided by the Great Midland Railway Company of Ireland. The capital of this company is £2,596,666, or more than 12,000,000 of dollars.

This company has a direct interest to subserve by inviting the travel between this country and Europe upon its road. The same is true also of the Chester and Holyhead and the London and Northwestern Railway Companies. These companies, with their various branch lines — under one management — embrace nearly one eighth of the entire traffic of the United Kingdom. The London and Northwestern Railway Company, August 1, 1849, owned $478\frac{1}{2}$ miles of road already finished—built at a cost of £30,617,620, or $150,000,000—$60\frac{3}{4}$ miles more in progress, and held the leases of over 200 miles more—including the Chester and Holyhead Railway, representing a capital of at least 200,000,000 of dollars. Amid all the depressions of railway stocks and business, for the past few years in England, the stock of this company has never been sold except above par; and by the recent advices from Europe, was selling at an advance. The influence of this capital will be brought at once, in aid of any line that shall bring across Ireland to Dublin the travel of this continent. The same motive which induced the British Government to aid the construction of the Britannia Bridge,—to obtain the most direct route from London to Ireland,—will lead them to favor the plan herein proposed.

Believing, therefore, that the state has only to display to the business community the practicability and advantages of this great route through Maine, to insure at the proper time its completion, we respectfully ask your honorable body to cause the line from Bangor to St. John to be surveyed at the expense of the state, and such further measures adopted as will give proper encouragement to the undertaking.

June 12, 1850.

STATE OF MAINE.
HOUSE OF REPRESENTATIVES, *June* 15, 1850.

Ordered, That 500 copies of the foregoing petition be printed for the use of the Legislature.

The printed copies of this petition and map reached the Provinces of New Brunswick and Nova Scotia by a most fortunate concurrence of circumstances, through the agency of A. C. Morton, Esq., the distinguished engineer of the Portland and Montreal Railroad, at or about the time of the receipt of the following despatch of Earl Grey, Colonial Secretary, which negatived forever the request for government assistance to the Quebec and Halifax Railway.

DOWNING STREET, *June* 19, 1850.

SIR :—I have to acknowledge your dispatch No. 168, of the 2d ult., enclosing a resolution of the Legislative Council, that an address be presented to yourself, requesting you again to call the attention of her Majesty's government to the subject of the proposed railway from Halifax to Quebec.

Her Majesty's government have not failed to give their best attention to a subject in which so deep an interest is taken by the inhabitants of Nova Scotia. But I am bound to state, that they are not prepared to submit to Parliament any measure for raising the funds necessary for its construction, considering the great amount and pressure of the exigencies which continue to weigh on the Imperial treasury.

[Signed]   I have, &c., &c.,
GREY.

Lieut.-Governor Sir JOHN HARVEY, &c.

The receipt of the plan for the proposed railway through the Provinces and Maine, followed by the despatch of Earl Grey, aroused at once to the highest pitch of excitement the people of the lower British Provinces in favor of the scheme, and awakened a corresponding feeling in the minds of the citizens of Quebec. The plan of a convention at Portland, Maine, to consider the various schemes which had been proposed to connect the upper and lower British Provinces by railway, was at once agreed upon, and the necessary measures put in progress toward its accomplishment.

An invitation in the form of a circular was issued by a committee of the citizens of Portland, addressed to the Governor, the Council, and the Legislature of Maine, the railroad companies, and friends of public improvement throughout the United States and the several British Provinces. The purposes of said convention were set forth in the circular of said committee, as follows:

CIRCULAR.

The plan of extending a line of railway through the State of Maine to the lower British Provinces, and to some good harbor on the eastern coast of Nova Scotia has long been regarded as a measure of the highest importance to the commercial interests of this continent and Europe. Events which have occurred on this side the Atlantic within the last few years, in the British Provinces and the United States, have led the most discerning minds of both countries to concur in the belief that the time is rapidly approaching, if not already arrived, when an effort should be made, by all parties interested in such a result, towards its consummation.

The region of this continent lying to the East of Lake Champlain and the Hudson River, and between the river and the Gulf of St. Lawrence and the Atlantic Ocean,—in reference to its geological features, its topographical and physical geography,—presents many striking characteristics, inviting the attention of the naturalist and the scientific inquirer. Its soil, climate, and commercial advantages indicate that it possesses the greatest natural advantages for the development of the highest physical and social condition of man, and point it out as the future abode of the most enterprising portion of the race.

This region of country, from the circumstances of its early settlement and the political changes it has undergone, has witnessed the most exciting scenes in the history of this continent, has been the theatre of the fierce contests of different races, and shared in all the eventful changes with which for more than two centuries the nations of Europe have been disturbed.

The final predominance of the English race throughout this region had scarcely become established, when new relations awakened an equally embittered hostility between England and her former subjects, leading both countries into bloody and destructive wars.

The spirit of peace has at last prevailed—national animosities, sectional and political hostility, have disappeared between the English races since the establishment of the boundaries of Maine and Oregon, and the contests of war have been succeeded by a noble and generous rivalry for the promotion of the arts of peace.

The introduction of the steamship and the railway has made former enemies friends, and the citizens of Montreal and Portland, of Halifax and Boston, of St. John and New York, are to all intents and purposes one people, speaking a common language and struggling for the same destiny. National hostility has given way to commercial and social intercourse, and under whatever form of government they may hereafter exist, they can never again become hostile or unfriendly.

An effort is now made to increase the means of communication between different parts of this extended region. In aid of this purpose, a convention is to be held at Portland, on the 31st of July instant, at eleven of the clock in the forenoon, at the City Hall, at which time and place it is proposed to consider the various schemes which have been proposed for the accomplishment of this result. The immediate object of this convention is to agree upon the most feasible plan for prolonging the line of railway from the state of Maine to the lower British Provinces, to some good harbor best fitted to become the entrepôt and terminus for the most direct line of Transatlantic navigation, and form a connection by railway between the upper and lower British Provinces through the state of Maine.

Such a line of railway extended from New York and Montreal to a point of connection in Maine, and from thence to Halifax, would undoubtedly prove the most popular and most frequented highway for all travellers between Europe and America, and a great thoroughfare both for the old and new world. The Atlantic can be most readily crossed from the eastern coast of Nova Scotia to the western coast of Ireland, thence by railway to Dublin, and by steam to Holyhead, whence the Menai Strait is crossed by the Britannia Tubular Bridge, and so to London or Liverpool, or any part of Great Britain or the continent of Europe. One great central line for European communication once laid down, into which the various branch lines could enter on either side as required, connected also by lines of railway with Montreal and Quebec, would secure a system of railways surpassing in value and importance any that has yet been proposed.

* * * * * * * *

We are encouraged to believe that the completion of this great work can be secured within a reasonable time, without withdrawing any portion of the means of the people along the line, wanted by them for the ordinary purposes of business. A liberal grant of public lands, and of public credit, from Nova Scotia, New Brunswick, and Canada, equal to that tendered in aid of the Quebec and Halifax Railway, with suitable compensation from the British and American governments for the carrying of the mails, will, we believe, at once invite into it private capital from Europe and the commercial interests of this country fully adequate to its early completion.

But whatever may be the pecuniary merits of the enterprise, it has social and commercial relations of the most delicate and patriotic character. Whatever shall tend to allay national prejudice, and harmonize national differences, contributes to advance the highest interests of humanity, and promote the welfare of the race.

The most sublime spectacle which the history of the world has ever disclosed, is being enacted in our day by the advancement of the English race towards universal supremacy,—a supremacy not maintained by tyranny or force, but resting upon the solid foundations of intellectual superiority—a love of freedom and of social order. Regardless of artificial lines of demarkation, or of the political divisions of this continent, we desire that intercourse between those who speak a common language, and are striving for the same destiny, shall be as free as the thoughts of the mighty race who have become the masters of the world.

PORTLAND, *July* 13, 1850.

THE NORTHEASTERN BOUNDARY.

REPORT OF THE SELECT COMMITTEE OF THE HOUSE OF REPRESENTATIVES.

SUBJECTS of the gravest character are necessarily involved in the resolutions and other legislative proceedings of the state of Maine submitted to the committee; calling for inquiry into systems of military defence, the value of railways as a means of attack and defence in time of war, and a careful consideration of the force of national obligation and of public faith growing out of the complex relations of federal and state governments under our national Constitution. With every desire to present the matters referred to them intelligently to Congress, the committee have sought to abridge into the narrowest limits possible the statements of fact and of argument which have influenced their judgment in reaching the conclusion that the general government should co-operate with Maine in its efforts to provide defences for the northeastern frontier.

The northeastern boundary dispute has been one of the most embarrassing subjects of American diplomacy, and has filled a large space in the public discussions and in the annals of the State Department, more so, perhaps, than any other public question since the foundation of the government. It will always forcibly recur to the thoughts of public men and to the minds of our people on the suggestion of a possibility of a disturbance of our friendly relations with Great Britain. The political disclosures of the last twenty years, the gradual modification of the colonial policy of England, and the increasing intimacy of the people on each side of the line along the eastern and the northern border, enable us the better to understand the motives of England in seizing upon that northeastern section of the Union. The possession of this territory afforded her the means of communication between her upper and lower provinces in the war of 1812-15, and she held it with unyielding pertinacity, menacing a war, until she induced our government to acquire the consent of Maine, and to surrender a military route through the valley of the river St. John, and yield up to her this key to her North American possessions.

Maine held this territory by an unquestioned title. Without her consent there was no power to agree on a conventional line of boundary which should secure to Great Britain this greatly coveted advantage. Such was the explicit statement of our government in all its negotiations with Great Britain, asserted by Hon. Edward Livingston, Secretary of State in General Jackson's administration, in his despatch of July 21, 1832, to Charles Bankhead; and by Hon. Mr. Forsyth, and others, from the time of the failure of the award of the King of the

Netherlands, to the conclusion of the treaty of Washington, August 9, 1842. The facts, therefore, set forth in the preamble to the resolutions of Maine, of March 25, 1864, in the words following, to wit: "Whereas it is made the duty of the federal government, under the Constitution of the United States, to protect and preserve the integrity of the Union, and defend each state in the maintenance of its sovereignty over its lawful territory; and whereas the original boundary of Maine extended northward to the dividing ridge that separates the St. Lawrence waters from those of the St. John River, the title to which was clear and unquestionable; and whereas the United States government neglected and refused to maintain and enforce the right of this state to the upper basin of the St. John River, permitting British troops to march across said territory in the war of 1812, and at the time of the Canadian rebellion in 1837, and afterwards to hold military possession of the country; and whereas the state of Maine, in 1838 and 1839, attempted to repossess herself of her lawful territory, and to protect her soil from spoliation by Provincial trespassers; and whereas the United States government interposed its paramount authority, calling upon Maine to withdraw all armed forces detailed for the protection of its territory, and assumed the duty and insisted on its right to exclusive control over all matters of needful defence of the same; and whereas this duty of defending the territory of Maine was so imperfectly performed by the United States government, that the territory was stripped of its most valuable timber before Maine could get possession of what remained to her after the ratification of the treaty of Washington, whereby a just and valid claim now exists against the general government which has been practically recognized by the federal authorities at Washington," cannot be called in question.

The matters involved in that controversy have often been presented, but their importance could not be realized at the time, and cannot be measured now without estimating the value of our institutions and forms of government in contrast with those of that nationality that now divides and holds dominion with us upon the continent of North America; and comprehending in some adequate measure the future of the race under two independent governments speaking a common language and striving for the same objects and the same destiny upon this broad theatre of the New World.

Vast as is our present national domain, it is less in extent than that of the colonial empire of Great Britain under the government of her North American Provinces, and that empire is in possession of such elements of strength as might lead her people to aspire to supremacy upon the continent, had they commercial advantages such as would be secured to them by the possession of the sea-coast of Maine. This sea-coast was the chief object, as it was also the principal theatre, of the terrific struggles between France and England from the first occupation of the country by the European races, till its final surrender to Great Britain at the close of the French war.

Waiving, for the present, all discussion as to the comparative advantages of the two systems of government now brought prominently into contrast by the expansion of the colonial empire of Great Britain in North America, and looking only at the chances of war, we must estimate the importance of the question before us, in view of our exposure to danger by the wresting from us of a further section of the eastern frontier—affording thereby, as it would, increased means of offence to an enemy, and diminishing our own strength, in the event of a European war. All external dangers to our country —all dangers arising from the possible diminution of our territory—lie at the east and north, along our eastern and northern frontiers. An enemy might burn and destroy the cities and towns of the seaboard in the Central and Southern States for the purpose of inflicting injury, as done, to some extent, in the war with England in 1812-15, but no one would think of penetrating very far into the interior of the country. No foreign power will ever wage war on us for the conquest of the heart or central portions of the country. The eastern seaboard, the northern lakes, and portions of the Pacific States, would be seized upon as worthy objects of conquest. The possession of these, or either of them, would give strength to our northern neighbor, whether the country continued under the dominion of England or were transferred to France.

A war between France and England would naturally lead to a struggle for the control of Canada; and in the event of a war between the

United States and Great Britain, Maine, all British North America, and the entire frontier from the mouth of the St. Croix to the Pacific Ocean, would be directly involved in the struggle.

The upper or interior provinces of Great Britain, originally belonging to France, with over a third of the present population of French origin, speaking their original language, and inheriting all the prejudices of their race, are situated, in reference to the commerce of the world, like the empire of Russia, dependent on the frozen Baltic or the narrow confines of the Black Sea. These British Provinces form a vast empire at the north of our boundary, extending across the breadth of the continent. Shut up in winter from active participation in the traffic of the Atlantic Ocean, the great theatre of the commerce of our day, it was long since perceived that they must have better access to the sea than is afforded by the natural outlets of the country. The merchants of Montreal had long realized this necessity, and they naturally fell in with the views of their neighbors in Maine in 1844, and embarked their means in a common enterprise—a railway from Montreal to Portland. This railway has given Canada an open seaport, inviting thither, by means of this new avenue to the St. Lawrence, the capital and trade of British North America. Portland is made the winter port of Canada, and the packet station, for twenty-four weeks of the year, of its lines of ocean steamers.

This line of railway is as important in its military aspects as in its commercial bearings; yet it had never entered into the military calculations of our government till attention was called to it by the authorities of Maine. All former plans of the War Office and of the Engineer Bureau were based on the idea that the route by the valley of Lake Champlain was the only one between the St. Lawrence and the seaboard till the valley of the Kennebec was reached; while the *prescience* and *forecast of commerce* connected the St. Lawrence and the Atlantic seaboard, in a favorable latitude, at the points where the navigable waters of each approach nearest—Montreal and Portland. One of the boldest and most successful of the commercial enterprises of modern times was the construction of this line of railway, with its extension across the Victoria Bridge at Montreal, and to the foot of Lake Huron, affording an uninterrupted line of railway, of uniform gauge, for the transit and transfer of freight, without change of cars, from all the lake ports from Sarnia to Montreal, into ocean steamers and sailing vessels at Portland harbor.

This magnificent river of commerce, though but a few years in operation, has already influenced the direction of business, if not changed the course of trade. Western produce, destined to Boston and other eastern New England ports, comes, to some extent, already, by way of Portland, over the Grand Trunk Railway, while Eastern Maine, and the lower provinces look more and more to this route every year for their supplies. Montreal is commercially situated, in reference to Portland, as Albany and Buffalo are to New York City, or Paris to Havre, in

France. With the growth of the Northwest, and the development of the lake trade, this comparison will be the more striking, for at this point on the St. Lawrence, during the season of navigation, the transfer of goods from sail-boats to sea-going vessels is effected. Hence, Portland and Montreal will naturally seek one commercial law for themselves, if not for the entire English-speaking and English-governed people of the continent. The commerce of these two cities has been rapidly developed by the railway. The import trade of Montreal increased from $9,245,884 in 1852, to $20,529,893 in 1862. Her exports were $2,119,228 in 1851, and $10,415,738 in 1861. The foreign imports into Portland in 1849 were $498,346. In 1863 they amounted to $9,034,520, including $8,419,005 passing into Canada, without the payment of duties. The exports of Portland to foreign countries were valued at $643,529 in 1849; in 1863 they reached a valuation of $5,018,356. These recent triumphs of the arts of peace, disclosing more distinctly the natural relations of the two countries, must influence the action of our national government—called upon to meet the new necessities which the experience of the hour and the civilization of the age call forth.

While extending national dominion, by the rapid expansion of our population, wealth, and material power, on each side of the continent, on the north and east by the surer conquest of the arts of peace, and the more intimate relations of commerce and trade, unmindful of political dangers at home, the people of the Northern States are summoned to new duties by the stirring scenes of civil war. Called to meet this new order of events, it is their duty to contemplate the certainties of the future. The future that lies before us is not that golden age anticipated and heretofore predicted by a hopeful view of past history. Our golden age is past. The future of our government must be one of stern responsibility, in view of the accumulated experience and burden of this hour of trial.

Our nation must soon be called upon to take the responsibilities of a great military and commercial power among the nations—duties heretofore unknown to American statesmanship—instead of yielding a blind submission to manifest destiny—a half-formed trust in accident and Providence.

British North America, holding the chief command of the North American fisheries, and all the outports of the continent east of the St. Croix, has to-day an extent of territory greater than was ever included in the boundaries of the American Union; and though its frontier on the Atlantic Ocean and the northern seas above the St. Lawrence is of comparatively little value for settlement, the eastern districts are full of all the elements of wealth; and the vast interior above our northern border, including the Pacific slope and the region drained by the rivers of the north, contains more arable wheat-growing land than the entire region of the United States lying between the Missouri River and the Pacific Ocean. This country is destined, in time, to sustain a population as dense as that inhabiting the same latitudes on the eastern continent, in

Northern Europe and Asia, and could sustain a population as great as that now under the dominion of the government of Russia. Wheat is raised over a breadth of more than eleven degrees of latitude north of the forty-ninth parallel, and Indian corn can be grown north of the forty-ninth parallel of north latitude, over the vast and well-watered table-land plains of the Northwest.

Dividing with us the empire of the great lakes; holding the outlet of that vast mediterranean sea, the St. Lawrence, from the forty-fifth parallel to the ocean, they can control the trade and transportation of all the Northwest, competing with us for the trade of the entire lake basin. Ships of a size capable of navigating the ocean can pass through the canals to Chicago and Superior City; and there in no reason to doubt that railroads and canals will yet connect Lake Superior with Lake Winnipeg, and the 750 miles of the navigable waters of the Saskatchewan send its traffic through this route to the Atlantic. There are those far-seeing enough to predict that in time, through these great watercourses of the Northwest, by connecting Frazer's River with the Saskatchewan River by canal, goods may be waterborne from the St. Lawrence to the Pacific seas.

British statesmanship, if not British diplomacy, has for the last fifty years concerned itself mainly with questions of colonial empire. The war of 1812 revealed the weakness of her North American possessions, and confirmed the opinion of King George the Third, who objected to the St. Croix in 1783, and insisted on the Piscataqua as the boundary; England agreed to a peace, as she saw our government gathering strength for a continuance of the struggle. Maine penetrates like a wedge from the Atlantic seaboard to within almost cannon-shot distance of the St. Lawrence, practically severing the communication between the upper and lower British Provinces. The only route between them, from the harbor of Halifax, her great naval station on the continent, to Quebec, the military fortress of the St. Lawrence, was across the territory of Maine, through the valley of the St. John. Troops were landed at Halifax in midwinter, pushed through to Canada by this route, enabling her to strike our forces on the northern frontier, with her glazed veterans from the battle-fields of Europe, before our forces in the Northwest were aware of their danger. The value of the St. John valley for military purposes was then fully understood by her, and she closed the war by the treaty of "peace and amity," concluded at Ghent, December 24, 1814. By the 2d article of this treaty it was agreed that every thing was to be restored to the *status ante bellum*, except certain islands which were to be made the subject of examination and future settlement. By this treaty, however, we were completely overreached and outgeneraled.

Prior to this no question was ever raised as to the boundary between New England and the British possessions, for, to use the language of the best English geographer, Professor Long: "No language could have been made use of, with the then existing knowledge of the physical geography of the country, more clearly establishing the right of the United

States to the entire territory than that employed in the treaty of 1783."—(See Library of Useful Knowledge, History of North America.)

The treaty of Ghent, article 5th, provided for the appointment of commissioners to run the line, etc. It further provides that: "If the said commissioners shall agree, etc., such decision shall be final and conclusive."

"And it is further agreed, that in the event of the two commissioners *differing upon all or any of the matters so referred to them, or in the event of both or either of said commissioners refusing or declining, or wilfully omitting to act as such*," etc., "some friendly sovereign or state to be then named for that purpose who shall decide," etc.

By this language Great Britain found a chance to escape from her treaty obligations. She set up a show of good faith; appointed her commissioner, under the 5th article of the treaty, to run and mark the boundary line, from the source of the St. Croix to the head of the Connecticut River; appointed her commissioner to determine the channel of the St. Croix, as provided for in the 4th article of the treaty, and another commissioner to establish the line in the channel of the St. Lawrence River, as required in the 6th article of the treaty. The two latter commissions were executed; one on November 24, 1817; the other on June 18, 1822.—(See Statutes at Large. vol. 8, pp. 250, 274.)

But the attempt to execute the commission for the running of the line, under the 5th article of the treaty, failed. The commissioners were named in

1816. Our government appointed Mr. Johnson; the British government selected Mr. Bouchette; they met at St. Andrew's, September 23, 1816, and the work was undertaken and partially performed in the years 1817 and 1818. Mr. Bouchette was removed, and Mr. Odell, a more pliant surveyor, substituted, and under imperial instructions the contingency provided for in the 5th article of the treaty of Ghent happened, by the *refusal* of the British commissioner October 23, 1820, to carry out the work; and our government was forced into an agreement for an umpire—a reference to a friendly sovereign or state. Such an opportunity for the exhibition of bad faith was never suggested as a possibility to the minds of the honorable American gentlemen who negotiated the treaty, any more than the thought that it was possible for Great Britain to demand in our day the surrender of the rebel emissaries, Mason and Slidell, contrary to all her previous declarations, the uniform hereditary policy of her government; or, what is still more recent, an apology from our government for the seizure of the pirates of the Portland steamer *Chesapeake* in a Provincial harbor.

Maine always comprehended the question and insisted on maintaining possession of the territory. The state of Massachusetts holding, at the time of the treaty of 1783, jurisdiction over the district of Maine, granted the townships of Eaton and Plymouth in 1807 and 1808, both lying north of the Aroostook River, and within the territory subsequently brought into dispute.

Hon. Mr. Stevenson, writing to Lord Palmerston on this subject of the British claim, under date of April 21, 1838, says : " It has only *been since the treaty of 1814, and the failure to obtain the territory by cession and purchase*, that the claim has been set up," etc.—(Parliamentary Papers of 1838, appendix, page 80.)

The instructions to the commissioners in 1816 were to run due north till they reached the waters flowing into the St. Lawrence, which carried the line far north of the St. John River.

From the time of her refusal to run and mark the boundary line, to the ratification of the treaty of Washington, the conduct of Great Britain was alike distinguished for the absence of honorable dealing, and the abundance of expressions of her distinguished consideration. Our government dreaded war on what was esteemed so slight a pretext as the loss of a portion of our territory; and hesitated, instead of insisting on a choice of line, even if the adoption of such a line should bring about an interruption of friendly relations. Had they insisted, there is no doubt that the line would have been run and established, and the whole matter closed, twenty years earlier, without loss of territory, of honor; or the shedding of blood.

The appointment of the King of the Netherlands, under the convention of September 29, 1827, as arbitrator, failed to settle the controversy. He awarded the bed of a river, in the execution of a commission to find the highlands separating the waters that flowed in opposite directions, from the northwest angle of Nova Scotia to the head of the Connecticut River. The absurdity of such an award served only to excite ridicule, and the Senate of the United States, by a vote of 35 to 8, rejected the award, as not responsive to the submission. But Great Britain gained time. While agreeing to abstain from exercising jurisdiction over the territory, she hesitated not to violate this contract. Sir Howard Douglass, as Governor of New Brunswick, in 1824, gave licenses to cut the timber, and assumed jurisdiction over land. Our government protested against these proceedings, as extracts from public documents will show.

From President's Message, December 4, 1827.

"While these questions [boundary, etc.] have been pending, incidents have occurred of conflicting pretensions and of dangerous character upon the territory itself in dispute between the two nations. *By a common understanding between the governments, it was agreed that no exercise of exclusive jurisdiction by either party, while the negotiation was pending,* should change the question of right to be definitely settled."

Mr. Clay, Secretary of State, to Mr. Vaughan, British Minister, November 17, 1827.

After reciting instances of British jurisdiction on the Aroostook River, Mr. Clay concluded his note in these words: "The proceedings which it discloses *being incompatible with the rights of the United*

States, at variance with that forbearance and moderation which, *it has been understood between us, were to be mutually observed*, and exhibiting the exercise of rigorous acts of authority within the disputed territory which could only be justified by considering it as constituting an incontestable part of the British dominions, I have to request such explanations as the occasion calls for." Subsequently Maine was ousted of all jurisdiction.

Mr. Van Buren, Secretary of State, to Governor Smith, March 18, 1831.

"I am instructed by the President to express his desire that, while the matter is under deliberation, no steps may be taken by the state of Maine, with regard to the disputed territory, which might be calculated to interrupt or embarrass the action of the executive branch of this government upon the subject."

Mr. Livingston, Secretary of State, to Governor Smith, October 5, 1831.

"In directing me to make this communication, the President has instructed me to ask for such information on the subject as you may possess, and to add the expression of his earnest wish that no measures may be taken by the state authorities that will change the state of things, before the whole subject can be acted upon at the ensuing session of Congress."

Same to Same, October 21, 1831, *in Reference to a Note to the British Chargé d'Affaires.*

"You will observe the extreme desire of the Executive of the United States to conform with scrupulous good faith *to the arrangement made with the minister of Great Britain* for preserving the state of things as it then existed on both sides until a final disposition could be made of the question."

Governor Smith to Mr. Livingston, November 10, 1831.

"In your last letter I am informed that an arrangement was made with the minister of Great Britain for preserving the state of things as it then existed on both sides, until a final disposition could be made of the question, and that the arrangement was communicated to me. I can only state, in reply, that until your last letter no notice of such an arrangement was ever received by me, and no copy of it can be found among the archives of this state. Though allusion is made to such an arrangement in the correspondence between Mr. Clay, former Secretary of State, and my predecessor, the late Governor Lincoln, it was then stated to have been violated by the British authorities. . . . During the whole progress of this negotiation Maine has continued respectfully but decidedly to remonstrate against proceedings directly involving her rights and interests as a state, and to which her assent was never requested. She contends that the United States have not the power, by the federal Constitution, to alienate, by negotiation or otherwise, any portion of the territory of a state without the consent of such state. She opposed the submission of the question to arbitration."

The ascertainment of the line of boundary in the manner provided for in the treaty of Ghent was exhausted by the reference to an arbiter and the rejection of his award. The only mode left for carrying out the treaty was the appointment of a new commission and the running out of the line. Great Britain declared this to be impossible and so pertinacious was Great Britain in insisting on holding on to the territory, that our government was induced to enter into negotiation for its purchase. It is a source of mortification to an American citizen to read the correspondence and to observe the paltry quibbles and silly subterfuges by which, for years, our government was deluded and led off from the question in issue, till at last the unthinking mass of the people of the country got tired of the dispute and favored a settlement on any terms. In all her negotiations the British government kept this one idea in view; to use the language of her minister at Washington, Sir C. R. Vaughan, of July 4, 1833, to Lord Palmerston: "*Great Britain must contend forever for an uninterrupted communication by the usual and accustomed road between Halifax and Quebec.*"—(Parliamentary Papers, p. 36.)

Our government proposed new lines of boundary for the sake of peace. It offered to treat on other matters in connection. This inspired England with courage, and our national government finally listened to proposals for "*a conventional line.*"

Maine was offered one million of acres of land in Michigan by General Jackson's cabinet, selected by her and located in a square form, in case she would submit to the award of the Dutch king. This offer she declined, and by resolutions unanimously adopted, called on the federal government to run and mark the boundary line.—(See Resolutions of Maine, of March 25, 1837.) Great Britain renewed her demand for a conventional line. On April 28, 1835, Mr. Forsyth, United States Secretary of State, informs Mr. Vaughan, the British minister, "*that the President does not possess the power to establish a conventional boundary without the consent of the state of Maine.*"—(Parliamentary Papers, p. 83.)

Lord Palmerston, in his reply of November 19, 1837, daunted by nothing, notices this statement of the rights of Maine, and combats it to avoid giving an answer to the direct proposal made by Mr. Forsyth for a new commission "to trace out the line." The proposal made by our government, "that a commission of exploration and survey should be appointed for that purpose," is evaded and finally declined. Lord Palmerston proposes the removal of "*the constitutional difficulties*," by "a new agreement for a conventional line," and says, "*it would be indispensable that the state of Maine should be an assenting party to the arrangement.*"—(*Ib.*, p. 98.)

Maine, seeing the stripping and waste of her lands, renewed her request year after year. Our government would do nothing. New Brunswick, without any shadow or pretence of title to the territory, lying, as it did, west of the due north line from the

St. Croix, which had always been the western limit of the territory of Nova Scotia, and in later times of New Brunswick, was giving permits to cut the timber; appointed a warden over it, and hesitated not to grant titles to the lands.

Maine sought to protect the territory from spoliation by force in 1838 and 1839, and brought on what is known as the Aroostook war. The general government then interposed its paramount authority, and forced Maine to retire from the territory, or encounter a war with the United States.

Great Britain achieved her object. She made Maine the party on one side, and the government of the United States the nominal party for her benefit on the other, ready to agree to any terms that could be extorted from Maine.

Mr. Webster found the controversy thus made up when he became Secretary of State in 1841. He was not inclined to regard it in any other light than as one belonging to Maine, rather than one affecting the highest interests and honor of the nation. The country demanded at his hands a settlement of the question, for which task no one of his predecessors had been equal. His great power, and his vast influence over the minds of the people of New England, alone enabled him to force a settlement of the dispute. The general government, during all the previous negotiations, had declined to look at its merits, to demand a settlement on the ground of title, and to face England on the true issue: though the Senate had declared the title of Maine "clear and unquestionable."

Maine, deserted by the national administration, was forced to yield to the demands of power, or wage war single-handed for her rights, not only against the British government and her colonies, but against the government of the federal Union. She was, in this way, robbed of 5,012 square miles (3,207,180 acres) of territory, larger in extent than the State of Connecticut, or rather forced to yield it; or dispose of it for the paltry sum of $300,000: a sum not one tenth the value of the timber taken off the territory by Provincial trespassers.

Great Britain would, no doubt, have paid millions sterling for the acquisition of this territory, but such an idea as making a bargain for money never entered the minds of the people of Maine. They knew the value of the territory (for it was covered with timber), its rich soil and favorable position for purposes of settlement, and its military importance to the country, and they scorned the idea of making money out of it by a surrender. In the heated secret debates of the Legislature of Maine, on the proposal of General Jackson to pay the value of the land taken by the Dutch king's award, no man ever dared to raise the suggestion of making money out of the question. He would have been forever execrated as a traitor. The feeling throughout Maine was universal, that it was a crime to sell it; parting with an invaluable military outpost would be a political offence, akin to the treason of Arnold. The United States government, with the same reason, might, as they believed, give up by treaty and surrender the right to levy duties on imports, to appease the commercial cupidity of Great Britain.

To make a show of title, England, after 1817, set up a claim to, and exercised jurisdiction over, the entire St. John basin, including that part of Maine lying west of the due north line from the source of the St. Croix, containing 12,027 square miles, equal to 7,697,280 acres, though she only wanted a military road across it. The treaty of Washington gave 5,012 square miles of this territory to England, and left 7,015 square miles to Maine, equal to 4,489,600 acres, from all which the more valuable timber had been taken off.

A brief historic sketch, showing the origin of the title to the territory, will establish all that has been asserted in reference to the bad faith of England and the disingenuousness of her diplomacy. This history goes back to the earliest efforts at European colonization.

France and England started together in their efforts to possess this empire of the New World. Disregarding the Pope's donation to Spain and Portugal, they watched, with the same jealousy as now, every movement of each, and of every other power, to gain title to the country. Agreeing in the doctrine of Elizabeth, in 1580, that *possession* was essential to the establishment of title, France granted to De Monts the New World, from the 40th to 46th degree of north latitude, November 8, 1603, reserving " any lands therein held by any other Christian prince or people."

England granted, in like manner, or with similar reservations, to the company of Virginia, the country from the 34th to the 45th parallel of north latitude, April 10, 1606. The French took possession at the

St. Croix, in Maine, in 1604; the English at Sagadahoc, in Maine, in 1607; both claiming to the extent of their charters. The French monarch, Henry IV., through the influence of the Jesuits, was induced, in 1607, to revoke the charter of 1603 to De Monts, a Protestant nobleman and a member of his household, after the settlement of the English at Sagadahoc; thus letting in and giving priority to the English title over the subsequent French charters to Champlain and Poutrincourt. Champlain took possession of the St. Lawrence in 1608, and discovered and gave his name to Lake Champlain. But on finding it south of the 45th degree of latitude, the northern limit of the English grant, he retired above that line, and in this way this most ancient landmark became established. The charter of New England of 1620 extended its line as far north as the 48th degree, but it met at the 45th parallel the possessions of the French on the St. Lawrence.

The future of France and England in America was practically determined by these events of 1607; and all men now see that the most important event of modern times was the establishment of the title of the English to the New World. England traces the growth of her empire by the expansion of her commerce, to that of her North American colonies.

The struggle for the sea-coast of Maine between England and France, commencing in 1607, ended with the peace of Ryswick, in 1697, and the future of the continent seemed all this time in suspense. In 1613 Argall found the Jesuit Fathers, Baird and Masse, at Mount Desert, with their faithful followers from the monasteries of France, living in peace with the native tribes. He promptly destroyed their settlement, killing or carrying them into captivity. This shedding of blood, the second act in the drama of empire in North America, aroused all Europe to the consequences of the measure, and called forth angry diplomatic controversy. France yielded again to the domination of England, who held the country to the 45th degree of north latitude. Champlain, from 1620 to 1635, insisted to his sovereign that whoever held the basin of the St. Lawrence should hold the open sea-coast of Maine; and although Cadillac, the future governor of Louisiana, and the founder of Detroit, after the commencement of the long war of 1687, known as the ten years' war, submitted a plan, in 1692, for conquering the English posts and holding the seaboard of Maine, he failed to receive adequate support from his government—till, in 1697, the peace of Ryswick, establishing by treaty stipulation the right of England to the seaboard east of the river St. Croix, again defeated the hopes of France for supreme control in the New World.

The struggles of France and England on this continent—perhaps stimulated by differences of religion and race—had their origin in an intuitive faith in the leading minds of both nations, in the future greatness of the country, and the hope of dominion. The French leaders, far ahead in theoretic ideas, found less support than the English in the disposition and character of their colonists.

Maine belonged to England, and was partially peopled after the St. Croix became the eastern boundary of New England; but with all these acquisitions from France, England had but a small portion of the continent. Prior to the conquest of 1759, according to Bancroft, dividing North America into twenty-five parts, France held twenty, Spain four, and England but one. Quebec was captured by Wolfe, in 1759. The treaty of peace of 1763 gave New France to England. A new government was to be established. In the royal proclamation of October 7, 1763, the line of boundary between the newly acquired province of Quebec and New England ran " from Lake Champlain, in 45° of north latitude, along the highlands which divide the rivers that empty themselves into the St. Lawrence from those which fall into the sea," etc. The same line was established by the Quebec act of 1774.

In the commission of Governor Wilmot as governor of Nova Scotia, dated November 21, 1763, the western boundary of that Province was established as follows: " Westward by a line drawn from Cape Sable across the entrance of the Bay of Fundy to the mouth of the river St. Croix, by said river to its source, and by a line drawn due north from thence to the southern boundary of the Province of Quebec." All this territory, belonging to Great Britain in 1763, was divided into New England, Nova Scotia, and the new Province of Quebec, whose lines of boundary could not be more clearly stated.

In the war of the Revolution, neither Canada nor Nova Scotia took part with the other thirteen colonies. In the definitive treaty of peace of 1783, notwithstanding the efforts of the king, George III., to make the Piscataqua instead of the St. Croix the boundary, the lines were established as follows: "From the northwest angle of Nova Scotia, to wit, that angle which is formed by a line drawn due north from the source of the St. Croix River to the highlands, along the highlands which divide the rivers that empty themselves into the river St. Lawrence from those which fall into the Atlantic Ocean, to the northwesternmost head of the Connecticut River," etc.

"East by a line to be drawn along the middle of the river St. Croix from its mouth in the Bay of Fundy to its source, and from its source directly north to the aforesaid highlands."

By the 5th article of Jay's treaty of November 19, 1794, there was an agreement for a joint commission to ascertain "what river was truly intended under the name of the river St. Croix, mentioned in said treaty of peace" (1783), etc. The duties of this commission were performed in 1798, the St. Croix was agreed on, and the source thereof marked and established by a suitable monument. This adjudication solved every remaining doubt, and left nothing open for dispute. To run and mark the line "from the source of the St. Croix" to the head of the Connecticut River, following the words of the treaty, was as easy as to find the summit of Mount Washington.

The lines agreed on in the treaty of 1783 coincided with the lines of boundary of 1763, then established for the convenient government of an empire, whose ports belonged to the same power. No language could be more explicit, and no ingenuity of statement could ever throw a doubt over the matter.

From 1817 to 1842 our national government sought to avoid war with Great Britain. They could not fathom the depth of that duplicity that led them into new negotiations for the possession of the northern part of Maine. The absurd pretence that it was "impossible to execute the treaty of 1783," asseverated by Lord Palmerston with the assumed positiveness of conviction, almost ripened into an admission on the part of our government, in the specious diplomacy of Lord Ashburton in 1842. At the end of twenty-eight years after the treaty of peace and amity concluded at Ghent, which was to close all disputes and give repose to the eastern border, at the end of the war of 1812–1815, Maine found peace only in yielding up every thing for the sake of the country. Her municipal charters, granted in good faith to her few settlers who had gone into the territory, were vacated by the act of cession; her citizens who had been imprisoned for adhesion to the American cause were left to seek new homes: and that portion of the territory mainly valuable in money for its timber, containing a rich soil suitable for settlement and fitted for raising wheat, left to them at the end of the struggle, which they had hoped soon to fill with enterprising citizens, was stripped of its more valuable timber. The locking up of the country from settlement for the space of twenty-eight years was itself a cruel and disastrous blow to the prosperity of the state. Maine complained, and she has since been treated with harshness and neglect.

But the conduct of Maine has been consistent. She would have vindicated her rights by the arbitrament of arms but for the interference of the federal government. Her commissioners in 1842, in giving their reasons for rejecting the terms proposed by Lord Ashburton, were overborne by threats of war. In their communication of July 22, 1842, they say:

"The state of Maine has always felt insuperable repugnance to parting with any portion even of her disputed territory for a mere pecuniary recompense from adverse claimants. She comes here for no mere bargain for the sale of acres, in the spirit or with the arts of traffic. Her commissioners have been much less anxious to secure benefits and recompense than to preserve the state from unnecessary curtailment and dismemberment."

The Governor of Maine, in his annual message to the Legislature, January 7, 1843, says:

"I transmit herewith a report, with accompanying documents, of the commissioners appointed under resolve of May 26, 1842, to confer with the authorities of the general government upon the subject of a proposed settlement of the northeastern boundary of this state, and for other purposes.

"The result and final adjustment of this question, even if it should be regarded by the people of this state as preferable to further procrastination and another foreign arbitration: under present auspices, I am persuaded, is far different from what they had anticipated. For myself, I can truly say that I have been deeply disappointed, to use no stronger term.

By this, however, I would not be understood as intending to cast censure upon the commissioners of this state. They were selected by the Legislature as gentlemen of elevated standing—commanding in a high degree the confidence of the public, and as eminently qualified for such a service. The correspondence on their part was conducted with signal ability, and the embarrassments of their position, and the circumstances by which they were ultimately induced to submit the question to the determination of the Senate of the United States, are fully appreciated. But however their course may be regarded, the result is, nevertheless, a subject of deep disappointment. The course of the British government, so far from having been, as was anticipated, conciliatory and liberal, was marked by an unyielding and grasping spirit. Its liberality, if any was evinced, was in unmeaning diplomatic compliments, while its exactions were in acres and substantial privileges; for this state can never admit that the case presented was one of doubtful title, in which the adversary parties might reasonably be expected to compromise by 'splitting the difference.' The relinquishment of a claim, therefore, by the British government, to a portion of what has been denominated the disputed territory, cannot be regarded by us as in any sense a concession. If a portion of this territory was necessary for the convenience of the British government, this state had a right to expect, on its being yielded, that a full and ample equivalent in other territory would have been freely tendered. Towards the fulfilment of such an expectation there has not been the slightest approximation.

"The indirect overtures on the part of the British government for an amicable adjustment of the boundary question, it is well known, were met on the part of this state in a spirit of magnanimous forgetfulness of the past, and with a generous regard to the supposed interests and wishes of her sister states. Earnestly entreated by the general government, and pressed as she was by circumstances, she could not hesitate to place herself in a position admitting of an amicable and honorable settlement of the question, confidently trusting that the government of the Union, in some of its departments at least, would secure her from sacrifice. For this step she has no cause of self-reproach. It was taken under circumstances that would fully justify its repetition. How this generosity and confidence on her part has been rewarded, is seen in the result! But I forbear to dilate upon the subject, especially as it would be unavailing. If in this Maine 'has not been treated as she has endeavored to deserve,' it is far from being the first instance. All her injuries, however, cannot shake her sense of duty. As a member of the Union, she will continue to be what she has ever been, faithful and true. And if she could be satisfied that the sacrifice was necessary for the good of the country, she could in that find ample consolation. To insolent and unfounded pretension she can yield nothing; to the cause of patriotism and the Union, every thing."

An able committee of both branches of the Legislature in their report of March 21, 1843, say:

"That the terms of the treaty of Washington, concluded on the ninth day of August, 1842, so far as they affect the state of Maine, are not satisfactory to the people thereof.

"That the hopes and expectations under which the state of Maine consented to participate in the negotiation which eventuated in the treaty of Washington, are greatly disappointed by the result of that negotiation.

"That the true meaning and intent of the resolves passed by the Legislature of Maine on May 26, 1842, entitled 'Resolves in relation to the northeastern boundary of this State,' did not authorize the commissioners elected under said resolves to surrender any portion of the territory within the line of the treaty of 1783 as claimed by Maine, without a full equivalent therefor."

The sum of $300,000 was paid over to Maine and Massachusetts, in equal moieties, "for the lands relinquished to the United States, and excluded from the dominion of the Union" by the new line of boundary. This is the only condition of the treaty that has been performed. But, for the fulfilment of this condition, the faith of both governments, Great Britain and our own, was pledged; and so great was Lord Ashburton's anxiety on this point, that he made the payment of this money a subject of public correspondence with the Secretary of State of the United States.

The advantages proposed to Maine, for this surrender of territory, were the free navigation of the river St. John and the payment over of the proceeds of the timber robbery, which was to go into a "disputed territory fund," to be kept by New Brunswick.

That provision of the treaty for the free navigation of the St. John, in the following words, "All the produce of the forests grown on those parts of the state of Maine watered by the river St. John *shall be dealt with as if it were the produce of the province of New Brunswick*," was shamefully evaded and defeated by the abolition of stumpage dues in New Brunswick, and the imposition of a high export duty on all lumber floated upon the St. John River—a plan substituted in place of the old method of selling lumber.

The disputed territory fund, it is true, reached a large sum, which Maine expected to receive; but it was all consumed by the claims for expense, and *not a dollar of it* was ever paid over to Maine.

Mr. Webster lived long enough to see the boasted advantages he had "secured to Maine by the treaty" vanish into thin air.

How persistently Maine has always, and since the ratification of the treaty, asserted her rights, the documentary history of the United States will show; with what success, the various bills and other matters on the files of Congress will establish. A bill reported in 1862, and again in 1864, from the Committee on Foreign Relations of the Senate, compensating Maine and Massachusetts for lands assigned to occupants under the fourth article of the treaty of Washington, lies undisposed on the table of the Senate.

That Maine has not been disloyal, her whole history and the records of the last three years will abundantly show. After reciting, in brief terms, her claims on the government; by the resolutions of 1864 she reiterates and renews her demands in the language of the resolves of the Legislature, approved by the governor, January 31, 1863, "that 'Maine expects and earnestly demands that measures be taken at once by the general government for the protection of its northeast frontier'; that this can be accomplished only by a military railroad from Bangor to the St. John River.

"*Resolved*, That the people of Maine, zealously attached to the principles of the Constitution and and loyal to the government of the United States, surrounded on three sides by the territory of a foreign power, its other side fronting the ocean, where it is at all times exposed to attack by a superior naval power, by force of its position of incalculable importance to, and steadily coveted by, the people of the British North American Provinces, cannot fail to perceive their danger in case of war with any one of the great powers of Europe; and they appeal to Congress for such aid and support as will enable them to protect their territory from foreign invasion, and secure them against further diminution of their ancient domain.

"*Resolved*, That the government of the United States having forced a reluctant assent from the state of Maine to the treaty of Washington, by which treaty the most valuable portion of the territory of the United States for military purposes was surrendered to Great Britain, securing to her a military route in the St. John valley, between Canada and New Brunswick: the only adequate measure of compensation that can be awarded to Maine is the construction by the federal government, or through its aid, of a military railway from Bangor to the St. John River, as suggested in the resolutions of Maine of January 31, 1863; that in order to secure this result, the state releases and assigns to the European and North American Railway Company of Maine all claims on the federal government accruing prior to the year 1860, in case the United States government affords such aid to said railway company as will enable it to carry out its line of railway from the city of Bangor to the St. John River, or to such point in the northern part of Maine as may accomplish the objects and purposes sought for by the government of this state and the United States."

Maine practically asks nothing of the United States government. The objects she seeks to accomplish are national in their character in every sense of the term. The defence of Maine is more essential to the maintenance of the national government than that of any other section of the country; and this can only be effected by a line of railway, extending from the central and more densely populated portions of the country, to the northeastern frontier. An interior line of railway, free from the interruption of an attack by sea, from New York, Boston, and Portland, to the St. John River, would enable our government to concentrate an overwhelming force upon it, and cut the line of communication between Halifax and Quebec. This accomplished, the line of railway from Portland to Canada in our hands, and the city and harbor of Portland made impregnable, British North America could not resist one winter campaign in a war with us. Ability on our part to strike the power of England from the continent is our best guaranty of perpetual peace with her.

June, 1864.

AN AMERICAN ZOLL-VEREIN.

LETTER TO THE SHIP-CANAL CONVENTION.

GENTLEMEN:—I am honored by your invitation to attend a convention at Chicago, on the second of June next, of those in favor of the enlargement of the canals between the Mississippi and the Atlantic. And I am further requested, in case I cannot attend said convention, to communicate my views in writing upon the matters embraced in the call.

Until to-day I had expected to have been able to attend as one of the delegates of the Board of Trade of Portland, Maine, some of whom are on their way, and whose intelligent interest in the success of your efforts will faithfully represent the prevailing opinions of our people.

Your call seems to limit the object of the convention to the single purpose of an enlargement of the existing canals between the valley of the Mississippi and the Atlantic Ocean—works of obvious value, if not of immediate necessity; yet it may fairly open the entire question of the internal commerce of the country, and the means of transit between the grain-producing regions of the interior of the continent—the great Northwest—and their place of market.

Questions of this character are of interest to all, and must, for years, if not for generations, to come, become the most engrossing topics of public concern, from the physical configuration of the North American continent, the limited capacity of its natural channels of trade, and the political difficulties in the way of all efforts at the opening of adequate avenues, by artificial means, to meet the wants of a rapidly increasing business.

Great as is now the internal trade of the country, it is a tithe only of what it will, in a few years, attain to. The production of food is not, at this time, equal to one tenth of the capacity of the Northwestern states, without resort to the artificial stimulants that are common in the British Isles. Besides this, one half of all the grain raised in the United States is produced at points so remote from market that its value would be consumed in the mere cost of transportation by the ordinary channels. With the aid of all existing canals and railroads, a bushel of wheat in the Northwest is only worth one half its value in Liverpool, so enormous is the cost of present transportation. The question is: How shall this difficulty be overcome? And it is this question alone that will engage the time and thoughts of the members of the convention.

It has seemed to me that the great difficulty lies in the way of outlets *from* Chicago, Milwaukee, and other lake ports, rather than in the lack of means to bring produce to the lake shores. Cheaply built and economically worked lines of railway, with other means of transit, bring into these great granaries— the lake ports—more produce than the outlets can economically take away.

What are wanted are cheap and expeditious means of transit from the upper lakes to the open sea. To secure these most effectually, we must make the St. Lawrence waters *an open Mediterranean Sea;* so that, from the head of Lake Superior and from Chicago, ships of useful size for navigating the ocean can pass, free of duty and with despatch, to the Atlantic ports and Europe, and backward to the same places, fully laden. By this means, you could diminish by one half, the cost of transit, for the benefit of the farmers of the Northwestern states; and indirectly, for the advantage of the entire population of the country.

This is a matter of easy accomplishment, if undertaken in the right spirit and temper. The *English-speaking people* of this continent are, for all commercial purposes, *one people*, holding a territory twice the size of the continent of Europe, capable of sustaining as dense a population as that which now occupies that favored portion of the globe.

This territory is held in nearly equal shares by the people of the United States and of the British North American Provinces, lying mainly on opposite sides of this great Mediterranean Sea, formed by the waters of the lakes and the St. Lawrence.

The laws of commerce disregard political boundaries, and the people of the Northwest should have their choice of routes to the open sea. Ships should load at Chicago for any port into which an Atlantic sailer can enter, and by as many routes as can be created: from the St. Lawrence, by the way of Lake Champlain into the Hudson, by the Ottawa, and by

Lake Ontario. The advance in the price of *a single crop of wheat* would pay for making all these routes, from Chicago to the Atlantic, navigable for ocean-going sailing-ships and steamers.

Montreal harbor could be made for the trade of New York what Albany is now ; and that, too, while the St. Lawrence basin, below the Victoria Bridge, would be crowded, like the Thames in our day, from London to the sea, when this continent is as fully peopled as Europe.

From Chicago to the Atlantic, for nearly the whole distance, navigation is as cheap as on the ocean. Short canals and lockage would not detain ships more than the average adverse winds of the Atlantic, so that the transit of goods, to and from Chicago and Liverpool, would be nearly as cheap as to and from New York. At one tenth of the cost of transportation by railway, such a line of navigation would supply an outlet to the trade of the Northwest. To transport a ton of goods, by ordinary highways, costs on an average twenty dollars per hundred miles. The railroads will perform this service for two dollars, the sailing-vessel for one tenth of this, or twenty cents, per ton. Open a ship-canal by the way of the St. Lawrence to Chicago, and the cost of freight per mile will scarcely, if at all, exceed the cost of transit on the ocean, or the lakes.

Our great difficulties in this country are political ones ; greater than the limited amount of capital in business. Public improvements are mainly dependent on local jurisdictions, Provinces or States, governed rather by sectional aims, than by regard to the higher law of commercial convenience. In the United States, nationality has scarcely been regarded as an object of statesmanship, while state governments have seized upon the more valuable attributes of sovereignty. The regulation of the currency and of the channels of internal commerce which should, beyond all other matters, be under the control of the government of the Federal Union, have been assumed by the states.

To this undue assumption of rights by the states, incompatible with the national sovereignty, can be traced the origin of the present atrocious civil war, upon the part of rebellious states. This war, however, has already taught us a mode of supplying a national currency which will never be superseded—a discovery worth more than the cost of the war to the present time. Should it enable the national government to disregard political boundaries in the construction of public works, looking only at physical and commercial laws, this war may yet prove to our nation a blessing.

The highest statesmanship of our day regards *the English-speaking people* of both hemispheres as one in purpose and in destiny. Such an opportunity for greatness, as that enjoyed by the head of the British ministry, has not before this time been offered to any minister of state. He has only to recognize the obvious duties of consanguinity and good-fellowship, to make the union of all who speak the English tongue complete in every thing that tends to the advancement of civilization, as they are one in purpose and desire. In this spirit let us act. Let political boundaries form no restraint upon commercial enterprise; and the continent, which it is our good fortune to inhabit, shall display exhibitions of material greatness worthy of a superior race, descendants of the heroic men who wrested this new world from the grasp of their less enterprising rivals, and planted over this broad belt of the temperate zone, from the Atlantic to the Pacific seas, institutions and laws favorable to commercial freedom and constitutional liberty.

If, however, the time has not arrived when we can treat the English-speaking people of the continent as properly subject to one commercial law—a result not far distant from our day, when an ocean tariff shall extend, with uniform provisions for the collection of duties, from Quebec to the Rio Grande, and upon the Pacific coast, with unrestricted internal trade,—or, in other words, if the British North American Provinces are not ready to adopt with us *an American Zoll-Verein*, we must make use of our own independent advantages. We can, more cheaply than the Canadians have built theirs, construct a ship-canal around Niagara Falls, and from Oswego to the Hudson, that shall, for years to come, take away from the lakes the surplus produce of the interior. We should further, with the same broad view, deepen the channel of the St. Clair, and extend this water-line, with a capacity equal to the passage of an ocean steamer, from Chicago to the navigable waters of the Mississippi, so that produce can pass by either route to the sea.

The people of the Great Republic of North America have been unexpectedly called upon to deal with great enterprises, vast and undefinable in their extent; and while expending, without discontent or embarrassment, large sums in suppressing insurrection and guarding against foreign invasion; they have found time to contemplate, as necessary practical measures, a railway from the Missouri to the Pacific, and a line of ocean steamers from San Francisco to the shores of the densely populated continent of Asia. A further knowledge of the capacities of our country and of the capabilities of its people will insure for these, and all the enterprises named, full and complete success.

With the highest regards, your obedient servant,

JOHN A. POOR.

May 30, 1863.

THE TRANSCONTINENTAL RAILWAY.

ADDRESS DELIVERED AT RUTLAND, VERMONT, JUNE, 1869.

Mr. President, and Gentlemen of the Convention:

I count myself fortunate in being able to participate in the proceedings of this convention, by your kind invitation. It is a business meeting. I came with my associates from Portland to report progress at the eastern end of the route, rather than to take active part in its labors. But for an important political state convention in Maine to-day, other friends from our state would have been with you, to show their appreciation of the enterprise you have under consideration.

I am happy to meet so large and so earnest an assemblage of business men, engaged in a work which is to connect you in business, by railway, with the harbor of Portland,—the line that is to form a chief link in that golden belt which is to span the continent of North America at its widest part, under the name of *The Transcontinental Railway.*

Evidences of thrift and prosperity are around me on all sides. This beautiful opera-house in which we are assembled attests the wealth of Rutland. But this visit to your flourishing town is a new experience, for it is, I believe, the first time that the men of Maine have been invited to speak for railroads in Vermont. It is pleasant to me to recall the railroad history of New England for the last twenty-five years, and to note the great changes in that time in the business of your region of the country.

It was my fortune to meet some of the leading railroad men of Vermont at Montreal, in somewhat of an adverse character in 1845, urging the claims of the Passumpsic Railroad, as an outlet for St. Lawrence trade by way of St. Johnsbury and Concord to Boston; against our favorite direct route from Montreal to the sea at Portland. You know how events turned. Every thing went in our favor. It is enough to say, that at Montreal Portland influence prevailed; the Legislature and people of Canada, with scarcely a dissenting voice, gave their support to the Portland line over all other projects, against the remonstrance of the leading capitalists and business men of Boston, presented at Montreal by one of your prominent citizens, Hon. Erastus Fairbanks, afterwards Governor of your state. He persevered at home in pushing his railroad, after his defeat in Canada; presented his project to the people of Boston, with a favorable response in the way of subscriptions to his stock. We moved on also, and in 1848, as our road to Montreal extended northward toward your State line, it became my duty as one of the directors of the Atlantic and St. Lawrence Railroad Company, with my friend and associate, Hon. P. Barnes, of Portland, to ask of the Legislature of your state a charter for our road across your northern counties. With generous unanimity the Legislature granted our request. Many at heart, or secretly, opposed our project. Others regarded it as a mere paper corporation. Others, alleging that the road would never be built, consented, but afterwards stoutly resisted further grants required. As our line advanced from Portland toward the Vermont border, every thing had to give way to the necessities of business,—the line was forced on, and opened through, so that cars came from Montreal to Portland on July 18, 1853, inside of twelve hours' time.

Maine is no longer dependent on Boston. Since then things have changed. Portland has risen into commercial importance, and become a shipping port and market for western produce, the packet station in winter of the Montreal and other lines of ocean steamers, and a better market than Boston for provincial trade.

The European mails are carried in winter direct by way of Portland to Montreal and the West, without paying tribute to Boston, or calling there, as in the olden time.

The Cunard steamers have retired from Boston since she lost the carrying trade of Canada, and the foreign importations into Boston have fallen from $45,988,545 in 1854, the highest point they ever reached, to $37,039,771 in 1868,—while the importations into Portland have risen from $3,124,676 in 1854, to $17,100,957 in 1868, and its exports in like proportion.

Portland, from its geographical position, is the natural Atlantic port and market of a large portion of New Hampshire and Vermont. Portland, Bristol, Woodstock, and Rutland are on the same parallel. Portland is 89 miles north of Boston, and only 25 miles east of it. More than three fourths of the territory of Vermont lies north of a due west line, on the parallel of 43° 39', the latitude of Portland, of Meredith, of White River Junction, of Woodstock, and the head of Lake Champlain, Whitehall. Before the advent of railways or canals, Northern Vermont came to Portland to market. The Northern Canal from Lake Champlain, 73 miles from Albany, was completed to the Hudson, at Waterford, 64 miles, in 1819, by the state of New York, which drew at once the trade of Western Vermont to New York City.

From 1820 to 1830 Boston made slow progress. In 1830 she began railroad agitation, and in 1835 stretched out her iron arms in the form of railways. She looked upon Maine commercially as still her province, and paid little regard to railroads east or north of Portland. She turned northwest and west, and with railway lines crossed the states of New Hampshire and Vermont to Lake Champlain, and to the St. Lawrence at Ogdensburg, and drew to her harbor the bulk of trade of both these states, and of Northern New York.

But Maine awoke from her lethargy in 1844, and Portland started her line to Montreal, which has largely changed the course of the grain trade of the West. The supplies of western produce for Lowell, Lawrence, and other places are left on the way, and do not come to Boston as of old; Boston herself drawing some of her domestic supplies from the West by way of Portland. Flour comes down the St. Lawrence and the canals and by the Grand Trunk Railway to Montreal; thence to Portland and to Boston by railway and steamer.

Finding her plans frustrated in 1845, to anticipate the completion of our railway from Portland to Montreal, to supersede it in point of fact, Boston started off on a new crusade—abandoning almost entirely the Boston, Concord, and Montreal project,—a railway to Ogdensburg, and completed it through by Boston capital in October, 1850. Then came Boston's great Railroad Jubilee, in full expectation that she would, by her superior attractions, intercept, at Ogdensburg, the produce of the West on its way to Montreal. But the whole project has, so far, as a commercial speculation, proved a failure, as the Boston Board of Trade returns fully show. The *Boston Daily Advertiser*, under date of June 9, 1869, admits that of the 43,415 barrels of flour which came into Boston in the month of May, 1869, 3,200 barrels only came by the way of Ogdensburg. The entire quantity of flour which came by way of Ogdensburg and reached Boston over the Northern and Fitchburg, and Boston and Maine roads in 1868, was but 90,004 barrels, against 704,070 barrels over the line of the Western (now the Boston and Albany) Railroad. In 1863, the northern roads delivered 326,900 barrels of flour into Boston, coming from Ogdensburg, against 543,227 barrels by the Western Railroad. In the same year, 1863, 271,530 barrels of flour were sent from Portland into Boston, and in 1865, 454,421 barrels of flour were sent into Boston by the Portland route. These figures illustrate the tendencies of Western trade.

Our railway from Portland to Montreal was proposed in 1844 as an outlet for western produce, a direct connection by the shortest line of railway between the navigable waters of the St. Lawrence and an open Atlantic port, in a distance of 203 miles on an air line. The work of construction was entered upon in 1846, and the railroad line estimated at 250 miles in length. As built, it deflected materially from the most direct route, after it had reached northwest from Portland to Island Pond, making the distance 292 miles from Portland to Montreal. A connection between Quebec and Montreal, and the necessity of keeping so far east of the direct line from Montreal to Boston as to prevent diversion of trade to that city, no doubt influenced its location. Without this deflection, the means for building the line could not at that time have been obtained.

The pressing and immediate necessity of Portland to-day is a direct line from Island Pond to Montreal, saving 46 miles over the present route by way of Sherbrooke and Richmond. This is fully admitted, and no one *now* fears Boston competition.

Attempts have been made in former years to secure this Island Pond cut-off, but without success,—the funds of the Grand Trunk Railway having been absorbed by extension of other lines further west. If a direct line of railway was extended from Island Pond to Montreal, it would cheapen, at least by one fourth, the cost of transit between Montreal and Portland.

At no very distant day, as I believe, this will be accomplished, as a necessity to Montreal and the Grand Trunk Railway, to retain their present importance.

The railway from Montreal to Portland (the first great international undertaking of this character) has given Portland commercial importance, with favorable results upon the social, political, and commercial notions and relations of the two countries. The beginning of that new order of things developed by our international lines of railway and steamer, is making the English-speaking people of this continent one in sentiment and in commercial undertakings. And it is pleasant to meet on this platform to-day a gentleman from Ontario, in the Dominion of Canada, representing one great link in this chain of iron that is to bind the people of this continent in bonds of perpetual peace.

But the progress of improvements in twenty-five years has somewhat modified our opinions as to the future of trade. Great changes have taken place in the navigation of the St. Lawrence and the lakes since 1844, and our views as to the value of the navigation of the St. Lawrence, below Lake Erie, have been somewhat modified.

The Welland Canal, begun in 1824, and opened in 1832, was found insufficient to pass the largest vessels navigating the upper lakes, and in 1841, the enlargement was undertaken by the government of United Canada, and completed in 1848 or 1849, with eight and one half feet of water on the mitre sills of the locks, one hundred and fifty feet of chamber between the gates, and twenty-six and one half feet in width in the clear. The locks would allow the passage of any vessel that could then pass the St. Clair Lake and the flats in that river, but less than 500 tons, in burden.

Mr. Thomas C. Keefer, an accomplished engineer, in his prize essay on the canals of Canada in 1850, says: "The depth of water provided for in the St. Lawrence and Welland canals is ample, being more than is afforded in many of the harbors upon the upper lakes, more than there is over the St. Clair flats, and as much as the general features of the St. Lawrence navigation will warrant." But since then the United States government has opened a ship channel through the St. Clair flats, 300 feet in width, protected on each side by heavy walls raised five feet above the highest waters of the lake, carrying fifteen feet of water from Lake Huron into Lake Erie. Propellers of over 1,400 tons burden now pass from Buffalo to Chicago.

Freight formerly taken off at Collingwood and Sarnia, now goes through to Buffalo, which has become the great depôt of the grain trade of the Northwest.

The result witnessed within the last few years was not foreseen in 1844, nor in 1852 when the Grand Trunk Railway scheme was inaugurated, and our line, the Atlantic and St. Lawrence Railroad, absorbed into, or annexed by perpetual lease to, the Grand Trunk Railway of Canada. The theory on which our railroad to Montreal was built has, in one respect at least, proved erroneous.

It was predicted, too, in 1844, that Montreal would become one of the three great cities of the continent, from the commercial advantages of its position, no one at that time anticipating the possibility of this deep ship channel between Lake Huron and Lake Erie. Montreal has great advantages as the commercial metropolis of Canada, has grown to be a great city; her population has risen from 57,715 in 1850, to 101,602 in 1860, and to 160,000 at the present time. Yet Montreal has not kept pace with the city of Chicago.

The growth of Chicago is without example. Settled in 1822, in 1850 it had a population of 29,463; in 1860, 110,793, and in April of this year, 265,000.

In looking over the Chicago Directory for 1868, I found it contained 94,000 names. The New York City Directory of this year, 1869, contained 189,443 names, or twice the number only of those found in the Chicago Directory for 1868. Her trade, wealth, and commercial importance have gone forward in greater proportion than the population.

Compilers of commercial statistics put flour forward as a representative of trade, and it would be interesting to look at the progress of the grain trade of Chicago.

The President of the Chicago Chamber of Commerce said, in a late commercial convention this present year: "When railroads shall carry grain cheaper than lakes and canals, and when these go out of use, the grain from a great country, which is now diverted to Chicago, will seek a direct route to the seaboard." He had reference, no doubt, to the lines of railroad terminating at Baltimore, Philadelphia, and New York, competing for the grain trade of the West, of which I shall hereafter speak, which took off a portion of the Chicago trade of 1867–8. The recovery in 1868–9 is due to the great enlargement of trade on account of better crops the past year.

In 1860 the quantity of grain moved eastward by all routes was 78,632,486 bushels. We cannot give as full statistics for the year 1868. The cost of shipping a bushel of grain from Chicago to New York, according to statement of the *Chicago Tribune* in May last, was 32¼ cents, divided as follows, viz.:

Inspection (in and out)	¼
Storage	2½
Commissions	1½
Freight to Buffalo	6½
Insurance	1¼
Elevator at Buffalo	2
Handling	¼
Commissions at Buffalo	1½
Freight by canal to New York	13½
Expenses in New York	3
Total expenses	32¼

It costs, therefore, 16½ cents a bushel to transport grain by canal from Buffalo to New York City, somewhat less than the charges by railway, showing an actual cost of $11,029,690 to the grain trade of Chicago, for the transportation of its products from Buffalo, or by other routes, to New York City, in 1868–9, which were as high in 1868 as in 1869. The great practical question, therefore, at Chicago and Buffalo is, how can we reduce the cost of transit to the Atlantic seaboard?

The supply of Western produce for Maine comes by way of Montreal, and if we had free trade in breadstuffs, this supply could in a few years equal the wants of New England.

Montreal is now a great city. She has secured a deep ship channel to the sea through Lake St. Peter. Vessels of light draft only came to Montreal from the sea in olden time, or prior to 1851. But in 1865 a depth of twenty feet was obtained, with a three-hundred-feet channel, while there was only a depth of eleven feet originally in the flats; so that after fourteen years of labor, from 1851 to 1865, the largest steamer of the Transatlantic Montreal mail line came regularly to the wharves in Montreal during the season of navigation. This work is similar to that executed by our government through the St. Clair Flats and Detroit River, already spoken of. The effect of this measure on Montreal is shown in the fact that the exports from Montreal have risen from $2,319,228 in 1851, to $7,792,776 in 1867; her imports from $9,178,840 in 1851, to $28,378,117 in 1867.

The Montreal ocean steamers known as the "Allan Line," commenced in 1856 with four steamers, having a capacity of 6,536 tons, are now increased to sixteen steamships in number, with an aggregate of 32,606 tons register.

Portland owes every thing to her harbor, and her present commercial importance to the Grand Trunk Railway, and she should be jealous of all attempts to disparage or underrate the Grand Trunk line. I am sorry to say advantage has been taken of its trials during our civil war, and others consequent on it, to disparage and injure it in public estimation, in which some of our public officials have been but too prominent. The claims of the Portland and Ogdensburg Railroad have been urged in hostility to that great line, whose fault lies mainly in an inadequate amount of local business travel, and an insufficient supply of equipment or rolling stock for the autumn trade. She has passed through her troubles as other roads have done, and is coming out all right.

What has the Grand Trunk line done for Portland? Portland in 1844 was literally a deserted village, rich in retired capital, but poor in enterprise and public spirit. The suggestion of a railway to Montreal was like an alarm-bell in the night, struck by the hand of a stranger. It aroused her sleepy ones to a consciousness of their condition, and drew into active energy whatever of dormant, or of patent public spirit there was left in the entire population. With generous emulation, forgetting past differences, men vied with each other, not only in extravagant hopes and predictions of its success, but in hard work and substantial aid, and it went through in its own way in spite of those most interested in its success. Portland has risen into wealth and comparative commercial importance since 1844,—her valuation from $4,365,788 in 1844, to $18,962,514 in 1854, to $26,953,939 in 1864, and to $28,572,748 in 1868, and in business and wealth in vastly greater proportion. Her valuation has kept up notwithstanding she lost $10,841,525 by fire in 1866, with a return of $3,528,180 only from insurance. Portland is comparatively free from embarrassment, but with an inevitable scarcity of money, which comes of such a vast loss. Insurance, public and private generosity have done much to relieve the distress attendant on such a calamity, and her courage and activity are greater than ever before.

In their impatience for new business, some of the people of Portland, or the more hopeful of them, were encouraged to look for it in the building of a line of railroad through the White Mountain Notch, by way of St. Johnsbury and Lamoille valley to Rouse's Point, aiming to make Ogdensburg the objective point of their scheme upon the St. Lawrence waters. You know the history of this project. St. Johnsbury wanted an outlet independent of the Passumpsic Railroad, and proposed a railroad to Montpelier, for which a charter was granted. Montpelier declined to bond her town as St. Johnsbury had done, and the measure hung fire. The St. Johnsbury interest started off to Portland in advance of the Montpelier people, and proposed a line from Portland west, agreeing to build it, if Maine would give them a charter. The Vermont Central were standing ready, as they said, to take a lease of the line to Portland at *six per cent.* on its cost. Afterwards, finding the scheme impracticable, they cut loose from the Central line, and started a new scheme, —a line from Portland to Ogdensburg by the way of the White Mountain Notch.

To the support of this project I could never bring the convictions of my judgment, and I have met no little opposition, as some of you well know, for standing out in opposition to the Notch route. I do not believe the line an easy one to build, and I do not think it will bring an adequate return of business for the outlay, if it is built. Hence I cordially fell in with your scheme and with the views presented by the president of this convention, who, with his friend, General Washburn, and other influential citizens of Vermont, visited Portland, for this purpose, in February, 1868. I shall never fail to thank you, Mr. Chairman, in behalf of Portland and of Maine, for your broad statesmanship and enlightened views on this question, and for bringing the claims of the Rutland and Portland line to the knowledge of our people.

To understand the value to Portland of the Rutland route, over other projected lines to the West, I have said to our people, it is essential to know something of the physical geography of the country between Lake Champlain and the Hudson River valley, and the territory of New England.

From New York City to Montreal, a distance of about 400 miles along the route of the Hudson River and Lake Champlain, is a comparative level,— Lake Champlain being but 90 feet above tide-water; and the highest summit between Hudson River and Lake Champlain is 132 feet above tide-level. The Green Mountain range, running nearly north and south, parallel with Lake Champlain, extends from the south line of Massachusetts to the St. Lawrence waters, forming a continuous ridge, with occasional depressions, but without any of the deep gorges and pointed summits which characterize the granitic formation lying east of the Connecticut River in New Hampshire. Three lines of railway now cross the

Green Mountain range; the Western Railroad of Massachusetts, now the Boston and Albany line, with long-continued heavy grades; the Rutland Railroad, over Mt. Holly summit; and the Vermont Central Railroad, by way of Roxbury and Northfield.

The Rutland and Central Railroads cross the state of Vermont diagonally by means of long ascents, over lofty summits, the exact height of which are not known to me. The proposed Ogdensburg line, further north, is understood to be surrounded with a still greater engineering difficulty in reaching the Lamoille valley. The most favorable route for a railroad across your state, south of Island Pond, as far as grades are concerned, is by way of Montpelier, where the Green Mountains can be passed, by easy grades, at an elevation of 1,340 feet only, above the level of the sea. The Nulhegan and Clyde summit, on the Grand Trunk line, is only 1,158 feet above tidewater. Neither the Rutland nor Central lines, already built, or the Montpelier and St. Johnsbury lines proposed, afford, or can afford, a direct line across the state. If one of your representatives wants to reach Rutland from Montpelier, the state capital, he must either go northwest to Burlington 40 miles, thence south 67 miles to Rutland, 107 miles in all; or run down 104 miles to Bellows Falls, thence 53 miles to Rutland, a total of 157 miles, when the distance between Montpelier and Rutland is only about 40 miles.

A line directly across the state from White River Junction to Rutland would shorten, by one half, the distance by railway to the state capital, and afford a natural and easy connection between all the railroads in that state. It would concentrate at Rutland a large amount of business, making it a great commercial town. I am told, among other projects in contemplation here, is the building of a canal from Lake Champlain. The experience of the last twenty years, in connection with railroads, has demonstrated the fact that Rutland is a point, if not the only point in the state of Vermont, capable of becoming a great inland town, by force of natural laws. Such, at any rate, is my conviction. One feels, on reaching Rutland, that he has got outside or beyond the commercial drift of New England, and that Rutland belongs to the New York system of railroads, and within reach of Western connections. Trains of cars from New York City at 8 o'clock A.M. reach Rutland at 5 o'clock P.M., and there is a great movement, both of passengers and of freight, north and south, as well as across Mt. Holly to the Connecticut River and the east.

It is obvious, therefore, that Rutland is the objective point for all successful railway movements from Portland, west. Such a line would follow the natural route from Portland to Lake Champlain, and on reaching Whitehall, the nearest point from Lake Champlain to the Atlantic, would not only meet the present wants of business, but be prepared to receive the accumulations which are sure to come to it by the extension of a line on the western shore of the lake from Plattsburg, and of a direct line of railway to Oswego, on the completion of ship canals from Lake

Erie into Ontario, and from the St. Lawrence into Lake Champlain, the favorite project of Chicago and the exporters of Western produce.

The Northern seaboard cities have strongly sympathized with the West in their desire for the Niagara Ship Canal, and this idea has at times had great apparent strength throughout the country. Six years ago, or in 1863, a call for a convention at Chicago to aid the canal project was numerously signed by members of Congress, near the head of which stood the name of our present Minister to France, the Hon. E. B. Washburn, of Illinois, a native of Maine. In 1869, Mr. Washburn led off in the movement to postpone and defeat the canal project, and it seems far less likely of accomplishment now than it did six years ago. The great Middle States, Pennsylvania, Ohio, and Missouri, and all the country south of them, oppose the grant of money from the national treasury to aid the building of this canal. The state of New York is opposed to it, and insists if money is expended by the general government for canal purposes, it should be applied to the enlargement of the Erie Canal,—giving it sufficient capacity to float the largest propellers upon the upper lakes. The expense of such an enlargement would be enormous, and the canal could not compete with the railroads in transportation. If such a canal had an unbroken level, so that boats or vessels could cover its entire surface, it could carry cheaper than the railroads; but the delay of locks destroys the efficiency of canals, and they could never compete successfully with railroads with large quantities of business. The capacity of a canal is limited by its locks. A railroad is a canal without locks, and you may cover the whole length of the lines with trains, provided there is an adequate supply of business. Looking, therefore, at the canal question in its economical aspects, as a practical one, it is obvious that the day for the enlargement of canals is far off, if not already gone by. While serving useful purposes in connecting by short links great basins of navigable water, like Lake Huron and Lake Superior, or Lake Huron and Lake Erie, canals can never compete with lines of railway in long transportation. The canals of Ohio, connecting Lake Erie with the Ohio River, serve a useful purpose in their own neighborhood, but they cannot compete for a moment with railroads.

It is obvious, therefore, to my mind, that railroad plans based upon the idea of the early completion of the Niagara Ship Canal must fail,—that a line of railroad from Ogdensburg to the seaboard at Boston or Portland must, as in the past, prove a failure. It will be cheaper to take freight from Buffalo to Portland by a direct line of railroad, than to pass it through a canal into Lake Ontario to Ogdensburg, and then transport it by rail to the seaboard; or, at any rate, cheaper to transport it by way of Oswego to Portland, by a continuous line. Produce once put upon a railroad should follow that track to the seaboard without further handling, and if moved slowly at only twice the speed of a canal boat, it can go about as cheaply, if not cheaper, by rail than by water, and be landed at the most convenient point at its place of destination. It is a knowledge of this that moved Buffalo and Chicago to desire an independent railroad, and a shorter line from Buffalo to the sea. Cheap navigation is now found between Buffalo and Chicago in summer; and could a series of canals be provided, free to all the world, from Lake Erie to the ocean, allowing the largest vessels now known upon the lakes to pass from Chicago to the open sea, the St. Lawrence route might in time grow into favor; but the St. Lawrence navigation below Quebec is an object of dread in autumn; at the West many believe it impossible to make use of the St. Lawrence below Montreal to any great advantage, when the grain crop is pressing forward to market, owing to the early closing of navigation. The Portland outlet by railway is the great feature in the commercial policy of Canada.

If a ship canal, equal to the passage of propellers carrying 1,500 tons burden, could be constructed from Lake Erie into Lake Ontario, and from the St. Lawrence into Lake Champlain, making Lake Champlain an *inland basin*, the produce of the West would undoubtedly flow into it in unmeasured abundance, to be drawn off by railway, as wanted, for shipment or home consumption, to Portland, Portsmouth, Boston, and New York, in distances varying from 180 to 240 miles,—such a canal policy might solve, in some measure, the question of transportation for Western produce. A long line of canal of 322 miles from Buffalo to Albany, or of 70 miles from Lake Champlain at Whitehall into the Hudson at Troy, cannot now, and never can, compete in transportation with railroads along its route. Here, then, comes the answer to the question, how can we reduce the cost of transit from Buffalo to the Atlantic seaboard? By building a new line of railroad from Buffalo by the most direct route to the Atlantic at Portland. This line will serve as the cheapest outlet for produce from Buffalo to the seaboard at the present moment, and meet the further wants of trade, when ship canals are constructed from Lake Erie into Lake Champlain.

But the most formidable of all the obstacles to a canal policy on the part of the government is the opposition of the great railroad companies and great railroad combinations, the mere statement of which excites a feeling of alarm. These recent combinations are an object of jealousy, almost of terror, at the West, as they are sapping the trade of the western towns for the benefit of the Atlantic cities. The first of these great combinations terminates at Baltimore, of which the Baltimore and Ohio Railroad forms the base. It owns a continuous line from Baltimore to Wheeling, a distance of 379 miles, with a branch of 104 miles from Grafton to Parkersburg, on the Ohio River, which is being spanned by a bridge—giving a continuous line to Cincinnati by way of Marietta, a distance of 205 miles. This company is constructing another bridge across the Ohio at Benwood, between it and Bellaire, to accommodate the Ohio Central Railroad, extending from the Ohio River to Columbus, 137 miles, which is a part of her chain; and they have recently purchased the intersecting road from Newark to Sandusky, 116 miles in length—giving them a hold upon Lake Erie, as well as upon Ohio at Cincinnati. The nearest outlet from Cincinnati to the Atlantic is at Baltimore, by way of Marietta, Parkersburg, and Grafton, a distance of 588 miles.

The second grand consolidation rests upon the Pennsylvania Railroad, with its various absorptions and combinations, including the Pittsburg, Fort Wayne, and Chicago line; and the Chicago and Rock Island and Pacific road, reaching to the Missouri River—already embracing 1,530 miles of completed railroad, with a capital equal to $122,110,164, whose gross earnings in 1868 to $36,260,213. It is now understood that this company have also secured the control of the line from Columbus to Indianapolis, and of the Miami Railroad, from Columbus to Cincinnati. At Cincinnati, a company under their control is bridging the Ohio from the Miami station to Newport, which owns the new line from Cincinnati to Louisville, a distance of 104 miles opened to traffic in June the present year. These movements have excited alarm among the business men and the people of Cincinnati, which city has lost almost the entire trade of the country lying east of it,—goods being freighted through from the Atlantic seaboard to all intermediate towns as cheaply, or even cheaper, than to Cincinnati; while the railroads running east, north of Cincinnati, and between it and the lakes, have carried the great stream of travel east and west, away from her city, and taken from her a large portion of the trade of Northern Ohio, Indiana, and Central Illinois, which formerly made Cincinnati their market. Cincinnati, aroused to the most determined action in an effort to restore her lost advantages, has voted to use the credit of the city, under authority of an act recently granted by the Legislature, to the amount of $10,000,000, to build a railroad on the most direct route from Cincinnati to Chattanooga; in the hope, if not with the certainty, of bringing the trade of Eastern Kentucky and Tennessee, and of the whole country lying west of the Blue Ridge, to her city,—a measure long in contemplation, and recommended by President Lincoln as a measure necessary to the carrying on of the war. But nothing could arouse Cincinnati to the necessary measures to complete this work, except the recent diversion of her trade to other places.

Coming to New York, the third great consolidated scheme is that of the Erie Company, whose line, on the six-feet gauge, extends northwest to Dunkirk and Buffalo, and by means of the Atlantic and Great Western Railroad to Cincinnati, from Salamanca on the Erie line, 415 miles from New York,—a distance of 448 miles, on the same gauge; where, in a distance of 863 miles from New York at Cincinnati, it connects with the Ohio and Mississippi Railroad, extending 340 miles from Cincinnati to St. Louis,— forming an unbroken broad-gauge line from the Mississippi River to New York, 1,203 miles. On this line cars now run for the entire distance without change. The plans of this company contemplate a line to Chicago, which was a portion of the scheme of Sir Morton Peto, interrupted for the time by his disastrous failure, when the great railroad revulsion took place in England, from which that country has not yet recovered.

But the greatest of all the combinations is that formed and carried on under the guidance of a single mind, that of Cornelius Vanderbilt, president of the New York Central Railroad; who has practically united into one company the Hudson River Railroad, the New York Central, the Buffalo and Erie, the Lake Shore, Cleveland, and Toledo, the Michigan Southern (from Toledo to Chicago), and the Chicago and Northwestern, reaching to Omaha, the eastern terminus of the Union Pacific Railroad,—embracing a length of 2,480 miles of lines in operation, costing $164,485,056, whose income in 1868 was $44,820,893; and other plans are on foot for still further absorptions and combinations.

These great railroad combinations in a measure control the trade, the public men, and the politics of the country. It is now understood that the Pennsylvania Railroad combination, under the lead of J. Edgar Thompson, are looking toward the Northern Pacific Railroad project, and this same Mr. Thompson, with Mr. Benjamin E. Smith, of Columbus, Ohio, are prominent contractors in the building of the European and North American Railway from Bangor, Maine, to St. John City, New Brunswick. When they come into control of the lines east of Bangor, they may turn their thoughts and their labors to the Northern Pacific, by a direct route from Bangor. The operations of the men engaged in these combinations are as vast and as unfathomable as the great deep,—the result of them, no man can estimate, foresee, or conjecture. They defeated the Niagara Ship Canal. To hold control of their present business, against all interference on the part of the national or state governments, they may possibly be compelled to reduce the cost of railroad transportation.

Of one thing we may be assured, that while the demands of trade and the necessities of business call for additional outlets, the building of this shortest practicable line from Chicago to the sea, will be called for before any great reduction of freights will or can take place. What direction shall this new line take? New Yorkers claim that they can find a new route as favorable as ours. But let the business men of Rutland take this question home to themselves, and they can now determine the route.

You, Mr. Chairman, have had experience in managing a railroad, in working a line with heavy grades and large expenditures. At present, your business is limited, yet you must charge enough to pay for doing this business, and giving a return of profit on the capital of your company. This business you can enlarge. In addition to great advantages of situation, sufficient to make you a great town, you are favored with treasures of wealth, as valuable as the coal deposits of Pennsylvania, in your marble quarries, a visit to which we have enjoyed to-day. Such a sight as I have witnessed is worth a visit of thousands of miles, and was to me, the most instructive lesson I have had for years. These marble quarries are enough to justify an expenditure equal to half your valuation, as shown by the grand list, or $2,000,000 of money to open the Transcontinental Railway, and give you the market of Chicago, and other cities in the West; and the open market of the world by a railway to the seaboard at Portland. Your line to Boston is inadequate to your wants. The elegant Post-office and United States Court room, in Portland, in process of construction, is of Vermont marble, taken from some of the quarries north of you; and if we had the direct line finished to Portland, this beautiful material would come largely into use for building purposes, not only in Portland, but in all the other Atlantic cities, as soon as the cost of transportation would justify it. There is room enough and space enough to work up here the material into public and private edifices, so that it could go forward to market in the most valuable form, shaped by the hands of your own artisans. The great labor should be expended here. You have in employ, probably, 1,000 laborers in the working of marble to-day. In a few years you will have ten laborers for every one now engaged, and a city of 50,000 people will be gathered within the limits of Rutland.

I have been speaking of a line of railway from Rutland to Portland in connection with the necessities of local trade. Is it not wise to go further, and examine into its claims as a portion of the Transcontinental Railway, or of that link of it which more immediately concerns us, the section between Portland and Chicago? The fact that flour would bear transportation by railway for 1,000 miles in competition with water-carriage by canal, was first demonstrated on the Grand Trunk line, extending from Lake Huron to Portland, since the completion of the Victoria Bridge at Montreal without a break or delay. This demonstration has forced competing lines to combine, and the rapid development of railway traffic against water transportation has been one of the great facts of the last ten years. In 1858, the New York canals carried 3,665,192 tons of merchandise, against 3,473,725 tons carried on the railroads of New York. In 1867, the tonnage of the New York canals has increased to 5,688,325 tons, against 10,343,681 tons carried by the railroads of New York, the canals now being worked to their full capacity. The increase and value of tonnage sent by canal and railway amounting to $486,816,505 in value in 1858,—increased, in 1867, to $1,723,330,207.

A great item of transportation is breadstuffs, and the question that the American farmers, whether Canadian or Republican, more especially the producers of Western wheat, must now consider, is, what will be their condition when the surplus produce of the West exceeds our necessary home consumption, and the demands of the English market? In order, therefore, to maintain our bread crop, our first duty is to cheapen the cost of transit to the seaboard, not only from Buffalo and Chicago, but from the the farm of the producer, two hundred miles west of Chicago, from the Mississippi and Missouri rivers to the northern Atlantic seaboard; while we devote our energies along the seaboard, and among the hills of New England, to the development of manufactures, as the necessary, natural, and only reliable market for the surplus produce of the West, and the proper employment of our native population. If we shall be able for the next few years to keep out of our market the cheap products of European labor, until our manufactures shall become established in New England; we may draw around our water-falls a busy population, and plant in every valley of New England thriving villages, with an industrious, independent, and highly educated people.

Public enterprise and commercial necessity, look upon this continent as one great field open to development, regardless of national boundaries or state lines. They conform their plans to *physical facts alone*. Lines of railway, starting from great commercial centres, or important commercial points, rely upon the level and the transit as the only safe guide to open the way to profitable investments. The restraints which hereditary customs and arbitrary laws throw in the way of railroads in the European countries are here comparatively unknown; and the enormous burdens which the people of the most favored of the European states are compelled to bear, are scarcely known to the people of this land, or those of British North America. In the discussion of railroad questions, as well as of all commercial undertakings, we are bound to look forward to the time, not far distant, when intercourse shall be *free*, among all the English-speaking people of the continent, as it is between different states of the Union under our federal Constitution, and among the several provinces now living under the new Dominion of Canada. Hence the necessity of looking at *commercial considerations alone,* in projecting our means of communications, whether of canal or railroad. And the great practical question meets us at the outset, as to what is the cheapest method for bringing Western produce from Lake Erie to the open sea. If it be cheaper, or if it can be made cheaper, to send produce to Europe through the St. Lawrence by the building of ship canals, so as to allow sea-going vessels of the size suited for economical ocean navigation to pass in and out of Lake Erie, and to the head of Lake Superior, fully laden—I must admit that such a work will yet be accomplished. But I am not prepared to admit that it will ever be found cheaper to take produce from the level of Lake Erie, 565 feet above tide-water, to the open sea, through ship canals into Lake Ontario, and along the St. Lawrence; than it will be to bring it all the way by rail, when we shall have a line by the most practicable route, thoroughly constructed and fully equipped, with *two,* or even *three* sets of tracks, from Lake Erie, at Buffalo, to the harbor of Portland, touching Lake Champlain at Whitehall.

This brings me directly to the question of the cost of transit by railway. This question was put to me at Chicago by the President of the Board of Trade. "What will ultimately be the cost of moving a bushel of wheat or a barrel of flour, per mile, or per one hundred miles and more, between great commercial points?" I sought to make the question plain by repeating the statements made to me years since by Moncure Robinson, esq., of Philadelphia, for many years the most eminent railroad engineer of the country. He projected the Reading Railroad, about one hundred miles in length, from Philadelphia, as an outlet to the coal trade, whose headquarters are at Reading. After thorough survey, he took his plans and estimates to England, and laid them before rich capitalists of London. His proposal was, a level line of railway, one hundred miles in length, capable of moving 3,000 tons per day, or 1,000,000 tons per annum—*with an inexhaustible supply of traffic for all time to come*—moved at the rate of thirty-seven cents per ton, for one hundred miles. This, he contended, would pay a six-per-cent. dividend on the entire cost of the road—its equipments, stations, wharves, and other business accommodations.

These plans and estimates were submitted by the capitalists, at his request, to the leading railroad engineers of England. After careful examination, these engineers reported the correctness of all the calculations; but declared the propositions absurd, as no such state of facts could possibly exist. Mr. Robinson showed them that his great line was so adjusted as to form a level or descending grade in the direction of the traffic—so that a locomotive would haul as many loaded cars from Reading to Philadelphia, as it would take back empty, from Philadelphia to Reading. This demonstrated the character of the line. The supply of business could only be ascertained by careful examination.

The capitalists then proposed that if the facts should sustain the theory, they would furnish the capital. A contract was executed on the terms above stated, and the most competent men, selected from all

England by the capitalists themselves, were sent over to examine the ground. If they reported adversely, Mr. Robinson and his friends were to pay for their time, and all the expenses of the exploration and examination. Parties came over, reported the correctness of Mr. Robinson's representations, and under this agreement the Reading Railroad was undertaken. The company was chartered on the 4th of April, 1833, and the work commenced in 1836; but the great revulsion of 1837 embarrassed some of the English parties, so that it did not go through as rapidly as contemplated. But it was finally accomplished, and was the first great work of the kind opened, and enjoys to this day the pre-eminence of being the most important work engaged in the coal-trade of the country. It made a profit on carrying coal at 37 cents per ton, and John Tucker, for many years president of the company, has declared, that they have carried coal at a profit at 25 cents per ton. At this time they charge somewhat more! [In 1861, their receipts for coal transportation were at the rate of $1.12 per ton, and in 1862, $1.12; in 1863, $1.75; in 1864, $2.75; in 1865, $2.82; in 1866, $2.25; in 1867, $1.85; and in 1868, $1.77 per ton.] In 1866, this company carried 3,714,684 tons of coal, receiving therefor $8,245,696. This business slightly diminished in 1867 and 1868 from causes purely temporary and accidental. The stock of this company averaged $140 to the $100 in 1864, was as high as $117 in 1866, and is at par at the present time. The mileage of the road, with its branches, being equivalent to 374 miles of single track, costing

$35,253,553, with gross earnings of $10,902,218 in 1866, and $8,791,937 in 1868, according to their published returns. This company employed, in 1868, 16,604 coal-cars. The average weight of coal-trains 779 9-100 tons; the weight of empty cars, per load, per train, 266 tons—showing a net load of 513 tons of coal moved per train, with a dead weight of return cars 266 tons only—showing conditions of trade unknown upon any other line of railway in the world. It never had a commercial success like the Pennsylvania Railroad, chartered April 13, 1846, now embracing a mileage of 538 miles, operated as a single company, costing $54,143,746, with an income in 1868 of $20,037,748.

These two companies, from their favorable position and location through productive regions and abundant business, and under systematic management, may be cited as examples to illustrate the working capacity of railroads. But there is no means of determining, either in this country or in Europe, the precise cost of moving freight under the most favorable circumstances. A railroad should be economically built, provided with suitable means of handling freight, and prudently managed, to accomplish the highest results. In our inexperience, the cost of construction has been greatly in excess of what is now required to build a good line, and we have experimented on the various methods of working, till we begin to see more clearly the errors of former years. Give railroads enough to do, and they will do your work cheaply. Where the business is small, cost of transportation is necessarily high, as the same machinery and equipments are required to do a small business as a large one. An increase of business increases, of course, the cost of working a road, but by no means in proportion to the increase of business; the additional cost of handling merchandise being the principal addition to the expense of moving freight upon a railroad, with favorable gradients. We can learn something practical, by looking at the coal-trade of England,—the coal-trade of the United States, at present, being small, compared with that of Great Britain. In 1843, 2,663,114 tons of coal were brought to London, and entirely by ships. In 1867, 6,329,550 tons were brought to London. A large portion of this, or more than 3,000,000 tons, was brought by railway. Transportation of coal by railway has all been developed in the last twenty years. Coal is now brought to London from Staffordshire, a distance of 150 miles, for one shilling, or twenty-four cents per ton; the miners or mining companies owning, loading, and unloading their own cars. We may anticipate as favorable rates in this country, with the progress now witnessed in improved machinery, and greater skill in management. We may, with profit, take lessons from England, where her railroads cost five times as much as ours per mile, and are operated for about one third the cost of working lines in this country.

Looking at the continent of North America in its physical aspects, we are impressed with the belief, that it is best fitted by nature of any of the great divisions of the earth for the abode of man; and that here will be achieved the highest results of a true civilization. It has all the elements of wealth and material power in convenient proximity, by the configuration of its mountain ranges and the drainage of its great rivers. Europe is broken up into small sections by mountain chains, naturally leading to several and separate states and nationalities. The centre of Asia is one vast desert, so elevated above the level of the sea, as to preclude the possibility of communication across it. The great empires of Russia at the north, of China at the east, and of India at the south, are completely separated from each other, having no available means of intercourse, except by distant voyages outside the surrounding seas. Africa and South America are prohibited, by the laws of climate, from great intellectual development, or active participation in the affairs of the world.

The most marked features of the North American continent are the great basins of the St. Lawrence and the Mississippi, the best grain-producing regions of the earth. The valley of the Mississippi and its tributaries has 1,244,000 square miles of territory, about the same area as China. The St. Lawrence basin has an area equal to 470,471 square miles. All of this territory, amounting to 1,714,471 square miles, is within the limits of the United States, with the exception of 357,812 square miles of the St. Lawrence basin, which belongs to Great Britain, within the Dominion of Canada. The markets of Canada alone are sufficient to concentrate a vast business, and build up a great metropolis at Montreal; and it would soon accomplish this result but from the fact that the St. Lawrence, below Montreal, is closed by ice for the several months of winter, compelling her to make use of Portland harbor for her winter business. But while Montreal remains under a different commercial system from our own, she can never expect to equal the commercial cities of the United States, or realize the great destiny that awaits her. If goods could be imported in bulk into Montreal, and sent to all the Western and Southern states as now sent from New York City, Montreal would at once become the great rival of New York, and compete successfully for the Northwestern trade. Her growth is now limited by the narrow confines of Canadian trade. She would become imperial, if her trade were continental.

Canada is comparatively well supplied with railroads, while Maine and the lower Provinces are suffering for lack of them. But railroads are springing up at the east, and promise to grow into importance and into mileage, in Maine, New Brunswick, and Nova Scotia, equal to what has been reached in the five other states of New England. Maine has now in operation 652 miles of railroad, and 218 miles more in process of construction: with 200 miles of additional line chartered, the construction of which will be entered upon at an early day. New Brunswick has 236 miles of railroad in operation, and 125 miles more in progress, without including any portion of the Intercolonial Railway line. Nova Scotia has 145 miles of railroad in operation, and 200 miles more in process of construction.

In projecting great lines of communication, Americans are relieved from the restraints of unfriendly physical laws. They can extend a line or lines of railway from the ports of the Atlantic to the ports of the Pacific. But our line will be the most valuable and the most commanding of all, for it will span the continent at its widest part; and, for its entire distance, pass through a region filled with elements of wealth, awaiting development, whose business shall equal any section of this continent,—portions of it already occupied by a busy and prosperous people. Great physical facts control its location. It may cross narrow straits more effectually to lengthen the land-route at the extreme east, because the whole idea rests upon the theory, that land conveyance is more expeditious than water carriage,—but it is compelled to touch Bangor, Portland, Rutland, and Whitehall on its way, before it reaches Rochester, Buffalo, and Chicago, the great centre of continental trade. This question has received the attention of the business men of the West. The Board of Trade of Chicago, after full consideration by the most active and sagacious men of the country, adopted a series of resolutions on this subject on May 21, 1869, as follows:

RESOLVED, That the construction of a line of railroad from Chicago to the Pacific Ocean invites attention to the necessity of securing a direct line of railway from Chicago to the most eastern shore of the continent of North America, at its widest part, so as to secure the shortest practicable line of transit between the commercial centres of Europe and Asia.

RESOLVED, That the immediate advantage to the commerce of Chicago, of a direct line of railway to the most eastern shore of the continent, touching the unrivalled harbor of Portland, Maine, running along the south shore of Lake Ontario, and from thence by way of Whitehall and Rutland, due east, to Portland, over a route recently chartered by the states of

Vermont, New Hampshire, and Maine, calls upon the Chicago Board of Trade to take action in favor of this line with a view to encourage the preparation at Portland of facilities for the receipt, distribution, and shipment of merchandise to and from Chicago, without the delays attendant on other Atlantic ports.

RESOLVED, That the city of Chicago, at the heart of the continent, midway between its eastern and western shores, at its widest part over any practicable route for a railroad, can only realize her greatest destiny by adhering to the policy of avoiding the circuitous route by way of New York for the transit of passengers, mails, and valuable merchandise; which by means of the longest land conveyance and the shortest sea-voyage, can be transported from Hong Kong to London in thirty-eight days, and from Yokohama to London inside of thirty-five days.

RESOLVED, That the citizens of Chicago and of the central portions of the continent will welcome the completion of a line of railway by the most direct route from Chicago to Portland, to Halifax, Nova Scotia, to St. John's, Newfoundland, already projected, built, or in progress, as a portion of the TRANSCONTINENTAL RAILWAY,—an event of the greatest importance to this city, second only to the line to the Pacific,—enabling pleasure tourists, men of business, and emigrants from Europe to reach the heart of the continent, and future seat of empire in the New World, without any of the delays, restrictions, or detentions which come of circuitous routes, multiplicity of companies, and governmental intervention.

RESOLVED, That the laws of commerce disregard national or artificial boundaries; that the free transit of passengers, mails, and goods over all natural and artificial routes in possession of the English-speaking people upon the continent of North America, is the FINALITY OF AMERICAN STATESMANSHIP; that canals, in connection with our great chain of lakes, must ultimately be provided, and of sufficient capacity to allow steamers suitable for economical ocean-navigation to pass from the ocean by way of the lakes, to the heads of Michigan and Superior, with inward and outward cargoes,—while the immediate duty of the hour is to secure ship-canals between Lake Erie and Lake Champlain of sufficient capacity to transport the produce of the West, seeking an Atlantic market, without transshipment between Chicago and Whitehall.

TIME AND DISTANCE.

The following tables show the distance from London to Hong Kong, via Newfoundland, Portland, Chicago, and San Francisco; also, the time consumed:

FROM LONDON TO CHICAGO.

Station.	Miles.	Days.	Hours.
London to Holyhead, rail	263	0	10
Holyhead to Dublin, steamer	63	0	4
Dublin to Galway, rail	125	0	5
Galway to St. John's, Newfoundland, steamer	1,656	4	10
St. John's to Cape Ray, rail	280	0	14
Cape Ray to Cape North, steamer	45	0	3
Cape North to Pictou, rail	120	0	5
Pictou to St. John, New Brunswick, rail	250	0	10
St. John to Bangor, rail	196	0	8
Bangor to Portland, rail	138	0	6
Portland to Rutland, rail	168	0	8
Rutland to Schenectady, rail	85	0	4
Schenectady to Buffalo, rail	287	0	10
Buffalo to Detroit, rail	230	0	8
Detroit to Chicago, rail	284	0	10
Total	4,190	8	20

CHICAGO TO HONG KONG.

Station.	Miles.	Days.	Hours.
Chicago to Omaha, rail	494	00	18
Omaha to Promontory Summit, rail	1,086	1	10
Promontory Summit to Sacramento, rail	690	1	00
Sacramento to San Francisco, steamer	140	00	6
San Francisco to Yokohama, steamer	4,520	20	00
Yokohama to Shanghai, steamer	1,085	3	00
Shanghai to Hong Kong, steamer	800	2	10
Total	8,815	28	20
Grand Total	13,005	37	16

And it is proper in this connection to say, that these resolutions were adopted on full consideration, to meet in some measure the suggestions of Portland, in proposing increased harbor accommodations, and ample facilities for handling Western produce; as shown by the Commissioner's report and map, made under the direction of the Superintendent of the United States Coast Survey. The present commercial business of Portland is all transacted within the inner harbor. The improvements contemplated will be an entire addition, giving us two and one half miles of additional water front; with docks sufficient for the lying afloat of forty ocean steamers, of 400 feet in length, at the same time. And the extension of Commercial Street, completely round the city along side of tide-water, for the distance of six miles, will give us such facilities for commerce, as can nowhere else be found north of Norfolk, Virginia. A leading New York paper stated a few years since that it was the opinion of the best commercial men in New York City, that she could well afford to pay $300,000,000, or an annual rental on that sum, if she could secure thereby a deep ship channel to the open sea. She was annoyed that the *Great Eastern*, without lighterage, could not enter her harbor, for want of the same depth of water as at Portland.

Let us look at it, then, in its practical aspects. One line of railway, from the Pacific to Chicago, is completed. The Northern Pacific Railroad, passing through a better country, over lower summits, with easier grades, is an admitted necessity, and will shorten, by 500 miles and more, the distance from Chicago to Japan.

From Chicago, in latitude 41° 52', and in longitude 87° 35' to Portland, in latitude 43° 39', and in longitude 70° 15', the distance is 871 miles, conforming, in its route, very nearly to the principle of great circle-sailing, adopting the lines already in contemplation. From Chicago to St. Clair River, by the Michigan Air-line Railroad and its connections, already in progress, the distance is but 280 miles, over a route with easy grades, in a distance that does not exceed by two and a half miles an air line. From St. Clair River to Buffalo, by the chartered route of the Erie and Niagara Extension Railway Company, represented here to-day by Wm. A. Thompson, esq., of Canada, the distance to Buffalo will be but 170 miles, over a most favorable line; making the entire distance, by rail, but 450 miles from Chicago to Buffalo.

Buffalo is the great city of Lake Erie. Its natural advantages gave it importance, but it received its great impulse of growth, as it became the western terminus of the Erie Canal. The country has outgrown the canal, and the ideas of Buffalo have not kept pace with the progress of railways. She failed to secure, at the right time, a bridge across the head of the Niagara River, at her own door, and is now compelled to witness, from a distance, the great stream of travel, east and west, across the Suspension Bridge, instead of through her own city. From this apathy Buffalo may yet recover; and by uniting with the friends of the Erie and Niagara Railway, restore her lost advantages. By a direct route from Buffalo to Oswego, uniting with the friends of the Lake Ontario Shore Road, she can secure a line to Whitehall, which shall make her independent of the New York Central, and a greater city than Montreal. The Chamber of Commerce of Buffalo, more interested than Chicago in the Transcontinental Railway, or in the section from Chicago to Portland, adopted resolutions on the subject on May 27, 1869, as follows:

RESOLVED, That the Board of Trade of Buffalo have observed, with satisfaction, the measures in progress in the states of Maine, New Hampshire, and Vermont, to secure the construction of a line of railway from the unrivalled harbor of Portland, Maine, to Buffalo, by the most direct and practicable route, by way of Rutland Vermont, Whitehall, and south of Lake Ontario; that such a line of railroad will command the trade of the lakes beyond any line practicable or possible, running from Portland west; and, operated in connection with lake steamers and sailing vessels from Buffalo, upon Lake Erie and the upper lakes, will give such additional facilities as are now required to take off the produce of the great West which accumulates at Buffalo, coming from Chicago and other lake ports.

RESOLVED, That the opening of a line of railroad from the commercial centre of New England, at Portland, to the West, touching the grand chains of lake and railroad transit at Buffalo; giving a new and more direct route for pleasure tourists, men of business, and emigrants, must attract the bulk of travel by this route from the East; not only from New England and the lower British Provinces, but from Europe, on the completion of the chain of railways now built, in progress, or projected, extending from this city east, to the most eastern shore of the continent,—as contemplated by the projectors of the "Transcontinental Railway;" which, by means of the longest land-route and the shortest sea-voyage, will reduce the transit between the commercial centres of Europe and Asia to the lowest limits of time and cost,—by traversing the continent at its widest part, by an unbroken line of iron rail from the Atlantic Ocean to the shores of the Pacific Seas.

RESOLVED, That, while as citizens of the state of New York, we have a just and becoming pride in the growth and commercial importance of the city of New York, we, at the same time, recognize the right and the duty of opening new outlets to other Atlantic ports, for the better and cheaper transit of the accumulating products of the Northwest, upon the great lakes; that we recognize the advantages of Portland harbor as a natural outlet and shipping-port for Buffalo, from its depth of water, ease of access, and completeness of shelter,—where facilities for handling merchandise can be indefinitely multiplied, as called for by the demands of trade, on the completion of a direct line of railway from the navigable waters of Lake Erie, at Buffalo, to the deep water of Portland harbor; which harbor will be reached in a distance of 540 miles by way of Schenectady and Rutland, as against 457 miles to New York City by the Central and Hudson River lines,—while by straightening the line from Whitehall to Buffalo, the distance from Lake Erie to Portland will be reduced to 480 miles; insuring low rates of freight, from the cheaper cost of construction, over the existing lines of railway from Buffalo to New York City.

And the gentlemen of this committee at Buffalo have written letters, already read to you to-day, expressive of their hearty concurrence in the measures you have now under consideration.

From Chicago to Buffalo will be but 450 miles; from Buffalo to Whitehall 280 miles, by the Lake Shore Railroad to Fulton, 10 miles south of Oswego; thence due east, north of Oneida Lake,—making a total of 730 miles from Chicago to Whitehall. From Whitehall to Portland the distance is but 151 miles on an air line, and if you add 33 miles more, on account of deflections, it would make the distance 914 miles from Chicago to Portland.

The great feature of our line from Portland to Chicago is its advantages as a natural route for immigrants to the West, so well stated in the resolutions of the Buffalo Board of Trade. This stream of immigration from Europe will touch the nearest American shore, and distribute itself along the line of the railroads to the West, according to the attractions held out to them. The manufacturing population, mechanics, miners, mariners, weavers, and spinners, forming an aggregate of 291,771 persons who came from Europe for the last thirteen years, will naturally find employment in the lower Provinces and in the Eastern States, which are to be rapidly developed under the new order of things, which the European and North American Railway is certain to introduce. One line of ocean steamers has already proposed to deliver five hundred immigrant passengers per week to the railroad at Halifax, on the completion of the line to the United States; and the railroad companies will be able to send a thousand immigrants per day from Halifax west, after suitable preparation, cheaply and more expeditiously than by any other means.

What, then, is the duty of the people on the route from Portland to Rutland? At this time they can determine the route of the first line built from Portland to the West. The distance from Rutland to Portland on an air line is only 136 miles. A railroad line will be probably at least twenty per cent. longer, following the openings through the mountains, which the God of nature in his wisdom has provided; and if this line exceeds in length our previous estimates, it will probably only require a line as long as that of the present one from Rutland to Boston. A line from Portland west is a necessity that admits of no delay; and probably no event has or can occur to Rutland so great in importance as that which shall make her a leading station on that transcontinental chain, that shall first sweep the long line of four thousand miles with the highest speed of the locomotive, and command the choicest traffic of the world. From Portland, east, the line is in progress. The eyes of the world are already turned toward the east, by way of the west, and we already perceive, in the movements of business, a foreshadowing of the great future that awaits the American republic.

Every portion of the world is becoming subject to the influence of railways; and as nations become advanced in civilization, they secure and enjoy their advantages. Those who make the most use of railroads surpass, in the same proportion, other nations and peoples in the race of progress. The states of Massachusetts and Connecticut, in the United States, and the kingdom of Belgium, in Europe, are examples worthy of especial note in illustration. Mr. R. Dudley Baxter, an able English engineer, in a paper read before the Statistical Society of London, in November, 1866, illustrates the influence and value of railroads in the creation of wealth and the enlargement of business, by comparing the railways of Belgium and Holland. He says:

"Belgium is one of the most striking instances of the benefit of railways. In 1830 she separated from Holland, a country which possessed a much larger commerce and superior means of communication with other nations by sea and canals. Five years later, the total exports and imports of Belgium were only

£10,800,000, while those of Holland were double that amount. But in 1833 the Belgian government resolved to adopt the railway system, and employed George Stephenson to plan railways between all the large towns. The law authorizing their construction at the expense of the state passed in 1834, and no time was lost in carrying it out. Trade at once received a new impetus, and its progress since that time has been more rapid than in any other country in Europe."

My advocacy of railroads has been devoted mainly to their moral, social, and commercial value, rather than as means of money-making or the investment of capital; while railroads have been the means of influence and wealth to those who built and managed them, and the foundation of fortunes to many; their great benefits have been received by the community at large,—adding more wealth to the holders of real estate than to any other class, while they have conferred their blessings to a greater or less extent upon all. No man has yet lived since the advent of the railway, adequate to conceive, much less to describe in words, the true greatness of its mission. While simplest of all the agencies of progress, it is the grandest of man's inventions. It gives to one community the opportunities, the enjoyments, and the refinements of every other; it equalizes the burdens which come of diversity of condition; and lifts individuals and communities alike in the scale of being. While genius, talent, and persistent enterprise grasp the highest rewards, the race is open to all, and those who win are those who try.

It is no stretch of the imagination to cover the broad plains of the beautiful valley in which we are assembled, with myriads of habitations of men, in the far-off future. A few years only will be required to change these sloping hill-sides now clothed in the deep verdure of the summer forests, into cultivated fields and smiling farms; to bring forth the rich treasures embowelled in the mountains for the uses of commerce and of art; and a busy population engaged in various departments of human industry, may enjoy in this healthful climate, in the land of their birth, surrounded by this magnificent scenery, the richest delicacies, the most costly refinements, and the proudest exhibitions of art. Laying aside lesser considerations,—looking only to the highest welfare of the community in which we live,—let us do all that in us lies to carry forward this great work.

Our beneficent Creator, by giving man the railway, has endowed him almost with powers of creation, in addition to those of development and improvement. If we cannot, in the shortness of our own earthly duration, enjoy in full measure all,—that those who shall come after us may,—we can, at any rate, enjoy much, and do much to bring to ourselves and to our children the richest of earthly benefactions. Our friend, Mr. Cain, president of your railroad company, told us at Portland that he witnessed in 1830 the opening of the Liverpool and Manchester Railroad; where England's colonial minister, Huskisson, terrified by the fearful spectacle of a railroad train in motion, rapidly approaching him, threw away his life by an act of insane fear,—strangely in contrast with our calmness, at this day, in witnessing the flight of trains at a speed outstripping the bird upon its wing,—with its precious freight sitting in the same security as around the family fireside. It is most wonderful to note the changes worked out by the railway in less than forty years, since Huskisson's death, or the first locomotive train was started. But I should weary you if I should attempt to describe the prodigious increase of commerce, the wonderful diffusion of wealth, the vast advance of human intelligence, and the spread of civilization, traceable to the railway, during these last forty years.

We are now entering the fourth stage of our existence as a nation. One hundred and fifty years were required to plant our people in North America, and expel therefrom other races that struggled for its dominion. The *colonization period* terminated with the capture of Quebec, in 1759; the overthrow of the power of France in the New World was peacefully consummated by the treaty of Paris in 1763. To give us *independence of European control*, fifty years more were required, terminating at the close of the last war with Great Britain in 1815. The last fifty years have been profitably spent in vindicating the principles of the Declaration of Independence, putting an end to chattel slavery, endowing all men with equality of political rights. This age of *internal political conflict* terminated with the overthrow of the slave-holders' rebellion, and the election to the presidency of the hero of that war, General Grant.

The fourth stage in our national career, on which we are just entering, is *the age of material development*, the limits of which no finite mind can foresee or comprehend.

A NATIONAL HIGHWAY.

MEMORIAL TO THE CONGRESS OF THE UNITED STATES.

THE Portland, Rutland, Oswego, and Chicago Railway Company, a corporation established by law, whose place of business is at Portland in the state of Maine, respectfully asks Congress to constitute the railway of said company, from the city of Chicago to Portland harbor, *a national highway ;* said company having the necessary authority to construct and maintain such a line of railway, by virtue of a charter for this purpose granted by the Legislature of Maine, between the city of Portland and the city of Chicago, with the approval of other state Legislatures ; arrangements having been already made for the formation of a company under this Maine charter, with a common interest, from the harbor of Portland to the navigable waters of Lake Ontario at the city of Oswego.

The admitted necessity of the country to-day is an improved system of transportation of Western produce to tide-water, for which the present system of public works is totally inadequate. The interior basin of the continent, drained by the waters of the Mississippi and St. Lawrence, containing an area of 1,714,471 square miles of territory, is the great grain-producing region of the globe, capable of supplying food for the entire human family; and it was stated by Messrs. Baring, in a communication submitted to the Oswego Transcontinental Railway Convention, in October, 1869, that 500,000,000 bushels of American wheat could annually find a market in Europe at the present cost of production, if adequate facilities existed for its transportation to tide-water. To a clear understanding of the relations of the proposed railway to the commerce of the country, it is necessary to notice the physical divisions of the United States, as follows:

	Square miles.
Atlantic slope	514,416
Northern Lake region	112,649
Gulf region	343,935
Mississippi Valley and tributaries	1,244,000
Pacific slope, south 49th parallel	786,002
Alaska, or Russian America	481,276
Total	3,482,278

The boundaries of the republic have expanded from an area of 815,615 square miles of territory, at the time of the formation of the government, to their vast present proportions, while the population has risen from three to forty millions in less than one hundred years. The increase of population from 1850 to 1860 was at the rate of 35.59 per cent., while from 1860 to 1870 the ratio of increase has been but 22 per cent. The grain-growing states of the West exhibited a falling off in the ratio of increase from 59 per cent. from 1850 to 1860, to 41.83 per cent. from 1860 to 1870.

During the last ten years, there was a large increase of wealth and of manufacturing industry in the northern seaboard states, without any corresponding increase of wealth in the interior grain-growing states of the country in spite of their increase of population; consequent upon the inadequate means of transportation for the bulky and perishable products of the West, in the shape of breadstuffs and provisions, which require the utmost possible rapidity and certainty of transit to their markets. Cheap food brought to the Atlantic seaboard states, would be the greatest incentive and stimulant to their manufacturing industry. The bracing climate and abundant water-power of the New England and other northern states give them facilities for manufacturing for the West; while the abundance of raw productions in the interior states demands the cheapest possible transportation on their way east, or at the seaboard. Northern New York and New England have found it more profitable to purchase breadstuffs by the products of the shop, than by the productions of the soil, one car-load of manufactures bringing ten of grain in return. A wise political economy, therefore, looks for such an adjustment of the means of transit between the interior and the seaboard, as will give to each, the greatest possible facilities in the way of transportation; looking to the European markets for the disposal of such surplus as the West may be enabled to supply.

The vast interior basin of the continent, so fitted by nature for the production of food, has natural outlets two thousand miles from the sources of their rivers, the Mississippi and the St. Lawrence, almost as widely separated from each other at their mouths as the breadth of the temperate zone; one closed by ice in the winter months, with an arctic climate, cutting off water navigation for nearly one half of the year; the other impeded by circuitous navigation, shifting channels, and shoal water, at its entrance into the Gulf of Mexico, with an unfriendly climate, subject to tropical diseases. Hence the efforts of the last fifty years have been the construction of artificial channels by canals, and outlets by railway to the sea, from the waters of the Mississippi Valley, and alongside the unnavigable water-courses of the St. Lawrence. These enterprises, vast and invaluable as they have been, are due to the enterprise of states and individuals, rather than to the general government; which abstained from the work of building or aiding railroads until the public necessities compelled its aid to the railroad to the Pacific.

Transportation is the great question of the day. It is well known to all business men that the present cost of transportation consumes one half the value of the breadstuffs raised in the West; while it is equally certain that by means of a freight railway, with two or three sets of double tracks with steel rails, iron bridges, and an adequate equipment, breadstuffs and provisions of the West could be delivered with certainty and despatch, and at uniform rates throughout the year, from the producer to the seaboard, or the consumer in the New England work-shops, far below the present cost of transportation; and enable the Western farmer to send his products to market without the present risks and fluctuations which demoralize agricultural labor, and subject the agricultural producers of the West to the condition of dependents upon brokers and speculators,—a combination of railroad men putting up the price of transportation at the close of water navigation at their pleasure.

The completion of the Pacific Railroad has changed the course of trade to the East, and is destined at no distant day to revolutionize the commerce of the world. The completion of the European and North American Railway, affording the shortest time of transit between the commercial centres of the United States and Europe, will contribute to effect a change in the routes of commerce, especially the lines of travel. All-through lines of railway now projected look toward the East Foreland of the continent as the plane over which to deliver and receive European passengers and valuable merchandise. The completion of the line from San Francisco to Chicago, a distance of two thousand three hundred and eighty-seven miles; and the completion of a direct line from Chicago to Portland, one thousand miles; connecting here with the European and North American Railway line, in rapid progress with its connections to Halifax, a distance of six hundred miles; to be ultimately extended to the eastern shore of Newfoundland, one thousand and three miles from Portland, renders it certain, that the passage from Hong Kong to London by this route can be made in thirty-four and one half days' time; and on the completion of the Northern Pacific Railroad, reducing the distance from Chicago to the Pacific Ocean at Puget Sound, by more than three hundred miles, and shortening the ocean voyage from Yokohama over eight hundred miles, the time of transit from Hong Kong to London will be reduced to thirty days; while from Lake Superior to Portland, by way of Mackinaw across the northern peninsula of Michigan to the St. Clair River, a shorter route will be found to the seaboard at Portland; and it is obvious at a glance upon the map, that a line through British territory from the Sault St. Marie to Montreal by the way of Lake Nipissing and the Ottawa, will afford the shortest possible route between the tide-waters of the Atlantic and Pacific oceans, above the 40th parallel of latitude.

The following table shows the distance and the length of time required to make the voyage around the world, on the completion of the several links herein contemplated, in the chain of railroads upon the continent of North America east of Chicago; reducing the journey around the globe to sixty-nine days and eleven hours, against eighty days, the time now required.

FROM LONDON TO HONG KONG.

Station.	Miles.	Days.	Hours.
London to Holyhead, rail	263	0	8
Holyhead to Dublin, steamer	63	0	5
Dublin to Galway, rail	125	0	4
Galway to St. John's, N. F., steamer	1,656	5	0
St. John's to Cape Ray, rail	250	0	10
Cape Ray to Cape North, steamer	60	0	4
Cape North to Pictou, rail	120	0	4
Pictou to St. John, N. B., rail	250	0	8
St. John to Bangor, rail	205	0	6
Bangor to Portland, rail	138	0	4
Portland to Chicago, rail	1,000	1	6
Chicago to San Francisco, rail	2,387	4	0
San Francisco to Yokohama, steamer	4,520	16	0
Yokohama to Shanghai, steamer	1,085	4	0
Shanghai to Hong Kong, steamer	535	2	0
Total	12,707	34	11

FROM HONG KONG TO LONDON.

Station.	Miles.	Days.	Hours.
Hong Kong to Calcutta, steamer	3,500	12	0
Calcutta to Bombay, rail	1,229	3	0
Bombay to Port Said, steamer	4,060	14	0
Port Said to Marseilles	1,440	4	0
Marseilles to Paris, rail	475	1	0
Paris to London	252	1	0
	10,956	35	
	12,707	34	11
Grand total	23,663	69	11

Of the 23,663 miles of transit around the globe by way of San Francisco, and through the great cities of Europe and Asia, 6,300 miles are by rail, and 17,342 miles by steamer; and while by the American route from London to China there is an increase of distance over the Red Sea route, 4,345 miles of the distance are traversed by rail, against 1,956 miles by way of the East. While, therefore, it is obvious to every one that the shortest line of transit in point of time, around the globe, will eventually be secured, no matter how many delays occur before reaching final success; and while we regard all the advantages of the Transcontinental Railway as sure to follow in the train of its accomplishment; our immediate purpose is so to construct the line in question as to reduce at once the cost of bringing the productions of the interior to the open markets of the sea, where they can be handled to the greatest advantage, and at the cheapest rates.

If the producer of Western breadstuffs and provisions can be assured of ample facilities for bringing his products to tide-water at all times, at reasonable rates, *permanently fixed and uniform throughout the year;* with opportunities to enlarge the means of transit, as the demand for transportation increases, there is no limit that can yet be assigned for the growth and development of the United States. By the building of a trunk line of railway from Chicago to Portland, capable of delivering 500,000,000 bushels of wheat annually, or 15,000,000 tons per year at tide-water, the cost of transit of wheat might be reduced to ten cents per bushel; and deliveries made on shipboard at Portland, within one week's time of its receipt, and generally within four days. The price of transportation by water from Portland to Liverpool would regulate itself and reach the lowest rate of ocean transit ever known, from the abundant supply of freights going forward, and the certainty of return cargoes, to the extent of merchandise offering in Europe, for the American markets.

In constructing lines of railway upon the continent of North America, regard should be had to geographical and commercial laws, rather than to lines of state or national boundary. The spirit shown by the people and government of Maine and the British Provinces in the carrying out of the Grand Trunk Railway, and of the European and North American Railway, indicated a strong tendency toward closer commercial unity between the United States and the continental Provinces of British North America; and the extraordinary spectacle of an Intercolonial Railway "entirely through British territory," forced upon the new Dominion of Canada by the imperial government of England, regardless of commercial laws and of natural routes of travel, by a circuitous route through an uninhabited country, to subserve imperial wants and necessity, imposing a cruel burden upon the resources of the Dominion; is evidence of a disposition on the part of Great Britain to excite and foster a spirit of hostility toward the people and government of the United States, at war with the spirit of the age. The United States government cannot shut its eyes to this obvious purpose of the imperial government, and it should be prepared to meet any threatened military advantage. A line of railroad "entirely through" American territory, from its great harbor in the East, by the most direct route to the basin of the great lakes, ready to meet upon our own soil and maintain with equal efficiency, military preparations along our entire northern frontier, from our eastern boundary at the St. Croix to the farthest west of parallel, and competing military works, is an obvious necessity; for the building of the Intercolonial Railway, imposed upon the Dominion government, as a condition of union, was urged upon military, and not upon commercial, grounds. While it is our duty to meet this menace of England face to face, a far higher purpose than national antagonisms leads us to seek to carry out this United States American Transcontinental line. Its construction will enlarge commerce, promote civil order, soften national asperities, and give to all men under different governments greater means of individual enjoyment, and new facilities for the acquisition of property. This is the true purpose of the railway. Men and nations can in no other way, so effectually promote public interest and private advantage, as by the extension of railways, owned and operated in the interests of business, and for the equal advantage of all.

Portland harbor has great natural advantages for European trade over any other Atlantic port, from its great depth of water, completeness of shelter, and nearness to the West and to Europe. The foreign commerce of Portland has increased so that her exports to foreign countries in 1870 were $15,659,407, greater than those of Boston by $3,566,774 in that year. According to the statement of the Commissioner of the Land Office, in his elaborate map of 1868, showing the commercial relations of the United States with various parts of the world, the distance from Philadelphia to Liverpool is 3,260 miles, from New York to Liverpool 3,050 miles, from Boston to Liverpool 2,930, from Portland to Liverpool 2,770 miles, while from Montreal to Liverpool by the St. Lawrence route it is 2,814 miles, from Quebec to Liverpool 2,634 miles, and from Halifax to Liverpool 2,500 miles. The accommodations for business in the way of wharves and docks at Portland are altogether superior to those of any city of the United States, while preparations have here been made for a great enlargement of wharf and dock accommodations by means of a marginal street, for miles, upon tidewater, for the accommodation of railroad tracks.

Looking at the demand for American breadstuffs in Europe, and the vast capacity of our interior states to supply this demand, lacking only a proper outlet; by securing cheap transportation from the interior to the seaboard, we are constrained to believe that the increased value of a single crop, added to it by the construction of the proposed railway, will more than equal the entire loan to be afforded the company to carry out this project. But the company does not ask the United States government to advance a dollar from its treasury, or risk a dollar in the form of a loan, except with the most ample security; while the company itself, by uniting the interests of the East and the West upon this grand national and international enterprise, will relieve the West from the great burden that now bears upon its prosperity, and benefit alike every section of the country.

January, 1871

A BILL TO SECURE CHEAP TRANSPORTATION OF BREADSTUFFS AT UNIFORM RATES.

Be it enacted by the Senate and House of Representatives of the United States of America in Congress assembled;

That the Postmaster-General is hereby authorized to enter into contract with the Portland, Rutland, Oswego, and Chicago Railway Company, for the use of its line in the carrying of the mails between the city of Chicago, in the state of Illinois, and the city of Portland, in the state of Maine, on terms and conditions, in this act set forth ; in case said railway company shall enter into contract with the government of the United States to construct and maintain a double-track line of railway, with an adequate equipment and with steel rails and iron bridges, from the navigable waters of Portland harbor, by the most direct practicable route due west or westerly, across the states of Maine, New Hampshire, Vermont and New York, to the navigable waters of Lake Ontario at the city of Oswego, and thence by the most direct practicable line to the city of Chicago in the state of Illinois.

SEC. 2. *And be it further enacted,* That whenever said company shall have completed forty consecutive miles of any portion of said line ready for the service contemplated by this act, as a first-class railroad, the President of the United States shall appoint three commissioners to examine the same and report to him in relation thereto; and if it shall appear to him that forty consecutive miles of said railroad have been completed and equipped, the Secretary of the Treasury shall issue to said company, bonds of the United States of $1,000 each, payable in thirty years after date, bearing 6 per cent. interest per annum, payable semi-annually, on the first days of January and July in each year, in lawful money of the United States to the amount of fifty of said bonds per mile; and so on in like manner as each forty miles of said line are completed, upon the certificate of said commissioners; which said bonds delivered to said company shall *ipso facto* constitute a first mortgage on the whole line of the railroad of said company, together with its rolling stock, fixture, and property of every kind and description.

SEC. 3. *And be it further enacted*, That the grants aforesaid are made upon condition that said company shall pay said bonds at maturity, with the interest thereon; and shall give said railroad a telegraph line connected therewith, in repair and use; and shall at all times transmit despatches over said telegraph lines, and transport mails, troops, munitions of war, supplies, and public stores, upon said railroad for the government, whenever required to do so by any department thereof; and the government shall at all times have the preference in the use of the same, for all the purposes aforesaid at fair and reasonable rates.

SEC. 4. *And be it further enacted*, That said railroad corporation may establish for its sole benefit fares, tolls, and charges upon all passengers and property conveyed or transported on its railroad at such rates as may be determined by the directors thereof, and may from time to time by its directors regulate the use of its road; *provided* that such rates of fare, tolls and charges and regulations shall at all times be subject to revision and alteration by Congress or such officers or persons as Congress may appoint for the purpose; and in case no such officer is appointed by Congress or under any law of Congress, the Postmaster-General is hereby vested with all the powers necessary to regulate the use of said road, and fix the rate of fares, tolls, and charges as contemplated by this act.

SEC. 5. *And be it further enacted*, That the government of the United States may at any time take and possess the road of said company with its franchises and property after one year's notice in writing; paying such compensation therefor as may be awarded by three commissioners appointed by the President of the United States, who shall be duly sworn to appraise the same justly and fairly; and upon the payment of any such award or the tender of payment thereof to said company, the title of said railroad shall vest in and become the property of the United States government.

SEC. 6. *And be it further enacted*, That on the completion of said line of railway from the navigable waters of Portland harbor to the navigable waters of Lake Ontario at Oswego, with suitable docks, wharves and appurtenances for the handling of merchandise and property, the Postmaster-General or other officer appointed by law, shall establish the rates of transportation both for passengers and freight upon all through business between tide-water at Portland and the city of Oswego; which rates shall not be changed without the consent of the Postmaster-General, or other officer appointed by law; and the same be uniform throughout the year.

SEC. 7. *And be it further enacted*, That whenever in the opinion of the President of the United States, the business of the country shall require the building and laying down of an additional double-track line alongside the existing road-bed of said company and within the limits of its right of way, or any portion thereof, and shall give notice thereof to said company, said railway company shall forthwith proceed to construct and maintain an additional double-track line in conformity with the notice as aforesaid; and on the completion of forty consecutive miles of said new line ready for the service contemplated by this act, fifty bonds per mile, of the tenor aforesaid, shall in like manner be delivered to said company, and so in the same manner as each forty miles are completed, upon the certificate of said commissioners; which said bonds shall constitute a mortgage on the whole line of railroad of said company, subject only to the prior mortgage of the United States, to require from time to time as the wants of business shall require additional double-track lines to be constructed and maintained by said company upon the terms in this act set forth; the government holding a lien upon said lines, its rolling stock, fixtures, and other property as contemplated in this act, with a right to purchase the same at the pleasure of the government as herein before set forth; and the rights of the government to the control of said line, and the rights of the company shall continue the same after additional double-track lines are built as provided by this act, in case a single double-track line is built.

SEC. 8. *And be it further enacted,* That whenever, in the opinion of the President of the United States, an extension or extensions of said line shall be required, beyond the limits mentioned in this act, it shall be lawful for the President of the United States to notify said company to complete and maintain such extensions, with one or more double-track lines, on the terms in this act set forth in reference to its main line. But said company shall not be compelled to build such additional lines, exceeding in all two hundred miles in length, without the consent of said company in writing, and it shall be lawful for said company to purchase any existing line of railway that may be found necessary or convenient in the carrying out of the provisions of this act.

SEC. 9. *And be it further enacted,* That before entering upon the work of construction of said line of railway, the location thereof shall be approved by a competent engineer, appointed by the President of the United States.

SEC. 10. *And be it further enacted,* That the railway of said company is hereby declared to be a *national highway,* and a post-road; and the government of the United States shall have the right to pass all needful laws for the protection of said road and the public; and it shall be the duty of each state through which said line shall pass to cede jurisdiction over the territory occupied by said railroad company, and said railroad company shall be subject to no state or municipal tax, and be subjected to no other burdens or obligations, except those imposed by its charter or by the laws of the United States. *Provided*, however, that nothing in this act contained shall relieve said company from any of its duties, liabilities, and obligations to the public and to the several states through which it passes, as set forth in its charter, or the respective charters under which the same is built.

SEC. 11. *And be it further enacted*, That in case of failure of said company to pay the interest due on the bonds issued by the government to aid its construction, or the principal thereof, as they severally mature, or fail to observe and fulfil the regulations prescribed as aforesaid by authority of the United States government; it shall be the duty of the Postmaster-General to take possession of said line, and all the property of said company, and report the same to the President of the United States to be by him laid before Congress; and it shall be the duty in that event of the Postmaster-General, to operate said line at the expense of the company, by proper officers by him appointed, for which authority is hereby granted; and it shall be the duty of Congress to pass all necessary laws for the protection of the government and the public, and make such disposition of the property of said company as to justice and equity may appertain.

SEC. 12. *And be it further enacted,* That after the payment of the bonds of the United States issued by the government to aid the construction of said railway, the government of the United States shall retain control of said road in the same manner as before, for the regulation of the transportation of passengers and freight; and all fares, tolls, and charges upon all passengers and property conveyed or transported upon its road shall be approved by the Postmaster-General or other officer appointed by Congress or under any law of Congress; so as to prevent any unnecessary increase in the price of transportation after such bonds are paid, and it is made the duty of the government to maintain and secure cheap transportation over said line at *uniform rates and throughout the year.* And it shall be lawful for said company at any time to pay the bonds of the United States issued to aid the construction of said line, or an equivalent amount of United States bonds bearing the same rate of interest, or any portion thereof, at its pleasure, and discharge to that extent its indebtedness to the government; and it may receive from the government bonds of the United States bearing a lesser rate of interest than six per cent., if such shall be the pleasure of the company at the time that any issue of bonds is made.

January, 1871.

THE FATHER OF ENGLISH COLONIZATION IN AMERICA;

A VINDICATION OF THE CLAIMS OF SIR FERDINANDO GORGES.

DELIVERED BEFORE THE HISTORICAL SOCIETIES OF MAINE AND NEW YORK,
1859.

Two events, of ever increasing importance, have marked the progress of this continent, destined hereafter to be regarded as the great epochs of its history —the grant of authority from the British crown, under which colonies were planted in America; and the final surrender of the continent to the English race, by the conquest of Canada from France,—the former obtained through the efforts of the sagacious and enterprising Sir Ferdinando Gorges, the latter achieved by the heroic valor of Wolfe. France, at one time, dividing with Spain the whole of North America,[1] saw its power broken, and its dominion in the New World extinguished, when at the charge of the British bayonet, the hitherto invincible columns

[1] On the evening on which this paper was read in New York, there was presented to the Historical Society a Spanish globe, dated 1542, engraved on copper, which shows the boundaries of Florida, and of " *Verrazzan or New France*,"—Florida extending as high as the 33° north,—New France reaching north to Terra Corterealis. This globe is one of the most valuable contributions yet made to the history of North America.

of Montcalm broke and fled from the Plains of Abraham, and the morning sunlight of September 18, 1759, revealed to the disappointed soldiers of De Levis the proud Cross of St. George, floating in triumph over the ancient citadel of Quebec. The dominion of a continent was changed by a single encounter; and English institutions are now planted, as the fruits of that victory, over a region of territory greater than all Europe, extending from the Northern Ocean to the Gulf of Mexico, and from the Atlantic to the Pacific seas. The future of this conquering race, no statesman or philosopher of this day is able to foretell. My purpose is, to trace the earliest practical efforts to plant it in America, and to vindicate the claims of Sir Ferdinando Gorges, the proprietor of my native State, to the proud title of FATHER OF ENGLISH COLONIZATION IN AMERICA.

The greatness of England is due to her colonization in America. She was but a second-rate power at the commencement of the seventeenth century, till raised to greatness by the iron will of Cromwell. After the destruction of the Dutch fleet, the conquest of Acadia from France in 1654; of Jamaica from Spain in 1655; the establishment of her navigation laws and her protective policy, she was admitted as an equal into the community of nations. The Venetians and the Swiss sought the friendship of the Protector. All the northern nations respected his power, and the great Mazarin acknowledged his authority as the lawful sovereign of Great Britain.

The necessity of encouraging the colonies previously planted in North America, led to the Navigation Act of Cromwell, in 1651, which was the foundation of the maritime superiority of England. That statute remained for nearly two centuries,[1] and secured to England the entire trade of all her colonies. It stimulated the commercial enterprise of her people. It allowed strangers no importations, unless of their own products in their own vessels. This act fell with crushing weight on the trade of Holland, and left England mistress of the commerce of Europe. The protective policy of Cromwell, also, gradually drew to her own shores the manufactures of Holland and Flanders, and finally those of France; after the revocation of the edict of Nantes, by Louis XIV., on October 24, 1685. This celebrated edict of Henry IV., in 1598, secured liberty of conscience and perfect toleration to the Protestants of France, with a right to share the public offices; and its repeal inflicted a blow on France from which it has never recovered. Over 800,000 of her best people fled from the persecution that followed, most of them to Great Britain and her colonies. The most skilful artisans of France sought refuge in England, over 50,000 taking up their residence in London. They established the manufacture of silks, jewelry, crystal glasses, and other fine works hitherto unknown in England, but since that time successfully prosecuted throughout the British realms. Such has since been the increase of the productive power of England that, according to the statement recently made by Lord Brougham in the British Parliament, the ma-

---

[1] The Navigation Act of 1651 was repealed with the Corn Laws, June 26, 1846. Ch. 22, 9 and 10 Victoriæ.

chinery of England, at this time employed in the various branches of industry, equals in effective power the labor of 800,000,000 of men, an aggregate threefold greater than the entire laboring population of the globe. Yet England was the latest of all the European powers to encourage its subjects who came to America by the direct aid of its government, or to take measures to plant its race in the New World. It was not so much the efforts of the government as the genius of the people and the enterprise of individuals, that gave to its sons the inheritance of this fair land; where free institutions have developed an expansive energy, that demands for its race supremacy of the sea and dominion over the land.

The discovery of North America by Sebastian Cabot, in the service of Henry VII., in 1497, seventeen months prior to the time when Columbus saw the mainland of the continent; and the exploration of its coast from latitude 67°, 30' north, to Florida, has often been urged in modern times, as giving to England, claim of title. But it was followed by no act of jurisdiction, or of occupation, for nearly a century,[1] while all the other maritime powers of Europe were engaged in schemes of colonization.

[1] The government of England was the first to lay down the true doctrine as to the right to newly discovered countries. They distinctly affirmed in 1580, in the reign of Elizabeth, that discovery and prescription are of no avail unless followed by actual occupation. "*Prescriptio sine possessione haud valeat.*" Camden, "Eliz. Annales," 1580.—Hearne's ed., 1717, p. 360.

" Occupation confers a good title by nature, and the laws of nations."— "Parl. Debates," 1620-21, p. 250.

Denonville's Memoir, on French limits in America. "N. Y. Doc. His.," vol. ix., p. 378.

"The first discoverers of an unknown country, not inhabited by Europeans, who plant the arms of their prince, acquire the property of that country."

Emmanuel, King of the Portuguese, whose subjects, at that time, were the great navigators of Europe, and whose vessels had visited the East by way of the Cape of Good Hope, mortified at his neglect of the offer of Columbus, determined to make up for it by new conquests in the New World. He despatched Gaspar Cortereal [1] to North America in 1500, who described its shores and forests, its stately pines, suitable for masts, etc. But traffic in slaves, then an established business of the Portuguese, being esteemed the more profitable, he sailed northward, took in, by kidnapping, a cargo of over fifty natives, whom he carried to Europe and sold for slaves. But the Portuguese did not maintain their claim to the country.

Juan Ponce de Leon, in the service of Spain, took possession of Florida in the name of his sovereign, in 1512, published a map of the country as far north as Newfoundland, and claimed it as a possession of the Spanish Crown. But the Spaniards chiefly sought at that time mines of gold and silver, and never extended their occupancy of the country north of Florida, at about 33° north latitude.

France, on the contrary, sent out fishing vessels manned by the Bretons and Normans, to Newfoundland, as early as 1504.[2] Those who came earliest

[1] The country of Labrador is laid down as "Corterealis" on the Spanish globe, spoken of in a previous note, and in contemporary maps of North America.

[2] "Relations des Jesuites." Contenant ce qui s'est passé de plus remarquable dans Les Missions des pères de la compagnie de Jésus dans la nouvelle France. Ouvrage publié sous les auspices du Gouvernement Canadien, 3 vols., 8vo., 1858. Quebec: Augustine Coté, editeur imprimeur. Vol. i., p. 1, "Relations," 1611.

"Documentary History of New York," vol. ix., pp. 1, 304, 378, 701, 781.

named the country first visited Cape Breton, from their own home. They discovered the Grand Banks of Newfoundland, visited all the creeks and harbors of the Gulf of St. Lawrence, gave names to the localities which they still retain, and published maps of the country. Jean Denys of Honfleur made a map on his return in 1506, and Thomas Aubert, of Dieppe, brought back natives and a plot of the country in 1508. The ocean they crossed was named the Sea of the West, 800 leagues broad in its narrowest strait from France. The Western Ocean they called the Sea of China. In 1524 Giovanni Verrazzani, a Florentine navigator in the service of Francis I., returned from his last voyage of discovery to America. According to Champlain,[1] he made two voyages to the New World, but we have no narrative from his own pen of more than one. He sailed to the coast of Carolina in a direct passage, where he found a native population more refined in its manners than that of any other country of the New World. It had never before been visited by Europeans. Verrazzani, sailing northward, explored the coast, penetrated its various harbors, entered the bay of New York, and spent fourteen days in the harbor of Newport, Rhode Island. At each place visited he made acquaintance with the native population, which proved more and more warlike and unamiable as he advanced northward. Following the general line of the shore, he sailed 150 leagues along the coast of Maine, clearly defining that great bay or gulf extending from Cape Cod to Cape Sable, known afterward as the Bay or Gulf of Maine. To the entire tract of country never before

---

[1] "N. Y. Doc. Hist.," vol. ix., p. 2.

discovered or frequented by Europeans he gave the name of New France. On reaching the 50th parallel of latitude he sailed to France, and published a most interesting narrative of his voyage.[1] France in this way established her claims to the country. It was not Cartier, as is commonly asserted, but Verrazzani, that gave the name of New France[2] to the country he discovered, which extended from the 30th to the 50th degree of north latitude. This claim France maintained, and named Carolina for Charles IX. During his reign in 1562 Ribaut built a fort there, which was called Charles-fort in honor of the king.[3] It is a singular fact that neither Spain, France, nor England had furnished up to this time any great navigator in the discovery of America. They were all Italians: Columbus a Genoese, Cabot a Venetian,[4] and Verrazzani a Florentine.

---

[1] "New York Historical Collections," vol. i., p. 39, *et. seq.*, *new series*, contains the full narration of Verrazzani's voyage, addressed to the French monarch, translated by J. G. Coggswell, esq., of the Astor Library.

[2] "Relations des Jesuites," vol., i., p. 14. Champlain, "N. Y. Documents," vol. ix., pp. 1–4. *Do*, vol. ix., p. 266. Harris' "Voyages," vol. i.

[3] Garneau's "History of Canada," vol. i., p. 118.

Curiosity has been awakened the past year in regard to the location of Charles-fort from the naval and military expedition to the same region under command of Commodore Dupont and General Sherman. No traces of the old fort have yet been found by those in the army of the Beaufort expedition. General Peter Force, of Washington, whose authority is most valuable, places the site of Charles-fort on the north side of St. Helen's Island.

[4] John Cabot, the father of Sebastian, undoubtedly was a Venetian. There is much evidence lately brought to light, tending to prove that Sebastian Cabot was born in Bristol. In Grafton's "Chronicles of England," page 1323, we find the following notice of Cabot of Bristol: "A native of that city, but who with his father removed to Venice at the age of four years."

Sebastian Cabot, son of a merchant of Cathay, in London.—Eden, 249.

Eden says: "Sebastian Cabot told me he was born in Bristol, and at four years of age went to Venice."—Page 255.

The French monarch, following out his plans for the colonization of America, sent out Jacques Cartier in 1534; who, sailing from St. Malo on April 20 with two ships and 122 men, on May 10, 1534, came in sight of Bonavista, Newfoundland, a spot discovered by Cabot in 1497. In the "Relations of the Jesuits," recently published under the patronage of the government of Canada, it is stated that Cartier had been on this coast ten years before, and it is fair to conjecture that he was in the expedition of Verrazzani. But we find no other account of any such voyage. Cartier was most fortunate in his expedition. He found the localities of the Gulf of St. Lawrence already known to the fishermen, having the names they now bear. He sailed around Newfoundland, took possession in various places, both on the mainland and the island of Newfoundland. Taking with him two young natives of Gaspé, by their full consent, he sailed for France and reached St. Malo on September 5, 1534.[1] The report of Cartier's voyage and discoveries excited great curiosity and interest; and with a more ample equipment in three ships, provided at the royal expense, he sailed on another expedition for the New World on May 19, 1535, carrying back to America his two young savages, who became useful as interpreters to the natives. Cartier on this voyage sailed up the Gulf and into the River St. Lawrence, where he spent the following winter at the fortified town of Hochelaga, to which he gave the name it still bears, Montreal.[2]

[1] Cartier's "Voyages"; Garneau's "History of Canada."
[2] Cartier's "Voyages"; Garneau's "History of Canada," vol. i., p. 21.

The next spring, erecting the cross in the name of his sovereign at various points, and taking with him the chief of the savages at Quebec, Donacana, and his two young interpreters, he returned to France on July 6, 1536. He made his third voyage in 1540, but no new discoveries were made; and for nearly fifty years, the more northern portions of North America were apparently forgotten by the governments of both France and England.

Spain, at that time the great European power, subjugated to her dominion, and planted colonies in, the rich countries of tropical and southern America, held the Gulf of Mexico, and Florida to the 30th parallel of latitude.

The spirit of adventure had only led the French and English to take fish in the northern seas, and fur and timber from the coast of Maine—though the coast of America, from Labrador to the Equator, was accurately delineated on maps published in Europe within fifty years of its first discovery by Columbus. The French sent Ribaut, in 1562, to Florida, and joined with him Laudonnière, in 1564, but no results of importance came of these expeditions, as the French were driven out by the Spaniards. The French asserted their right to the country north of Florida, for nearly one hundred years after its discovery, previous to any substantial claim to it being set up on the part of England.

The first act of the British Parliament, concerning America, was passed in the second year of the reign of Edward VI., in 1548, entitled "An act against the exaction of money, or other dues, for license to traffic into Iceland, Newfoundland," etc. England seemed more intent on religious disputes than on the extension of her dominions in America, during the reigns of Henry VIII., Edward VI., and Mary. No returns of the English fishery are found prior to 1577. Those of the French date back to 1527—three years after the expedition of Verrazzani. In 1577 there were found one hundred and fifty French fishing vessels on the coast of Newfoundland, engaged in the cod-fishery, and only fifty English ones. The heroic exploits of Drake, the first Englishman that circumnavigated the globe,—who, sailing on this voyage from Plymouth November 15, 1577, returned to the same port September 26, 1580,—and the "Discourse" of Sir Humphrey Gilbert, "to prove a passage by the northwest to Cathaia," printed in 1576, had filled the youthful mind of England with enthusiasm for noble undertakings, and stimulated the ambition of all classes; and Sir Humphrey Gilbert led the way in the plans of colonizing the New World. He obtained from Queen Elizabeth a charter "for planting our people in America," June 11, 1578, in the twentieth year of her reign. Under this grant he took possession of Newfoundland, and planted the city of St. John's, in the presence of thirteen Europeans, of various nations—fishermen, who accidentally, but not unfrequently, assembled in that secure seaport, at that early day. This port, long after this, retained the name of "the English port," and is so mentioned by the historian L'Escarbot, in his history of the voyage of De Monts to Acadia, in 1604. But the loss of Sir Humphrey Gilbert, at sea, proved fatal to his plans, and it was some years before Newfoundland became a permanent settlement, or colony.[1] In 1584, the queen granted letters-patent for the planting of a colony in Virginia to the gallant and accomplished Sir Walter Raleigh, whose heroic efforts for the honor of his country, and whose melancholy fate, excite at this day the sympathy of all generous minds. But the first colony he transported to Virginia returned—the second perished by some unknown means; and thus was reserved for another the glory of *first* planting the Saxo-Norman race in the New World.[2]

Such is, in brief, the history of European attempts at colonization in North America, to the close of the sixteenth century. There were not any European

[1] John Guy was sent out as Governor of Newfoundland in 1610, and began the colony at Conception Bay. The Newfoundland colony is the oldest of the present colonies of Great Britain.

[2] Since the writing of this paper, a work of great interest to the student of English history has been undertaken, "A Calendar of State Papers." Edited by W. Noel Sainsbury. London, 1860. Longman, Green, Longman, & Roberts. It is subdivided into three great branches, or divisions—"Domestic," "Colonial," and "Foreign." The first volume of each is already published. That containing an abstract of colonial documents embraces the period from 1574 to 1660, from which we condense the following, viz. :

1. 1574. Points stated in reference to proposed efforts to plant settlements in the northern parts of America. Petition to the Queen, dated March 22, 1574, to allow of an enterprise for the discovery of sundry rich and unknown lands "*fatally reserved for England and for the honor of your Majesty.*" Endorsed, Sir Humphrey Gilbert, Sir Geo. Peckham, Mr. Carlisle, and Sir Richard Grenville. p. 1.

Sir Humphrey Gilbert's commission and charter are dated June 11, 1578.

2. 1580. Fragment of a report of persons who had travelled in America, with John Barros, Andrew Thevett, and John Walker. Sir Humphrey Gilbert did confer in person. In 1580, John Walker and his company discovered "a silver mine within the river Norumbega." p. 2.

1600. Consideration on " a proposition for planting an English colony in the northwest of America. If the Prince would assist it, in part, his Majesty's merchants go liberally into it—the country be stirred to furnish men ; some gentlemen moved to be adventurers, and a worthy general chosen, qualified to judge by sight, of the strength of the places ; it might be a glorious

settlements from Florida to the Northern Ocean. Two hundred and fifty years ago England, a second-rate power in Europe, had not a colonial possession on the globe. France and Holland were then the great maritime nations; and well did Sir Ferdinando Gorges say in the House of Commons, when called on to show why he should not surrender the charter of New England, "*That so valuable a country could not long remain unpossessed, either by the French, Spaniard, or Dutch, but for his efforts here to settle a flourishing plantation.*"[1]

action for our Prince and country, honorable for the general welfare, and adventurers, and in time profitable." p. 4.

(This paper bears internal evidence that Sir Ferdinando Gorges was its author.)

1603, Nov. 8. Copy of patent by the French King to De Monts, of Acadia, from 40° to 46° of north latitude. p. 4.

(The early filing of this copy in the British State-Paper Office shows how complete was the information of the government as to the movements of the French towards colonizing the New World.)

1606, April 10. Grant of charter to Geo. Popham and als. by King James, from 34° to 45°. p. 5.

1607, March 9. Ordinance enlarging the number, and augmenting the authority of the council for the two several colonies and plantations in Virginia and America. Thirty members for the first colony, from 34° to 41° north latitude; and ten members for the second colony, between 38° and 45° north latitude.

1607, March 13. Letter of Gorges to Challong. (See later note.)

1607, Dec. 13. Geo. Popham to King James. "Maine Hist. Coll.," vol. v., p. 341.

1613, Oct. 18-28. Montmorency, Admiral of France to King James. Complains of Argall at Mt. Desert. Requests compensation, etc.

The following are found in the "Calendar of Domestic State Papers":

1603, July 26. Warrant, etc., to N. Parker ("Warrant Book," p. 102), take possession of the office and papers of Sir Ferdinando Gorges on his suspension from office.

1603, Sept. 15. Warrant to pay 56s. per annum to Sir F. Gorges, who is restored to his former post of Captain of the new fort at Plymouth. ("Warrant Book," fol. 18.)

1608. *Letter.* Sir F. G. to Thomas Gamel of Salisbury. Escape of Challoner (Challong) out of Spain. Bad feelings of the Spaniards towards the English.

1609, July 31. Warrant to deliver ordnance stores to Sir F. G., Captain of the forts at Plymouth Island.

[1] Gorges' "Briefe Narration," vol. ii., p. 36. "Maine His. Coll."

The throne of England was filled by Elizabeth from 1558 to 1603. That of France from 1589 to 1610 by the liberal-minded and chivalric Henry IV., who of all the sovereigns of his time seems most fully to have appreciated the importance of American colonization. In the autumn of 1602, an expedition was fitted out by the merchants of Rouen, under charge of Seigneur Du Pont Gravé, of St. Malo; and in the early part of 1603, Henry sent Champlain, the great French navigator, to the St. Lawrence; who visited on his return from Quebec, Gaspé, the Bay of Chaleur, and the other places occupied by the fishermen in the Gulf. He encountered icebergs of prodigious length, between the 44th and 45th degrees north latitude, and obtained from the savages a description of the St. Lawrence above Hochelaga.

On the return of Champlain in 1603, Henry had granted to Pierre du Gas, Seigneur De Monts, a French Protestant, and a member of his household, all that part of North America lying between the 40th and 46th parallels of north latitude, and confirmed it by letters-patent, November 8, 1603.[1] In this grant the king says: "Fully confiding in your great prudence, and in the knowledge you possess of the quality, condition, and situation of the said country of Acadia, from the divers voyages, travels, and visits you have made into these parts, and other neighboring and circumjacent, etc., etc., we do ap-

---

[1] L'Escarbot "Historie de la nouvelle France," 1609.
Champlain's "Voyages" (ed. 1632), p. 44.
Hazard's "Coll.," vol. i., p. 45.
Williamson's "History of Maine," vol. i., app.
Sainsbury's "Calendar of Colonial State Papers," vol. i., p. 4.

point you our Lieutenant-General, to represent our person in the country, coasts and confines of Acadia, from the 40th to the 46th degree of latitude." The design was *the occupancy of the country*. De Monts sailed from Havre de Grace March 17, 1604, with two vessels, in one of which, Captain Timothy, of New Haven, master, were De Monts, Champlain, Poutrincourt, and the accomplished scholar and historian L'Escarbot.[1] In the other, commanded by Captain Morell, of Honfleur, was Du Pont Gravé, the companion and associate of De

[1] L'Escarbot's "History of New France" is by far the most valuable of all the works on America of that date. His first edition, published in 1608–9, 12mo, contained a map of the country explored. This work was translated into English, and published by P. Erondelle, London, in 1609, as an original work, without any allusion to the author. A second edition was published in Paris in 1612, under the following title, which we translate from the copy recently placed in the Astor Library:

"HISTORY OF NEW FRANCE,

Containing the Voyages, Discoveries and Settlements made by the French, in the West Indies and New France, with the consent and authority of our Most Christian King; and the diverse fortunes of those engaged in the execution of these things, from a hundred years ago, till to-day.

In which is comprised the History Moral, Natural and Geographical of the said Province: with Tables and Pictures of the same.

By MARC L'ESCARBOT, Lawyer in Parliament; Eye Witness of a part of the things here recited.

Multa renascentur qua iam occidere cadent que.

PARIS:

JOHN MILLOT, in front of St. Bartholomew with the three crowns, and in his shop, on the steps of the great hall of the Palace.

1612.

WITH PATENT FROM THE KING."

In the Library of Congress is a copy of the third edition, published at Paris, in 1618.

The Dutch and the French adopted the names of the rivers and places given them by L'Escarbot.

I am aware that Warburton and others assert that L'Escarbot came out in the second expedition in the ship *Jonas*, in 1606; but I find nothing to justify this statement from his own writings.

Monts. They called at Isle Sablon, and reached the coast May 16, 1604, where they found a ship trading with the natives contrary to the directions of the king, which they seized and confiscated; giving the master's name, Rossignol, to the port, his only return for the voyage. The port is now called Liverpool, but a lake in the interior still bears the name of the unlucky master. Exploring the coast westward, De Monts reached Port Mouton, where they landed, waiting the arrival of Du Pont Gravé. The company of planters, those who designed to remain in the country, was one hundred in number; and here they erected tents, and planted the ground with grain, which two years later was found bearing a good crop.

Champlain, impatient at the delay, proceeded west in a shallop, explored the coast, and discovered the beautiful island, which he named St. Croix—from the fact that just above it the streams formed a natural cross, one on each side, entering at right angles with the main river—which river finally retained the name of St. Croix, or Holy Cross, and now divides New Brunswick from Maine. Champlain rejoined his companions at Port Mouton, after exploring as far west as the Penobscot. On the arrival of Du Pont Gravé and Captain Morell, both ships sailed west, entered the Bay St. Marie, discovered the Bay of Fundy; then sailing north reached Port Royal. Poutrincourt, who came out to select for himself a place of settlement, was so delighted with Port Royal, that he solicited, and obtained from De Monts a promise of a grant of it; and with Du Pont Gravé, returned to France, in the autumn of 1604, to arrange for his removal to this country, and for a fresh supply of planters.

Under the advice of Champlain, De Monts' company proceeded west, discovered the river St. John, followed the coast westward, and planted themselves in the spot he had selected, known at this day as Neutral Island, in the St. Croix river, within the limits of the state of Maine. This was the first settlement of Europeans north of Florida. Here they laid out a town, and planted the ground. During the autumn of 1604 habitations were erected, a fort built, a magazine constructed, and a chapel finished.[1] The winter of 1604-5 was long and severe, and thirty-five of their number died of the scurvy. In

[1] "Leaving the River St. John, they came, following the coast twenty leagues, to a great river—properly a sea—where they fortified themselves in a little island, seated in the midst of this river, that the said Lord Champlain had been to reconnoitre ; and seeing it strong by nature, and easily guarded ; and in addition, seeing that the season was beginning to pass, and the necessity of seeking a lodging without going further, they resolved to stop there. The Island of St. Croix is difficult to find for one who has not been there—there are so many islands and great bays to pass, before reaching it.

"But there was one difficulty. The fort was on the northern side, where there was no shelter, except the trees on the bank of the island. Without the fort was the lodgings for the Swiss, and other little houses, like a suburb of a city. Some had built cabins on the main land, near the brook. But in the fort was the house, or dwelling, of Lord De Monts, made of good carpenter work, with the flag of France floating above it. On the other side was the magazine, where reposed the safety and life of all—similarly made of good carpenter work, and covered with shingles ; and opposite the magazine were the houses of Lord Orville, Champlain, Champdoré, and other noble personages, and on the opposite of the dwelling of De Monts, was a covered gallery, for the exercise of play, and for workmen in rainy weather ; and between the said fort and the platform where the cannon was, all filled with gardens. Each one amused himself, or worked with a gay heart. All the autumn passed with this, and it was doing well to have lodged ourself, and cleared up the Island before the coming on of the winter."—L'Escarbot, book iv., ch. 4, p. 460, 2d edition, 1812.

the spring, De Monts, disappointed at the rigor of the winter, seeking a milder climate, proceeded to explore the country west and south, designing to settle four degrees south of St. Croix. He visited Mount Desert, the Penobscot, the Kennebec,[1] Casco, and Saco; and coasted as far south as Cape Malabar, twelve miles south of Cape Cod. Portland harbor, which he named "Marchin," from the Chief, or Sagamore, who then resided here, and who was killed in 1607, took the name of Machigonne. De Monts sailed into all the bays, harbors, and arms of the sea, from St. Croix to Cape Malabar, a distance of over four hundred leagues, "searching to the end of the bays." Saco still retains the name "Chouaquet," given to it by De Monts, in 1605. South of "Pescadouet," Piscataway (Portsmouth), the harbors were less and less satisfactory, and the country less and less inviting; and after reaching Cape Malabar, De Monts despaired of finding a suitable place of settlement, as he had designed. While at Cape Cod, in 1605, they carried on shore a large kettle for cooking, which the Indians seized in the absence of the cook. On discovering the theft, he attempted to rescue it from their hands; but he was slain by them, and the kettle carried off. This was undoubtedly the same kettle that Bradford speaks of, which the Plymouth people found in their first explorations in 1620.

[1] "Sailing west, 1605, to find a place of settlement they, De Monts, Champlain and Champdoré, came to Norumbega, the river of Pentagouet (Penobscot), and thence to Kinnibeki (Kennebec), which shortens the way to the great river of Canada. There are a number of savages settled there, and the lands begin to be better peopled."—L'Escarbot, book iv., ch. 7, p. 497.

In the spring of 1605, Du Pont Gravé arrived at St. Croix with supplies and a reinforcement of forty men, for the colony, which gave great joy. At his suggestion, the establishment was broken up at St. Croix, and they removed to Port Royal. Here, under the advice of L'Escarbot, they cleared and cultivated the lands, and built a mill for the grinding of their corn. Though Port Royal was destroyed by Argall, in 1613, it was rebuilt, and has ever since been peopled. A settlement was made on the St. John, above the Falls, by Du Pont Gravé, and St. Croix was also soon reoccupied. In 1611, when the Jesuits, Biard and Masse, visited the Kennebec, for the purchase of grain, but without success; Plastrier, who lived at the Island of St. Croix, gave them, on their return, two hogsheads of beans, which rendered important aid, in supplying Port Royal with food in the winter of 1611-12. Four French ships were at that time taking fish at the White Rock, twenty-two leagues west of St. Croix. The whole country was familiar to the French; Champlain and Champdoré the pilot carried back reports to Europe. In 1609, the work of L'Escarbot was translated and published in England. De Monts sailed up the Kennebec river, as is reported, in 1605, in the expectation of reaching Hochelaga, or Montreal, by water; led into this attempt by the reports given him by the Indians. Though claiming the country as far south as the 40th parallel of latitude, there is no evidence that De Monts ever sailed south of, or attempted to extend his jurisdiction south of, Cape Malabar. All east of this was claimed as within the control of France.

The country east of French Bay, or the Bay of Fundy, was called ACADIA; between that and Canada, NORUMBEGA.[1]

At the commencement of the seventeenth century the Dutch were the most commercial and the most powerful nation of Europe, if superiority in wealth and enterprise is to be regarded as the true measure of greatness. Small in territory and inferior in point of numbers to France or England, Holland had grown superior to either in all the arts of civilized life. Tolerant of religious opinion and enjoying unrestricted commercial freedom, the people of the Low Countries had accumulated wealth, reclaimed their marshes from the invasions of the sea, and cultivated the arts of peace. Their prosperity excited the jealousy of England, and they were finally compelled to yield to the iron will of the Protector, who infused new life into all pursuits, not only of commerce but of war. The people of Holland had learned to practise religious toleration long before those of any other nation, and were the first to recognize the commercial code, or what is commonly called the "law of nations." They were equally in advance of other powers in all commercial ideas and undertakings. As early as 1581 the Dutch merchants had established a profitable trade with the West Indies, and in 1597 had a still more lucrative one with the East Indies. In 1600 the realized wealth of Holland surpassed that of France, England, or Spain. Her Batavian provinces had yielded abundant returns to her merchants, though requiring long and tedious

---

[1] "Relations des Jesuites."

voyages around the Cape of Good Hope; and other nations sought to reach the same coveted treasure by a shorter route across the Atlantic, by the long-hoped-for *northwest passage* to Cathay. With this view the famous British East India Company was chartered December 31, 1600, with a capital of £70,000. In 1602 the Dutch East India Company was chartered with vastly greater capital. An expedition for the colonization of North America was one of the early objects of the Dutch government and people, and they claimed the country from the 41° to the 45° of north latitude. Their ship, in command of Henry Hudson, was off the mouth of the Penobscot river July 18, 1609, and from that year they had actual and permanent possession of Manatte, or New York Island. So that France, Holland, and England started almost simultaneously in a career of colonization in the New World.

At this time appeared on the public stage Sir Ferdinando Gorges. Born 1573, at Ashton Philips, in Somersetshire, he became a distinguished naval officer in the Spanish war prior to 1603, when, on the accession of James I., he was made Governor of Plymouth. How early he became interested in the colonization of America does not quite clearly appear, but being an intimate friend of Sir Walter Raleigh, though twenty-one years younger, it is fair to suppose that he possessed the same adventurous spirit: and in his "Briefe Narration," speaking in later times of the grant to himself of the Province of Mayne, which was dated April 3, 1639, he says: "Being now seized, of what I had travailed, for *above forty* (40) *years*, together with the expenses of many thousand pounds, and the best time of my age; laden with troubles and vexations from all parts, as you have heard, I will now give you an account in what order I have settled my affairs, in that, my Province of Mayne, with the true form and manner of the Government, according to the authority granted me by his Majesty's Royal Charter. First. I divided the whole into eight Bailiwicks or Counties, and these again into sixteen several hundreds; consequently, into Parishes and Tithings as people did increase and the provinces were inhabited," etc. Gorges speaks in familiar terms, at the commencement of his narrative, of the efforts of Sir Humphrey Gilbert and of Sir Richard Grenville to plant colonies in America, the last of which terminated 1585, so that his mind was evidently familiar, at an early day, with their plans for American colonization. It has been recently made to appear that he was directly concerned in the great voyage of George Weymouth, in 1605, regarded as the initial point in the history of New England; and probably, in the previous ones of Gosnold, in 1602,[1] and of Pring, in 1603.

[1] Interest has of late been awakened as to the route and the purposes of Gosnold's voyage, which at this time deserves notice. On March 26, 1602, Capt. Bartholomew Gosnold, in the forty-second year of the reign of Elizabeth, sailed from Falmouth, in the County of Cornwall, for a voyage into the north part of Virginia, in the bark *Concord*, with thirty-two persons on board—twelve of them sailors, and twenty "to remain in the country for population." So that the priority of the English in efforts to colonize the country is clearly established. The country that invited rival efforts at colonization by the Dutch, French, and English extended from Cape Breton to the head of Delaware Bay.

Of those who came out with Gosnold, who was chief in command, and who died in Virginia in 1607, the only names preserved to us are Bartholo-

The information, recently brought to light by a publication of the Hon. Geo. Folsom, "A Catalogue of Original Documents in the English Archives, Relating to the Early History of Maine," proves, what was before only a matter of conjecture, that Gorges was the chief promoter of Weymouth's voyage. In

mew Gilbert, second officer; John Angel; William Street, shipmaster; Robert Solterne, who came out with Pring the following year—afterwards a licensed clergyman; John Tucker; John Brereton, gentleman, and journalist of the voyage; James Rosier, the journalist of Weymouth's voyage in 1605, and Gabriel Archer, gentleman, and also journalist of the voyage, who subsequently went to Virginia.

The land-fall of Gosnold is thus described by Archer:

"On Friday, the fourteenth of May, early in the morning, we made the land, being full of fair trees—the land somewhat low—certain hummocks, or hills, lying into the land; the shore full of white sand, but very stony, or rocky. And standing fair along by the shore, about twelve of the clock the same day, we came to an anchor, where eight Indians, in a Biscay shallop, with mast and sail, and iron grapple, and a kettle of copper, came boldly aboard us; one of them apparelled with a waistcoat and breeches of black serge, made after our sea-fashion; hose and shoes on his feet; all the rest (saving one that had a pair of breeches of blue cloth) were naked. These people are of tall stature, broad and grim visage; of a black swart complexion; the eyebrows painted white; their weapons are bows and arrows. It seemed, by some words and signs they made, that some Basques of St. John de Luz, have fished or traded in this place, being in the latitude of 43°. But riding here, in no very good harbor, and withal doubting the weather, about three of the clock the same day in the afternoon, we weighed, and standing southerly off into the sea the rest of that day, and the night following, with a fresh gale of wind; in the morning, we found ourselves embayed within a mighty headland," etc.

This headland was Cape Cod, a name given to it by Gosnold, from the abundance of cod taken there, and which it still retains, despite the efforts of subsequent voyagers and writers to affix to it the name of Cape James, in honor of the king. John Brereton, the fellow-passenger and historian of the voyage, thus describes Gosnold's land-fall:

"The 13th day, we landed in seventy fathoms, and observed great beds of weeds, much woods, and divers things close floating by us, when as we find smelling of the shore as from some southern cape and Andalusia in Spain. The 14th, about six o'clock in the morning, we discovered land, that lay north, and the northerly part we called the Northland, in which to another rock, upon the same, lying twelve leagues west, that we called Savage rock; for six leagues toward the said rock is an outpoint of rising ground, the trees thereof were high and straight from the rock, east northeast. But finding ourselves short of our purposed place, we set sail westward, leaving them and their coast about sixteen leagues S. W.; from thence we perceived in that course two small Islands, the one lying eastward from Savage rock, the other to the southward of it. The coast we left was full

Gorges' letter, on file in the State-Paper Office, published in full by Mr. Folsom, dated March 13, 1607, addressed to Mr. Chalinge (Challong), he speaks of the return of the former voyage, of *but the five savages*," whom Weymouth took as "*the chief return* TO US, WHO FIRST, sent to the coast." [1]

of goodly lands, fair plains, with little green round hills above the cliffs, appearing unto us.
"The 15th day we had again sight of the land, which made ahead ; being, as thought, an Island," etc. This proved to be Cape Cod.

From these accounts, Dr. Belknap supposed Savage rock to be on the northerly shore of Massachusetts Bay, about Nahant. Drake, in his elaborate history of Boston, expresses the belief that "Savage rock" was in the vicinity of Great Boar's Head, in Hampton, and that Gosnold's land-fall was at Boon Island, on the Isle of Shoals, from the fact that they are nearer to the 43° of latitude than any island on the coast.

The late John McKeen, Esq., of Brunswick, a thorough and accurate observer and explorer, in a paper read before the Maine Historical Society, exposes the errors of modern writers, and shows that the statement of Strachey, that Gosnold's land-fall was at the mouth of the Sagadahoc, is the true one. Strachey was a contemporary, and undoubtedly wrote with the narrations of Archer and Brereton before him ; and in constant intercourse with those who shared this adventurous voyage. R. K. Sewall, Esq., in his able work, "Ancient Dominions in Maine," concurs in fixing the land-fall of Gosnold at Sagadahoc.

We think the evidence fully establishes the fact we assume, that Gosnold's land-fall was at Sagadahoc : that on the 13th of May, 1602, he sighted the islands from Seguinto Cape Elizabeth, and gave to the latter the name it still bears, in honor of his queen ; that the name of Falmouth, subsequently adopted for the site of the present city of Portland, was so affixed in compliment to the port from which the first voyage of exploration sailed. It was a favorite idea with the English, from the first, to give the name of their former home, or their place of embarkation, to the places visited in the New World, as in case of Bristol, Plymouth, Falmouth, Yarmouth, Portsmouth, Dartmouth, York, Wells, etc. The French, on the contrary, generally adopted the local names of the country, attempting to express in language the sounds gathered from the lips of the natives.

[1] 1607, Mar. 13. Plymouth. Letter of Sir Ferdinando Gorges to Mr. Chalinge.

Mr. Chalinge—I received your lrê sent me by the Mr. Nicholas Hines by whom I rest satisfied for your pte of the proceedinge of the voyadge and I doubt not but you will be able to answer the expectacon of all your freindes. I hoope you shall receive verie shortlie, if alreadie you have not, an attesta-

This voyage of Weymouth was nominally undertaken to find the long-sought-for northwest passage to India, and " as set forth " by the Earl of Southampton, and Arundell, Lord Wardour. But this was undoubtedly a pretence to mislead the French who claimed the country, and were, at this time, occupying the territory and coasting along the shores of Maine. De Monts and Weymouth were in the same waters in 1605. Weymouth sailed from the Thames, March 31, 1605, explored the coast of Maine, and west as far as Nantucket. As Weymouth had been familiar with the coast in a previous naval service of twelve years, and knew that any idea of find-

tion out of the highe Courte of Admiraltie to give satisfacon of the truthe of our intent, yt sett you out, let me advise you to take heede that you be not ov'shott in acceptinge recompence for wrongs received, for you know that the jorney hath bene noe smale chardge to us, *yt first sent to the Coast and had for our returne but the five salvages whereof two of the principal you had with you and since within in* two months after your depture we sent out an other shippe to come to your supplie, and now again we have made a nue preparacon of divers others, all of wch throughe your misfortune is likely to be frustrate and our time and chardge lost, therefore you^r demands must be answerable hereunto, and accordinglie seeke for satisfacon which cannot be lesse than five thousand poundes and therefore before you conclude for lesse attende to receive for resolucon from hence, if they answere you not thereafter, for if their condicon be not such as shall be reasonable, we do know howe to right ourselves, for rather then we will be loasers a penny by them we will attend a fitter time to gott us our content, and in the mean time leave all in their hands, therefore be you careful herein, and remember y^t it is not the buisness of merchants or rovers but as you knowe of men of another ranke and such as will not preferre manie complayntes nor exhibite divers petitions for that they understande a shorter way to the woode, soe comendinge you to God and continuing my selfe
        your most assured and lovinge friende
Plymoth 13 of   Ferdinando Gorges
Marche 1607
   Postcript
I pray you use the meanes that the salvages and the companie be sent over with as muche speede as is possible and yt you hasten yourself away if you see not likelihoode of a present ende to be had for we will not be tired with their delaies and endlesse sutes such as commonlie they use but leave all to time and God the just revenger of wrongs
            Ferdinando Gorges
[Endorsed]   The Coopie of Sr. Ferdinando Gorges his lrē to Mr. Chalens.
     Received ye 6 day.

ing, by this route, a northwest passage to India, was absurd; the conclusion is inevitable, that Weymouth's voyage was designed to lay the foundation of the Royal Grant, which secured the continent to Great Britain. In fact, Weymouth proposed to plant a colony, and Owen Griffin and another man had agreed to remain. A most interesting discussion is now going on by many able writers in Maine, as to the river visited by Weymouth, and which of the noble harbors of that wonderful coast was the Pentecost harbor, in which he anchored his ship *Archangel*, in 1605. Weymouth carried back to England, in 1605, five natives of Pemaquid, from whom Gorges obtained full "particulars of its stately islands, and safe harbors, what great rivers ran up into the land, what men of note were seated on them, what power they were of, how allied, what enemies they had, and the like." By his glowing descriptions of the beauties of the country, he satisfied the royal inquiry, and laid the foundation for the subsequent grant from the king.

It was through the efforts of Gorges that King James made the Royal Grant or Charter, dated April 10, 1606, granting to "the Council of Virginia" the continent of North America, from the 34° to the 45° of north latitude, and all the islands within one hundred miles of the shore. Sir Ferdinando Gorges and the Earl of Southampton petitioned the king for his charter, but no copy of this interesting document has as yet been brought to light. The attacks on Sir Ferdinando Gorges, for "grasping cupidity" in obtaining charters from King James and the Stuarts, are among the striking evidences of the intolerance of the times. He, or any one, who would sacrifice his private fortune to establish plantations in America, deserved the gratitude of the nation and the warmest commendations of modern times. Instead of this, the historians of New England—those even of our times, or such as follow Puritan authorities—unjustly represent Gorges as a man of a selfish and grasping spirit, whose only ambition was private advantage. The grants to Sir Humphrey Gilbert and to Sir Walter Raleigh by Elizabeth were as obnoxious to the charge of monopoly as those subsequently given to Sir Ferdinando Gorges and his associates, which the Puritans attacked; but no complaint was made against Elizabeth for these grants, although others, lavishly bestowed by her in various departments of trade and manufactures, were boldly attacked by the Commons.

This charter of April 10, 1606, is the foundation of the title of England to North America. It was followed up by immediate acts of jurisdiction and possession. In May, 1606, the Lord Chief-Justice of England, Sir John Popham, having become associated in the enterprise, sent out Captain Haines, "in a tall ship belonging to Bristol and the river Severne, to settle a plantation in the river of Sagadahoc"; but from the failure of the master to follow the course ordered, the ship fell into the hands of the Spaniards by capture, and the expedition failed of success. In August, of the same year, a ship, sent out by Sir Ferdinando Gorges, under command of Henry Challong, with two savages as pilots, for the same purpose—the two designed to form one expedition,—shared a similar fate. Another vessel, sent by the Chief-Justice, in command of Hanam, under charge of Martin Pring as master, sailed two months later, reached the coast of Maine; but not finding Challong, made a perfect discovery of all the rivers and harbors, and brought back a most exact description of the coast; which so encouraged the company, that they determined to send out a greater number of planters, with better provisions for the planting of a colony at Sagadahoc the next year. In consequence of these mishaps Virginia was occupied prior to Maine. The expedition of Captain Newport to the Chesapeake, which sailed December 19, 1606, landed at Jamestown May 13, 1607.

On May 31, 1607, the first colony to New England sailed from Plymouth for the Sagadahoc, in two ships—one called the *Gift of God*, whereof George Popham, brother of the Chief-Justice, was commander; the other, the *Mary and John*, which Raleigh Gilbert commanded—on board which ships were one hundred and twenty persons for planters. They came to anchor under an island, supposed to be Monhegan, July 31; and in two hours after, eight savages in European apparel came to them from the shore in a Spanish shallop, and after rowing about the vessels awhile, boldly came on shipboard, where three of them stayed all night. The next day the others returned with three women in another Biscay shallop, bringing beaver skins for the purpose of trade, so familiar had these people become with the habits and designs of their European visitors. The fish of Monhegan were already more esteemed than those of Newfoundland, and this spot was the common resort of all the trading vessels on the coast. By this means, undoubtedly, the Indians became possessed of French and Spanish shallops prior to 1607.

After exploring the coast and islands, on Sunday, August 9, 1607, they landed on an island they called St. George, where they had a sermon delivered unto them by Mr. Seymour, their preacher, and returned aboard again. On August 15 they anchored under Seguin, and on that day the *Gift of God* got into the river of Sagadahoc. August 16 both ships got safely in, and came to anchor. August 17, in two boats, they sailed up the river—Captain Popham in his pinnace, with thirty persons, and Captain Gilbert in his long-boat, with eighteen persons, and "found it a very gallant river; many good islands therein, and many branches of other small rivers falling into it," and returned. August 18 they all went ashore, and there made choice of a place for their plantation, at the mouth or entry of the river, on the west side (for the river bendeth towards the northeast and by east), being almost an island, of good bigness, in a province called by the Indians "Sabino"—so called of a Sagamo, or chief commander, under the grand Bashaba. August 19, they all went ashore, where they had made choice of their plantation, and where they had a sermon delivered unto them by their preacher, and after the sermon, the President's commission was read, with the laws to be observed and kept: George Popham, gent., was nominated President. Thus commenced the first occupation and settlement of New England, and from which date the title of England to the New World was maintained.[1]

This act of formal possession of the country under their charter, August 29, 1607, was the consummation of England's title to New England, and the foundation of her future greatness; and the day should be observed as an epoch wherever there exists a community who enjoy the common law of England or speak the mother-tongue.

This charter, of April 10, 1606, was *"for the planting of colonies or plantations in North America."* It placed the power in a council of thirteen. To

---

[1] The charter of De Monts was revoked by the king, in 1607, on account of the intense jealousy of his rivals. This loss of title by the French allowed the English charter of April 10, 1606, to take precedence of all French grants. In all subsequent contests with rival nations, the Dutch and the French, the occupation by the Popham colony, in 1607, was put forward as the ground of title. In 1632 the Dutch West India Company, in their address to the States-General, under date of May 5th, say: "In the year 1606 his Majesty of Great Britain granted to his subjects under the names of New England and Virginia, north and south of the river (Manhattoes), on express condition that the companies should remain one hundred miles apart. Whereupon the English began about the year 1607 to settle by the river of Sagadahoc. The English place New England between 41° and 45° of north latitude."—" Holland Doc. N. Y.," p. 51. The Dutch contended that they had the right to occupy the one hundred miles reserved by the charter as open territory.

Count de Tillieres, French ambassador, writing to Secretary Conway, under date of April, 1624, admits the claim of England to Virginia and to the Gulf of Mexico, south five hundred leagues ; but denies all right north. In answer to Tillieres, the charter of King James, in 1606, to the two companies is quoted to show that the claim of both is equally valid.—" Calendar of Colonial State Papers," i., p. 60. In 1631, Champlain, in his great memoir to the king, giving a statement of the rival claims of the French and English, says: " King James issued his charter twenty-four years ago, for the country from the thirty-third degree to the forty-fifth degree. England seized the coast

encourage competition and excite rivalry, it provided for the planting of two distinct and separate colonies, each having a local government, of North and South Virginia, the former subsequently known as the Plymouth, the latter as the London Company; each company not to colonize or establish a plantation within one hundred miles of each other. Neither Gorges nor the Chief-Justice had their names inserted, for fear of exciting, as it would seem, the jealousy of rivals. Eight persons only were named in the charter, four for each colony, who might be expected to join the expeditions.

The history of this Popham Colony is very imperfectly known. They called their settlement

of New France, where lies Acadia, on which they imposed the name of New England."—"French Doc. N. Y.," vol. ix., pp. 1 and 2.

In 1630, September 9, the Scotch adventurers addressed a letter to the king from the Council of Scotland—those claiming title under the grant to Sir William Alexander, afterwards Lord Stirling,—in which they assert that "the planting of New England in the north" was by Chief-Justice Popham. —"Cal. of Colonial State Papers," i., p. 119.

In a work entitled "An Encouragement to Colonies," by William Alexander, Knight, printed by William Stanly, London, 1625, it is said: "One of them, Sir John Popham, sent the first company that went, of purpose to inhabit there, near to Sagadahoc." P. 30.

Captain John Mason, writing to Sir Edward Coke, Secretary of State, under date of April 2, 1632, says: "Plantations in New England have been settled about twenty-five years."—"London Doc. N. Y.," vol. iii., p. 16.

In the work of Sir Ferdinando Gorges, grandson of the original proprietor of Mayne, entitled "A Description of New England,—America Painted to the Life," published in London, in 1659, he says: "New England is between 41° and 45° of north latitude. In 1606 the country began to be possessed by the English by public authority. . . . A peninsula at the mouth of the river Sagadahoc, where they built a fortress, which they named St. George." P. 18.

Sir John Popham was ridiculed in his time for his efforts to plant colonies in America. "Chief-Justice Popham not only punished malefactors, but provided for them, and first set up the discovery of *New* England to maintain and employ those that could not live honestly in the *Old*."—Lloyd's "State Worthies," p. 46.

Fort St. George, the remains of which are still in existence; from which place, George Popham writes to King James, under date of December 13, 1607, in the Latin language, in which he says: "My well considered opinion is, that in these regions the glory of God may be easily evidenced, the empire of your Majesty enlarged, and the welfare of Great Britain speedily augmented." They finished their vessel, of fifty tons, in the winter and spring, called the *Virginia* of Sagadahoc, in which they returned to England that year. They lost their governor, George Popham, during the winter, who died February 5, 1108. Captain Gilbert, who succeeded to the command, was compelled to return, to settle the estate of his brother, Sir John Gilbert, who had deceased, and to whose estate he was heir. Added to these, the death in England of the venerable Chief-Justice Popham, who died June 10, 1107, and the terrible severity of the winter through which they had passed, threw discouragements in their way, which they had not the courage to surmount.

This was the critical period in the history of the English race, in the New World. Both France and England were claiming title. The occupation of the territory could alone determine the rights of the parties. Poutrincourt, inflamed with all the zeal of the Catholic faith, kept his hold on Acadia, and returning to France, with De Monts, in 1607, obtained from him a grant of Port Royal. He came out at the instance of the king, with a new grant, in 1610, with Fathers Biard and Masse; and being free from the annoyance of the Huguenots, he despatched his son Biencourt to France, to bring further recruits to his colony. The flower of their youth were cheerfully engaged for this service, from all the Jesuit colleges of France.

As they were about to embark for Acadia, the merchants of Dieppe, who had furnished the supplies for the ship, refused the Jesuits admission on board, on account of their religion, so strong was the Protestant faith at that time in France. The zealous and enthusiastic Madame de Guerchville, moved to anger by this refusal of the merchants, raised the entire sum required for the voyage by contributions among the Catholic nobility; and despatched Biencourt, and his Jesuit missionaries, who arrived at Port Royal just in time to save Poutrincourt and his party from starvation. Meanwhile Champlain had in 1608 laid the foundation of Quebec, and held actual possession of the St. Lawrence under a new charter. Emboldened by the breaking up of Popham's Colony, at Sagadahoc, the French pushed forward their possessions, claiming the territory as far south as Cape Cod. Gorges knew the importance of maintaining possession of the country, and while "*all his associates gave up to these discouragements,*" his heroic spirit, so far from yielding, rose with the occasion that demanded still greater sacrifices; and, as he says: "Finding I could no longer be seconded by others, I became an owner of a ship myself, fit for that employment, and under color of fishing and trade, I got a master and company for her, to which I sent Vines and others, my own servants, appointing them to leave the ship and ship's company for to follow their business in the usual places. By these and the help of those natives, formerly sent over, I came to be truly informed, of so much as gave me assurance, that in time, I should want no undertakers, though as yet, I was forced to hire men, to stay there the winter quarters, at extreme rates," etc.[1]

We may therefore fairly claim that the occupancy of Vines and others under Gorges saved the country from falling into the hands of the French. We find the English at Pemaquid in 1608 and 1609.[2] Thither the Virginia colony sent annually for fish, from 1608 and onward. Sir Francis Popham, the son of the Chief-Justice, continued to send his ships to Pemaquid, and the same ship was found there by Captain John Smith, on his first visit to the coast, in 1614. Belknap says that Vines came over a long time before the settlement at Plymouth, and the authorities concur in fixing it in 1609. Sir Ferdinando Gorges, though he does not name the year, speaking of events in the order of their occurrence, places the settlement of Vines before the voyage of Hobson; and tradition has assigned to Vines the honor of holding Pemaquid, Monhegan, and Sagadahoc, from 1609 till he removed to Saco, where he spent the winter of 1616–17. Captain Hobson came over as early as 1611. Gorges says in connection with this voyage, "for some years together nothing to my private profit was realized, for what I got one way I spent another."

In 1613, Argall, from the Virginia colony, on visiting the coast for fish, learned that the French

---

[1] Gorges' "Briefe Narration."   [2] Relations des Jesuites.

had a trading-house at Penobscot, and a settlement at Mount Desert, or St. Saviour, another at St. Croix, and one at Port Royal. After procuring a sufficient force he broke up these posts and destroyed St. Saviour and Port Royal, carrying the Jesuits and some of their adherents to Virginia as prisoners; many of the French settlers fled to the woods, but returned and re-occupied the places thus laid waste by Argall. French fishing and trading ships were constantly visiting these places. In June, 1614, Captain Henry Harley, one of Popham's Colony at Sagadahoc, sailed in Gorges' employ with Assacumet, one of those natives first taken by Weymouth, and the famous Indian Epenow, of Martha's Vineyard, who proposed to show them valuable mines of gold. He was, as Gorges says, "a person of goodly stature, strong and well proportioned," but he escaped from them as soon as they came to the coast, and the expedition was productive of no useful results. It is not necessary to narrate all the events connected with the expeditions to the country, prior to 1614, when the eccentric but intrepid Captain John Smith appeared on the coast, in command of four ships.

This venture of Smith paid a profit of £1,500, "by traffic in otter and beaver skins, salt fish, train oil, and such other like gross commodities." Smith at this time made a plot or map of the country, since known as Smith's map of New England, published in 1616, and he was made Admiral of New England by the company. In 1615 Smith sailed again for New England, in two ships, which voyage proved disastrous. He lost his masts in a gale, returned to

Plymouth, and again sailing was taken prisoner by the French. One of the vessels, however, in command of Captain Dermer, made its way to New England and returned well laden. In the same year, Sir Richard Hawkins, President of the Plymouth Company, departed for these parts, and took in a cargo for Spain, principally fish, which proved a profitable business. In 1616, eight ships from London and Plymouth made profitable voyages to New England, and the value of the fisheries of Monhegan was fully established. There can be no doubt that Monhegan was occupied with a trading, though changing, population, many years before Plymouth was settled; and when Edward Winslow, of the Plymouth flock, visited it, in May, 1622, as he says, "*to obtain victuals for our famishing plantation*," he found there thirty ships. He also says: " I found there kind entertainment and good respect; with a willingness to supply our wants; through provident and discreet care, we were recovered and preserved, till our own crop in the ground was ready."

Such was the condition of New England affairs in 1616, before war had broken out among the Indian tribes, pestilence destroyed the native population, or the Pilgrim settlement been initiated. The country was well known along the coast, from the Bay of Fundy to Cape Cod, and the fisheries yielded abundant profit. It was comparatively full of people, a native population, subsisting not only on game and the products of the soil, but on oysters, salmon, and the choicest fish, in which the harbors, rivers, and coves abounded. The territory, now known as the state of Maine, with its numerous and well sheltered harbors; its noble rivers, swarming with the most valuable fish; its forests, of unrivalled beauty, surpassing, in the estimation of the navigators, those of the north of Europe; its soil, bearing readily the choicest grains of Europe, in addition to Indian corn, and the potato indigenous to this continent; the charming variety of scenery; its undulating surface; its climate, that for healthfulness and salubrity left nothing to desire,—attracted the most skilful of the European voyageurs to its shores. The region lying between Cape Porpoise (Kennebunk) and the Penobscot was the most frequented of all, for it is by far the most beautiful portion of New England, and the possession of it excited the ambition of the French and English alike. It was the seat of Indian empire, more populous than any portion of the continent, the home of the Bashaba, whose authority extended to Narragansett Bay. The Indians always occupied the best portions of the continent until driven from them by superior force, as seen in our day in the case of the Cherokees and Choctaws of the South, and the Penobscots of our own state. The French were the first to perceive this great fact, and their possessions followed closely the grounds held by the Indians. We have not time to pursue this inquiry, but we hazard nothing in predicting that the seats of empire on this continent, of the European races will eventually coincide with those of the aboriginal inhabitants.

The coast was at that time well delineated on maps in common use; the Dutch had a flourishing colony on the Hudson river; and on the same day that John Smith was exhibiting to Prince Charles, for his approval of the names upon it, his map of New England; the Dutch figurative map of New Netherlands, extending east to the Penobscot, was laid before the States-General for their inspection and adoption. The early navigators saw nothing inviting between Cape Cod and Manhattan, while all the harbors east of Cape Porpoise were filled with voyageurs from the Old World. In 1602, when Gosnold came to New England, the Indians, clothed in Indian apparel, visited his ships without any signs of surprise, as at Pemaquid, in 1607, the aborigines came fearlessly on board the vessels of Popham and Gilbert; and the famous Indian Sagamore Samoset went from Pemaquid to greet the Pilgrims at Plymouth, in March, 1621, with hearty welcome in their own language. "*Welcome, welcome, Englishmen,*" said Samoset, and proved his friendship to the end of his life. The welcome of Samoset was sincere, because the Indian tribes, who valued goodly rivers, fertile fields, and abundant forests, as the best hunting grounds; felt no jealousy of men who sought a resting-place on the barren and deserted sands of Cape Cod, where the native population had been swept off by the plague. And the French looked with equal indifference on that feeble band of fishermen whose location at Plymouth in no way interfered with their plans of dominion in the New World. About this time, 1616, a bloody war broke out between the Tarratines, who lived east of the Penobscot, supposed to be incited to it by the French, and the Bashaba of Pemaquid. He was slain, and his people destroyed. At the same time, a devastating pestilence swept off the Indian race without injuring the whites. Gorges says: "Vines and the rest with him, that live in the cabins with these people that died, not one of them ever felt their heads to ache."

The year 1616 brings us to what may be called the Pilgrim period; for at this time were initiated those measures that resulted in what Mr. Webster called the first settlement of New England. The history of the times would disprove the popular theory, that "religious impulse accomplished the early settlement of New England"; by which is meant the settlement therein of the Pilgrims. But the plan of colonizing America did not originate with them, nor were they in any sense the leaders of the movement. They resorted thither from necessity, and while they profited by the labors and enterprise of others, achieved nothing beyond those in a subordinate position. The settlement of New England was the work of many years, and was achieved by the same influences as those still at work to extend the Saxo-Norman race. It was the legitimate result of the commercial ideas and adventurous spirit of the times.

The Protestant faith was struggling to maintain its foothold in the British Isles in the reigns of Henry VIII., of Edward VI., and of Mary, and not till the reign of Elizabeth was it fully established. This consummation gave internal repose to the nation, and allowed the spirit of enterprise to expand and ripen. This spirit sought employment in the New World, and drew from Elizabeth the earliest charters. The English Puritans exhibited the restless spirit of change that had grown up in the English character, under the influence of the last fifty years; and not in the reign of the despotic queen, but in the reign of the weak James, those who had not property, or court favor, naturally preferred a life of adventure, with the hopes of profit or preferment in a new country. It was the age of private enterprise and of intellectual freedom. The East India Company was laying the foundation of English empire in the East; while the Council of Virginia was planting the seeds of a more glorious dominion over the wilds of nature in the West. The same spirit that has filled the valley of the Mississippi and the Pacific shore, with natives of New England and of Europe, within the last fifty years, led to the first emigration to America.

That "religious impulse" led the followers of Robinson to Leyden, in 1608, is undoubtedly true, but religious persecution in England soon ceased, and no one there suffered death, for that cause, after 1611. The forms of the church service were as harmless then as now, and were originally adopted, after long debate, by a majority of *one* only, in a full convention of the English clergy, in the reign of Elizabeth. The articles of the church were Calvinistic, and in no wise differed in doctrines from those of the Puritans. Elizabeth was a far greater stickler for observance of church ceremonies than any one of her successors. But the Leyden flock did not leave England in her reign.

It is time to vindicate the truth of history; to do justice to the claims of Gorges, and to repel the calumnious charges of the men who founded the Theocracy of New England,—who persecuted alike Quakers, Baptists, and Churchmen. Fifty years after the putting of men to death for errors of doctrine had ceased in Old England, from which the Massachusetts Puritans pretended to have fled " for conscience sake," they executed men of the most blameless lives for the slightest differences of opinion, or doctrine, in religion. On finding that Baptists and Quakers and Churchmen were only multiplied the more, by this means; as persecution grew more severe, they finally passed a statute, that Quakers should be treated as vagabonds, whipped from town to town by the magistrates, till driven beyond the boundaries of the colony. In point of fact, within the boundaries of the colony of Massachusetts Bay, from the time they first landed, till the arrival of Sir Edmund Andros as Governor in 1686, the government of Massachusetts Bay was more arbitrary and intolerant than any despotism from which they fled from England. Stripes, imprisonment, and even death itself were inflicted on those who regarded baptism as a sacrament, fit only to be administered to those capable of understanding its import. The banishment of Wheelwright and others for antinomian heresy, and his escape into Maine, show the character of the times.

The Plymouth flock, a portion of those whom Robinson had gathered at Leyden, were an amiable and pious people. They gladly sought the protection of Sir Ferdinando Gorges, the founder of the New England Company, prior to their removal from

Holland, and came out in view of his promise of a charter, from whom they obtained it in 1621. But they never, in fact, exerted any considerable political influence on the history of the continent. The colony of Massachusetts Bay, on the other hand, was guided by the boldest set of adventurers that ever set foot on American soil. The fathers of this colony, who first met in Nottinghamshire, 1627, and those who led the way afterwards, were men whom Charles had imprisoned for their too great freedom of speech in the House of Commons, and who gladly escaped to America to avoid a worse fate at home.

Sir Ferdinando Gorges readily gave them a charter, March 19, 1629. They came over the same year. One condition, as Gorges says, of the grant was, that it should not be prejudicial to the previous grant to his son, Robert Gorges, made in 1622, then in the actual occupation of his grantees. But writing secretly to Endicott, their first governor, under date of April 17, 1629, " the Governor and deputy of the New England Company for a plantation in Massachusetts Bay," residing in England, advise him, that Mr. Oldham had become the grantee of Robert Gorges, and that the Rev. Mr. Blackstone and Mr. Wm. Jeffreys had been duly authorized to put Oldham in possession of the premises; yet they held it void in law, and advised that " they should take possession of the chiefe part thereof," and thus destroy the value of the grant previously given to Gorges. This was done, and Gorges' grantees were driven out—a fair specimen of the sense of justice of that

Company. To mislead the people of England as to their true designs, after leaving England, while on shipboard, they publicly requested the prayers of the English Church, for their success in planting "the Protestant faith in America." But on landing, they forcibly expelled the two brothers Brown, who came over highly recommended by the Company in London, and against all protestations and reason they were sent back to England by the first vessel that returned, because they absented themselves from their meeting on the Sabbath. These men, in the privacy of their own chamber, were guilty of following, in their devotions, the form of the English liturgy. For this they were driven out of the country. The Massachusetts Bay Company sent their charter with the great seal of the king to America, to render its recall the more difficult; and when it was subsequently vacated by writ of *quo warranto*, refused to comply with the order of court for its return. The disputes at home, which resulted in the beheading of Charles and the Revolution of 1688 in England, alone saved the leaders and their followers from punishment. The Royal Charter, uniting the colonies of Plymouth, Massachusetts Bay, the Province of Maine and all the country east of it, under the governorship of Sir Wm. Phipps, a native of Pemaquid, put an end to the Theocracy of New England in 1691.

The modern popular history of New England has sought to conceal the exact truth, and to throw apology over the grossest offences. Those who trust to such early writers as the Cottons, the Mathers, and

Hubbards of former days; on whom the modern historians of Massachusetts seem mainly to rely, may find abundant means of correcting their opinions. We may, at this time, venture to speak of these men as they deserve. The accurate and accomplished historian of Rhode Island, in his recent history, speaking of the Massachusetts historians, justly says:

"The opinions of men who maligned the purity of Williams, of Clarke, and of Gorton, who bore 'false witness' to the character and the acts of some of the wisest and best men who ever lived in New England; who strove to blast the reputation of people whose liberal views they could not comprehend; who collected evidence to crush the good name of their more virtuous opponents by casting upon them the odium of acts wherein they were themselves the guilty parties; who committed outrages in the name of God, far more barbarous than the worst with which they ever charged 'the usurper';—the opinions of such men, we say, are not to be received without a challenge."
—Arnold's "History of Rhode Island," vol. i., p. 14.

The impartial and graphic Macaulay thus describes the Puritans of that day:

"The persecution which the separatists had undergone had been severe enough to irritate, but not severe enough to destroy. They had not been tamed into submission, but bated into savageness and stubbornness. After the fashion of oppressed sects, they mistook their own vindictive feelings for emotions of piety; encouraged in themselves, in reading and meditation, a disposition to brood over their wrongs; and when they had worked themselves up into hating their enemies, imagined that they were only hating the enemies of Heaven. In the New Testament there was little indeed which, even when perverted by the most disingenuous exposition, could seem to countenance the indulgence of malevolent passions. But the Old Testament contained the history of a race selected by God, to be witnesses of his wrath and ministers of his vengeance, and especially commanded by him to do many things which, if done without his special command, would have been atrocious crimes. In such a history it was not difficult for fierce and gloomy spirits to find much that might be distorted to suit their wishes. The extreme Puritans therefore began to feel for the Old Testament a preference, which, perhaps, they did not distinctly avow, even to themselves, but which showed itself in all their sentiments and habits. They paid to the Hebrew language a respect which they refused to that tongue in which the discourses of Jesus and the Epistles of Paul have come down to us. They baptized their children by the names, not of Christian saints, but of Hebrew patriarchs and warriors. In defiance of the express and reiterated declarations of Luther and Calvin, they turned the weekly festival by which the church had, from the primitive times, commemorated the resurrection of her Lord, into a Jewish Sabbath. They sought for principles of jurisprudence in the Mosaic law, and for precedents to guide their ordinary conduct in the books of Judges and Kings. Their thoughts and discourses ran much on acts which were assuredly not recorded as examples for our imitation. The prophet who hewed in pieces a captive king, the rebel general who gave the blood of a queen to the dogs, the matron, who, in defiance of plighted faith, and of the laws of Eastern hospitality, drove the nail into the brain of the fugitive ally who had just fed at her board, and who was sleeping under the shadow of her tent, were proposed, as models, to Christians suffering under the tyranny of princes and prelates."—Macaulay's "History of England," vol. i., p. 62.

The most odious features of Puritan intolerance were developed in Massachusetts, with the rise of that party to power in England; and when the Commonwealth passed away at home, the weak counsels of the Stuarts were unable to control the people of New England. We find the Massachusetts Puritans persecutors from the outset of their career, denying the rights of citizenship to all but actual church members, and refusing to others protection even against the Indians. When the first New England league was formed in 1643, for better protection against savage warfare, the delegates of Maine were excluded because they were Churchmen, and those of Rhode Island because they were Baptists.[1]

The settlement of Plymouth is clearly due to an act of Sir Ferdinando Gorges. His aim from the first was the settlement of the country, not advantage to himself. He sought, by putting other men prominently forward, and in every other way, to disarm the jealousy that always follows upright public action. As Gorges says: "The planting of colonies in America was undertaken for the advancement of religion, the enlargement of the bounds of our nation, the increase of trade, and the employment of many thousands of all sorts of people." The grant obtained on his request says, "*was never intended to be converted to private uses,*" and in answer to the Commons, who sought to abrogate his charter, he publicly offered to surrender it, "not only in behalf of himself, but of the rest of those interested in the Patent, so they would prosecute the settling of the plantation as was first intended. Wherein," he said, "we would be their humble servants in all that lay in our power, without looking to the great charge that had been expended in the discovery and seizure of the coast, and bringing it to the pass it was come unto." This was "after they had found, by our constant

---

[1] Bradford's "History of Plymouth Plantation," p. 416; Brodhead's "History of New York," pp. 361, 362.

perseverance therein, some profit by a course of fishing upon that coast." All writers agree that after 1616 the New England fisheries were successful and profitable to the English.

At this time, or prior to March, 1617, Gorges, in pursuance of his policy of settling the country, invited the Leyden church to emigrate to America. He says: "Before the unhappy controversy happened between those of Virginia and myself, they were forced, through the great charge they had been at, to hearken to any propositions that might give ease and furtherance to so hopeful a business. For that purpose it was referred to their consideration, how necessary it was that means might be used *to draw into those enterprises* some of those families that had retired themselves into Holland for scruple of conscience, giving them such freedom and liberty as might stand with their likings. This advice being hearkened unto, there were, that undertook the putting it in practice, and accordingly brought it forth," etc. "Such as their weak fortunes were able to provide," and they "with great difficulty recovered the coast of New England," etc., etc. The Council of Virginia still held the country under the original charter of 1606, and it was the work of Gorges to draw the Leyden flock to America. Bradford says: "They liked not the idea of going South." They had confidence in the success of Gorges' plan of a separate charter for New England. The Leyden flock early saw that they must soon become extinct if they remained in Holland. They could not remain longer in that country, or return to

England to reside. They had little or no means of support, and trusted to the chances of obtaining it, in the new employment of fishing and trading to New England, then so popular at home. Robert Cushman and John Carver were sent to the king, asking permission to "enjoy liberty of conscience in America, where they would endeavor the advancement of his Majesty's dominions, and the enlargement of the gospel." "This," his Majesty King James said, "was a good and honest motive," and asking "what profit might arise in the part we intended," (the most northern parts of Virginia,) 't was answered "Fishing." "So God have my soul," said James, "'t is an honest trade, 't was the Apostle's own calling." Winslow says: "Some one of the Plymouth Colony lent them £300 gratis, for three years, which was repaid." Winslow further says: "Some of the chief of the Plymouth Company doubted not to obtain our suit of the king, for liberty in religion." Bradford says: "Some others wrought with the Archbishop, and they prevailed in sounding his Majesty's mind, that he would connive at them, and not molest them, provided they carried themselves peaceably."[1]

A still greater difficulty remained, the raising of money for the expedition. This was finally done through Mr. Thomas Weston, a merchant of London, who with others, seventy in all, "some gentlemen, some merchants, some handicraftsmen; some ad-

---

[1] The date of their application was in 1618, as appears by the following:
1618. Seven articles which the Church of Leyden sent to the Council of England to be considered of, in respect of their judgments, occasioned about their going to Virginia. *Endorsed* "Copy of Seven Articles sent unto the Council of England by the Brownists of Leyden."—"Calendar of Colonial Papers," vol. i., p. 21.

venturing great sums, some small, as their estates and affections served." By the hard conditions agreed to, the whole Leyden Company adventured their persons, as well as their estates. Hutchinson says: "They had no notion of cultivating any more ground than would afford their own necessary provisions, but proposed that their chief secular employment should be, commerce with the natives." It was a trading company, not designing a community of goods, but a fair adventure in business. Any idea of founding a colony or of remaining in the country beyond the seven years of their partnership, nowhere appears in their earlier movements or writings. Having made up their minds to emigrate from Holland, they formed a partnership for seven years, to pursue fishing and traffic in the New World. They then applied to the Council of Virginia for a charter. Bradford says: "By the advice of some friends, the Patent was not taken in the name of any of their own company, but in the name of Mr. John Wincob, a religious gentleman, belonging to the Countess of Lincoln, who intended to go with them."[1] The statement explains fully the relations of the parties. This Countess of Lincoln had the most intimate relations with the New England settlements. Some of her children afterwards emigrated to America, and her daughter Frances was at that time the wife of John Gorges, the eldest son and heir of Sir Ferdinando.

Their departure from Deft Haven, their arrival in England, and their trials in getting to sea have been narrated with a minuteness and particularity

---

[1] Bradford's "History of Plymouth Plantation," p. 41.

that leaves nothing unsaid, and the voyage of the *Mayflower* is as famous as that celebrated one of ancient times, in quest of the Golden Fleece. Captain Smith says the Brownists found his chart or map "cheaper than his employment as a pilot," and with that in their hands they sailed to New England and sought Milford Haven, conspicuously laid down in it, now Cape Cod Harbor. Here they came to anchor, and sought New Plymouth, the precise spot designated on Smith's map four years before. When the Pilgrims sailed, Gorges had not obtained the charter for New England. On the return of the *Mayflower*, they sent to Gorges for their charter. In speaking of it, he says: "They found that the authority they had from the Company of Virginia could not warrant their abode in that place; . . . They hastened away their ship with orders to their solicitor to deal with me, to be a means, they might have a grant from the Council of New England's affairs, to settle in the place,—which was performed to their particular satisfaction, and good content of them all."

Their charter was dated June 1, 1621, granting to John Pierce, a clothworker of London, and his associates: One hundred acres of land to each settler, with a nominal rent, commencing at the end of seven years, the termination of their partnership; with liberal grants of land for public uses; and also certain rights of hunting, fishing, etc. It did not profess to grant any civil rights, or confer on them the power of making laws.[1] In that respect it differs from the

---

[1] This long-lost charter has been recovered, and is printed in full in vol. ii., series 4 of Massachusetts Historical Collections.

charter granted to Robert Gorges in 1622, which vested ample powers for governing the country by means of a Parliament,—one branch, like the Commons of England, chosen by the freeholders of New England, the other appointed by authority of the Crown, with an Executive under the name of Governor.[1] In this charter to Robert Gorges we find the model, or pattern, of the British colonial governments of later times. The division of the powers of government into three branches was unknown to the Pilgrims, or to the Puritans, for a long period, and this accounts for the despotic character of their governments. It was a quarrel in the General Court of Massachusetts about Mrs. Sherman's pig, that led to the breaking up of the General Court and its division into two branches, in 1645.[2] The Pilgrim government at Plymouth, which continued till the charter of William and Mary in 1692, never attained to the knowledge of a division of the legislative power into two independent branches. Their government was through the church.

The first charter granted to the Plymouth flock came, therefore, from the original Council of Virginia, who held at that time the entire country. Through Thomas Weston they had heard of the plan of Gorges, for a separate grant of New England, and they sailed for North Virginia, trusting to Gorges for a grant.

The petition of Gorges for the New England charter was dated March 3, 1620. An order in council

---

[1] This charter to Robert Gorges is found in full in Gorges' "Briefe Narration," p. 44; vol. ii., Maine Historical Collections.

[2] This amusing story is found in Winthrop's "Journal," vol. ii., p. 260.

was made July 23, 1620, directing the preparation of the new charter, and it passed the seals November 3, 1620. In this charter it says: "We have been humbly petitioned unto, by our trusty and well beloved servant, SIR FERDINANDO GORGES, Knight, Captain of our Fort and Island by Plymouth, and by certain the principal Knights and Gentlemen Adventurers of the said Second Colonye, and by divers other Persons of Quality, who now intend to be their Associates' divers of which have been at great and extraordinary charge, and sustained many losses in seeking and discovering a Place fitt and convenient to lay the Foundation of a hopeful plantation, and have years past, by God's assistance and their own Endeavors, *taken actual Possession of the Continent hereafter mentioned in our name and to our use as Sovereign Lord thereof, and have settled already some of our people in places agreeable to their Desires in those places;* and in Confidence of prosperous Success therein, by the Continuance of God's Divine Blessing, and our Royall permission, have resolved in a more plentiful and effectual manner to prosecute the same."

That Gorges had complete possession of the country before the Plymouth people came over, is also shown by the complaints against him for a monopoly in fishing. He had brought the country sufficiently into notice to attract thither the Pilgrim flock. To deny to Gorges, therefore, the glory of being the founder of New England because his own colony was overshadowed by that of Massachusetts Bay, is as unjust as it would be to deny to Columbus credit as the discoverer of America, and to assign the glory of it to Sebastian Cabot; simply because Cabot first discovered the mainland of the continent seventeen months before it was seen by Columbus. All fair minds agree that it was the far-sighted and gifted Genoese, who, by inspiration, looked through the darkness of ages, forecast the future, and pointed the way for Cabot and Vespucci to the New World across the ocean, though his modesty permitted the name of another to be given to it; that of Cabotia, which for a time gained favor, yielding to that of America. Still more clearly than Columbus did the instinctive sagacity of Gorges foresee and predict the fruits of his own great endeavor, and behold a rising state in America free from European control. And yet for the last thirty-nine years, or since Mr. Webster's great speech at Plymouth, on December 22, 1820, the truth of severe history has been overlooked in admiration of the creations of his genius.

As an epic poem, Mr. Webster's speech stands in the same relation to history as the Iliad of Homer or the Æneid of Virgil. The war of the gods on Olympus, and the flight of Anchises, regarded at one time as historic truths, were just as real and true to history as Mr. Webster's description of the landing of the Pilgrims. Among all the achievements of Mr. Webster, there is nothing that shows his real greatness so much as those efforts, by which, in the style and manner of the ancient historians, he embodies in an impressive form the great facts and ideas that are supposed to govern human affairs. It is fair to apply to this composition the definition of "Classical History," so clearly and beautifully expressed in his address before the New York Historical Society of February 22, 1852. This Pilgrim speech is a true specimen of classical history, "not," as he says, "a memoir, or a crude collection of acts, occurrences, and dates; it is a composition, a production, which has unity of design, like a work of statuary or of painting." As such, his Plymouth speech bears the impress of his creative mind. He transferred to the Plymouth panorama a representation of the heroic achievements of Gorges, of Popham, and of Vines. Mr. Webster's poetry has been regarded as history. But it is such history as are the writings of Livy, or the historic plays of Shakespeare. The mission of the poet precedes that of the historian, and the imaginary characters of a poetic mind continue for a while to walk the earth under the shadow of a great name. The Pilgrims have richly enjoyed this distinguished honor. The Hon. Edward Everett, evidently on the authority of Mr. Webster, says, in his Plymouth speech, four years later: "This, the source of our being, the birthday of all New England,—this grand undertaking was accomplished on the spot where we now dwell.... A continent for the *first time* explored, a vast ocean traversed by men, women, and children, voluntarily exiling themselves from the fairest portions of the Old World," etc. Modern historians of the Massachusetts school have since then taken these flights of poetic fancy for historic verities, and sought to elevate them into the dignity of history. They might as well insist, that a modern Fourth of July oration was the cause of our Revolutionary war, though uttered some years after that event had taken place.

Regarded as a political event, the Plymouth settlement was not of the slightest consequence or importance. It neither aided nor retarded the settlement of the country, and is of no moment except as the actors in that work were concerned, or those who claim thence their inheritance. As a tale of individual and personal heroism, in which patient resignation was mingled with superstitious confidence, it deserves sympathy and respect. But those who seek to give it political importance confound the Plymouth settlement with that of the Puritan Commonwealth of Massachusetts Bay: two events as independent of each other in every respect as was the settlement of New Netherlands from that of Lord Baltimore, on the Chesapeake. The Pilgrims had at the outset no idea of founding a colony. The idea may have been suggested to them by the language of the charter of June, 1621. It is true, they dignified their head officer with the title of governor, a term formerly applied to the head of any family or company. He had no civil authority whatever, and the fact that for the first seven years no records of any sort were kept, and not a scrap of written history made, prior to 1627, shows how primitive were all their ideas of government and of property.

Bradford began his history in 1630, and at a later date, rejoicing over the downfall of the bishops, in the days of the Commonwealth, he appends thereto the following comments: "When I began these scribbled writings, which was about the year 1630, and so peeced up at times of leasure, afterwards; little did I think their downfall was so near," etc.[1] The compact signed on board the *Mayflower*, under date of November 11, 1620, which has been eulogized as "the germ of republican freedom," was, as Bradford says, "a combination, occasioned partly by the discontented and mutinous speeches that when they came ashore, they would use their own libertie," etc.[2] In 1632, the first records of Plymouth Colony were commenced, but they had before them the example of the colony of Massachusetts Bay whose records are of the same date as their settlement. The famous Captain John Smith, a cotemporary, says: "About one hundred Brownists went to Plymouth, whose humorous ignorance caused them to endure a wonderful deal of misery, with infinite patience."

It was under the charter given to John Wincob, and in the protection of the original Virginia Company, with the map of Smith for their guide, they came to America, too poor to own their vessel, or to pay for the land they should here occupy; and

---

[1] Bradford's "History of Plymouth," p. 6.
[2] Bradford thus explains the matter: "I shall a little returne backe and begine with a combination made by them before they went ashore, being ye first foundation of their governmente in this place; occasioned partly by ye discontented and mutinous speeches that some of the strangers amongst them had let fall from them in ye ship. That when they came ashore they would use their own libertie; for none had power to command them; the patente they had being for Virginia, and not for New-england, which belonged to an other Government, with which ye Virginia Company had nothing to doe. And partly that such an acte by them done (this their condition considered) might be as firme as any patent, and in some respects more sure."

yet these obligations were never repaid, or acknowledged. The representations of Mr. Everett and others would lead us to suppose that the Pilgrims embarked for America across an unknown sea, to seek a resting-place in thickest darkness of ignorance, like that deep mystery that shrouded the Atlantic when the vessel of Columbus first turned its prow westward from the Canaries, one hundred and twenty-eight years before. Oratory, painting, and poetry have brought their richest gifts to the Pilgrim altar, and raised this feeble band of unlettered men to the rank of statesmen and heroes. The genius of Webster, the oratory of Everett, the industry of Bancroft, and the zeal of Palfrey have not failed to offer incense to the pride of Massachusetts as the leading community of the western world,—and in their devotion to her, overlooked the great influences that for a whole generation had been preparing the way for the secure occupation of her soil. And they have too readily followed the authority of those partisan writers, whose zeal for their own cause has outrun their sense of justice. And historic truth demands that the view of the character of Gorges, as drawn by the two latter, should be corrected by the light of more recently discovered information. Gorges' defence against the charge of having unjustly betrayed the Earl of Essex refutes it altogether, and should dispel the prejudice that Mr. Palfrey's recent work is calculated to perpetuate. The long-lost history of Bradford, recovered in 1855, and published in 1856, since the first issue of Mr. Bancroft's earliest volumes, will, undoubtedly, lead to a modification of the views expressed by him as to the claims of Gorges. It seems strange that the Pilgrims should have been advanced to the condition of heroes; while the services of Gorges in a long and illustrious life of duty should have been overlooked and forgotten. But this is not difficult of explanation. By force of accident, not now needful to relate, the colony of Massachusetts Bay became the leading one of New England; and its population have always, beyond any other people, indulged their pride of ancestry. Mr. Webster easily sympathized with that spirit of Massachusetts that demanded for her the proud title of "Parent Commonwealth." He enstamped on his time, beyond any man of this country, the impress of his own proud and heroic spirit. He inspired a love of country, a pride of home, a feeling of contentment and satisfaction favorable to industry, to religious sentiment, and the accumulation of property. The industrial superiority of that state, the growth of the last thirty years, is largely due to the elevated sentiments by him inspired.

With the progress of refinement and the increase of wealth in every civilized community of every age, there is a tendency to exaggerate the past, to undervalue the present, and to question all anticipations for the future. As weary age looks at existing facts as the limit of human experience, the poetic mind encourages future hopes, reproducing from the past all the varied forms of beauty or grandeur that the page of romance has foreshadowed—and every cultivated community must have its classic and romantic age, demanding a corresponding history. It glories in after years in the fabled greatness of a remote but heroic ancestry, till severe history dispels the poetic charm. The Egyptian tradition pointed in after years to the days of its earlier grandeur a thousand years before the great Menes, the founder of the temple of Karnac, whose dynasty commenced thirty-four centuries before the Christian era. The Grecian poets of its more modern times constantly dwelt on the fabled glories of the past, the age that preceded the days of Homer and Hesiod; and the Roman orators in the proudest days of its luxurious civilization pointed back to the foundation of Rome, whose fabled city was but the rudest structure of savage life. England glories still in the crude institutions of Alfred, while France with greater glory recounts the heroic deeds of Charlemagne.

New England has had her days of hero-worship, and brought her devout offerings in the same spirit to the shrine of the Pilgrims, and raised them from the humble condition of artisans and laborers to the rank of founders of empires; and the sentimental Mrs. Hemans, under the spell of Mr. Webster's genius, has thrown the charms of her poetic fancy around the rude homes of its early settlers. All this is a pure myth. The war of the gods on Olympus and the mythic tales of the love of Sappho, are just as real. Had the Pilgrims landed on the rocky cliffs of Sagadahoc, of Donaquet, or of Pemaquid, the poetic fancy of Mrs. Hemans might have had the color of the truth. But to talk of "the rock-bound coast" of Plymouth, amid the sands of Cape Cod; and of "the giant branches" of the scrubby pines on the south shore of Massachusetts Bay, is simply a flight of fancy. "The bleak and death-like desolation of nature" which, as Mr. Everett truly says, "met the eyes of the Pilgrims on their approach to land" is changed by the exuberant fancy of Mrs. Hemans into charming spots like those which the voyagers had found in the rich forests of that Norumbega, whose praises had been sung by John Milton. The beautiful retreats at Diamond Cove and Pentecost Harbor,—the rich forests on the banks of the Penobscot, the Sheepscot, and the Kennebec, had attracted thither numerous voyagers from the Old World, before the Leyden church had been gathered under the charge of the pious Robinson. New England had all the attractions described by the early navigators answering the poetic descriptions of Mrs. Hemans. It had "good harbors, very good fishing, much fowl, noble forests, gallant rivers, and the land as good ground as any can desire." But this does not apply to the region where the Pilgrims made their home.

Let every one read the poetic description of the landing of the Pilgrims by Mr. Webster, and study the picture of it by Sargent, with the simple history of Bradford in his hands; and he is lost in admiration, like that which the student of classic history feels, in the perusal of the works of the great master of epic poetry. According to Bradford, they embarked at Deft Haven, July 21, 1620, sailed from Southampton August 5, put back twice,—persevered in their plans, and espied Cape Cod November 9, 1620, old style, and came to anchor in Cape Cod harbor November 11, 1620, and on the same day signed their compact of government, and chose, or rather confirmed, John Carver, governor.

Their ship remained at Cape Cod till December 25, 1620, new style. Prior to this, Bradford, Standish, and others had explored the country, setting out on December 16. On December 21 they passed through Plymouth, and returned to the ship December 24. After much doubt and difficulty and days of wandering, on Wednesday, December 30, they determined on their place of settlement. On January 4, 1621, they went first on shore, and began to cut timber for a house. The *Mayflower* remained in the harbor till April 15, when she departed for England. Till then a large portion of them lived on shipboard, and there is no account of any distinct or specific act of landing. The winter was mild beyond example, and when Samoset, "the Sagamore of Moratiggon, arrived, March 26, he was stark naked, only a leather about his waist, with a fringe about a span long, or a little or more." Had the winter been as usual, or severe as that of 1607, when Popham wintered at Sagadahoc, not a soul of them could have survived. Modern historians have accidentally fixed on December 22 as the landing of the Pilgrims, and they attempt to justify it by the statement of Bradford, that on that day the explorers passed through Plymouth and pitched upon it as one spot, to be recommended for the settlement. But unfortunately for their accuracy, this day was the twenty-first, and the adoption of the twenty-second is not justified by any fact whatever.[1]

[1] "And this being the last day of ye week (Saturday, Dec. 19, n. s.) they prepared 'ther to keep ye *Sabbath*. On Munday they sounded ye harbor,

The great misfortune of Gorges was that, as a man of true honor, he felt compelled to support the fortunes of the weak and decaying Stuart dynasty, to which he remained true to the last. He also suffered in his fortunes in not emigrating to America. In a paper on file in the English State-Paper Office, quoted in the recent volume of Mr. Folsom, it is stated that Gorges came to New England with Mason in 1649,[1] but we find no confirmation of this statement elsewhere. He was commissioned, it is

and founde it fitt for shipping; and marched into ye land, and found diverse cornfeilds, and litle runing brooks, a place (as they supposed) fitt for situation; at least it was ye best they could find, and ye season, and their presente necessitie, made them glad to accepte of it. So they returned to their shipp again with this news to ye rest of their people, which did much comforte their harts.

"On ye 15, (25 n. s.) of Desemr, they wayed anchor to go to ye place they had discovered, and came within 2 leagues of it, but were faine to bear up againe; but ye 16, (26) day ye winde came faire, and they arrived safe in this harbor. And after wards tooke better view of ye place, and resolved wher to pitch their dwellings; and ye 25 day (Jan. 4, 1621, n. s.) begane to erecte ye first house for common use to receive them and their goods."—Bradford's "History," pp. 88, 89.

The above contains all that relates to the famous *Landing of the Pilgrims on Plymouth Rock*. The intelligent reader instinctively smiles at this recital, when he contrasts this simple statement with the gorgeous decoration of the event by Mr. Webster. When the anniversary of the Landing of the Pilgrims was instituted, in 1769, the authors added *eleven* days for difference of style, instead of *ten* the true difference. They fixed on Monday, the day "*they sounded the harbor and marched into the land*," as the one most deserving of commemoration. From this has grown the magnificent conception of the Landing of the Pilgrims!

[1] *The title and case of Robert Mason touching the province of New Hampshire in New England.*

A⁰ 1616 King James I. sends John Mason Esq. as Governor to Newfoundland, who after remaining there two years was ordered to New England and with *Sir Ferdinando Gorges made a voyage along the coast in* 1619, *account of which they furnished to his Majesty. A⁰* 1620 the King grants by Charter to some of the nobility under the title of the Council of New England the territory called New England with divers privileges &c.—Folsom's Catalogue, 1674-5, March.

true, by the king as Governor of New England in 1637, but from the accidental loss of the ship in which he was to embark he did not set sail for America.

But he persevered in his great work, and lived to see in New England prosperous communities, and his province of Mayne the best governed of all. He not only established the Pilgrims at Plymouth, but subsequently caused to be granted to them a large and valuable tract of land on the Kennebec, with an enlargement of their charter, January 3, 1629. Nova Scotia was also granted to Sir William Alexander, afterward Lord Stirling, in 1621. He established his son, Robert Gorges, by grant at Nahant and Boston, in 1622. After this he planted Agamenticus, and when Christopher Levett came over in 1623, for the purpose of fixing on a place of settlement, he found that Monhegan, Pemaquid, and Cape Newagan had been already taken up, and he selected the peninsula of Machegonne, now the site of the city of Portland, for himself. There he built his house, and gave, to what is now known as Fore River, his own name, calling it Levett's River. The Cape Ann settlement was made in 1625, under a charter from Lord Sheffield, but not continued; and finally, the Company of Massachusetts Bay came over in 1629, whose men of deed and daring finally overrun the whole of New England, and led Gorges to predict the final separation of their government from that of the British crown. He says: "Some of the discreeter sort, to avoid what they found themselves subject unto, made use of their friends to procure from the Council for the Affairs of New England to settle a Colony within their limits; to which it pleased the thrice-honored Lord of Warwick to write to me, then at Plymouth, to condescend that a Patent might be granted to such as then sued for it. Whereupon I gave my approbation so far forth as it might not be prejudicial to my son Robert Gorges' interests, whereof he had a Patent under the seal of the Council. Hereupon there was a grant passed as was thought reasonable; but the same was after enlarged by his Majesty, and confirmed under the great seal of England; by the authority whereof the undertaking proceeded so effectually, that in a very short time numbers of the people of all sorts flocked thither in heaps, that at last it was specially ordered by the King's command, that none should be suffered to go without license first had and obtained, and they to take the oaths of supremacy and allegiance. So that what I long before prophesied, when I could hardly get any for money to reside there, was now brought to pass in a high measure. The reason of that restraint was grounded upon the several complaints, that came out of those parts, of the divers sects and schisms, that were amongst them, all contemning the public government of the ecclesiastical state. And it was doubted that they would, in short time, wholly shake off the royal jurisdiction of the sovereign magistrate."[1] Gorges seems to have reached that conviction, common to our race, at this time, that it is capable of shaping its government to the wants of the people,

[1] "Briefe Narration," p. 51.

and that Episcopalian or Puritan theology, cannot for any length of time find cause of difference. He never persecuted; on the contrary, he welcomed those who escaped Puritan persecution in New England, or those who sought refuge from priestly domination at home. He granted lands in Maine to Rev. John Wheelwright and others, who fled from Massachusetts, first into New Hampshire, and then into Maine, banished on account of errors of doctrine; and was earlier than Rhode Island in the practical adoption of unlimited freedom of opinion. That he should have suffered in the estimation of the Puritans, and be denounced by them in opprobrious terms for being a royalist and a churchman, ought not at this time to diminish from the respect fairly due for his great services. But for Gorges the western continent must have fallen under the dominion of Roman Catholic France; and Keltic civilization would have changed its destiny, for all New England was in possession of the French prior to 1606. They had secured the favor of the savages and held the country from Cape Malabarre to the St. Lawrence. They do not seem to have been aware of the voyages of Gosnold, of Pring, or of Weymouth, though fully alive to the danger that threatened their possessions by the planting of the colony of Popham, at Sagadahoc.[1]

[1] In a previous note we have referred to the correspondence between the French ambassador, Count de Tillieres, and the British government. In Gorges' "Briefe Narration," p. 40, he thus speaks of this matter:

"The French Ambassador made challenge of those territories granted us by the King, our sovereign, in the behalf the King of France, his master, as belonging to his subjects, that by his authority were possessed thereof as a

With all the efforts of Gorges, the labors of the Puritans, and the zeal of the British race from 1606 to 1759, the French held twenty times the extent of the English territory on the continent, till the great struggle took place one hundred years ago on the Plains of Abraham, and the power of France passed from the continent forever.

Compare the services of Gorges with those of Wolfe; and all will agree that the claims of the former far surpass in real magnitude those of the latter. Yet the name of Wolfe is immortal, while that of Gorges is comparatively unknown. As the heroic soul of Wolfe was just ready to take its flight to the world of spirits from the field of battle, as the light had faded from his vision, his ear caught the words, "They fly!" "They fly!" "Who fly?" said the dying hero. "The French," said the attendant. "What, so soon?" said Wolfe; "then I die content," and expired at the moment of victory. He knew that he had gained an undying fame. The glory accorded to Wolfe for the conquest of Canada followed at once as the fruits of that victory. But those, like Columbus or Gorges, who labor for their country or for mankind in the less brilliant pursuits of peace, must wait the slow but ever faithful record of severe history to do them justice. When Columbus in old age, worn out in the service of his adopted country, died amid poverty and neglect, they placed over his grave these words:

part of New France. To which I was commanded by the King to give answer to the Ambassador his claim, which was sent me from the Lord Treasurer under the title of *Le Memorial de Monsieur Seigneur le Conte de Tillieres, Ambassadeur pour le Roy de France.* Whereupon I made so full a reply (as it seems) there was no more heard of that their claim."

"Columbus has given a new world to the kingdom of Castile and Leon." But, alas for human pride, the fame of Columbus has arisen higher and higher year by year in the admiration of men, while the empire of Spain has passed from the continent of America, and a weak and decaying dynasty fills the throne of Ferdinand and Isabella. When Sir Ferdinando Gorges closed his life, in 1647, his countrymen should have placed over his grave these words: "Gorges saved North America to England." Instead of this a cloud of obloquy rested on his name in both countries; at home because he supported the monarchy, and in New England because he had not done homage to the Puritan theocracy. And to this hour the meed of praise has been selfishly withheld. When George Popham, the able and accomplished governor of the colony at Sagadahoc, knew that the hour of his departure had come, he was consoled in the thought that his name would be imperishably connected with the history of New England, for he was the *first* of his race whose bones should be laid on American soil. Like Wolfe, he said: "I die content, for my name will always be associated with the first planting of the English race in the New World; my remains will not be neglected away from the home of my fathers and my kindred." And yet to this hour, two hundred and fifty-two years from the time that Popham died, the place of his burial is unknown.[1]

[1] While these pages are going through the press, measures are in progress to commemorate the first settlement of New England, and to preserve the memory of the man who led hither the first English colony.

Congress has made an appropriation for a fort at the mouth of the Kennebec—the ancient Sagadahoc,—which is to be called Fort Popham.

Mr. Webster said, "the record of illustrious action is safely deposited, in the universal remembrance of mankind," and while we admit the truth of this maxim, we cannot forget that the record is rarely exhibited till the generations that knew their actors had passed away. Homer's words were not listened to in his lifetime, nor till his history and even his birthplace were forgotten. He still lives, not in history, but in his own immortal writings. The greatest names of England, Milton and Cromwell, were a by-word and a reproach for years after their death. So it has been with the Father of English colonization in America. Loaded with reproach by all the Pilgrim and Puritan writers of his time, his only crime was that he never countenanced persecution. The narrow and illiterate Bradford, the arrogant and bigoted Winthrop, the leading cotemporary writers of the times of Gorges, were incapable of doing justice to his motives or his conduct. Within the last forty years, the growth and development of the English race in America, and the importance of the United States in the community of nations, have stimulated inquiry into its early history. The earliest settlement of the country, and the influences by which it was achieved, have become matters of the deepest interest. Events which we supposed to be of the least apparent moment, at the time, have influenced the direction of human affairs and permanently affected the history of the race.

Two hundred and fifty-six years ago, the first European settlement north of Florida was made at St. Croix, in our state, by the French with every assurance of permanently holding the continent. In that same year, 1605, George Weymouth returned to England, after having explored the coast of Maine and of New England, not made known before, by the voyages of Gosnold and Pring. The leading minds of England selected their place of settlement, looking simply at the natural advantages of the country. From Mount Desert to Cape Elizabeth was the fairest land, and the most inviting sea-coast, that had tempted an Atlantic voyage. There, they made their first effort to plant a colony, as the means of enlarging the dominion of their nation. The seat of empire accidentally passed farther west, for a time, to avoid the dangers of Indian and French hostility, and in the struggle for control of the continent between England and her colonies, a large portion of Maine was the subject of controversy. Her position became a subordinate one in the time of the Commonwealth, and not till our day has she been able to vindicate her just position. But we already see the initiatory steps that shall realize the idea on which the thrice-honored and renowned Warwick, and the sagacious Gorges, set on foot this Empire of the West;—and that chosen spot they selected become the seat of its power. Within the last sixteen years we have witnessed the great minds of England uniting with those of our own land, in cementing anew the ties of lineage which the folly of an unwise ruler less than a century ago had severed. Already the iron arm of the railway has joined States and Provinces into one community of interests, and the iron locomotive departs from Casco Bay on an unbroken line of iron to the distant waters of Michigan and Huron, yet to be extended to the far-distant shores of the Pacific. A giant work, greater than the Pyramids, now spans the waters of the St. Lawrence, while the ocean has been bridged by such lines of steamers that have practically annihilated space and time in the operations of business. It was the belief of those who first planted our state that it would be the fairest portion of America, and that the deep waters of our bays should float the richest treasures of an expanding commerce. The realization of these visions is not far distant from our day; and if the sons of Maine are true to themselves and to their state, the dawn of that day may be speedily ushered in.

As it was the foresight of Gorges that planted the Saxo-Norman race in America, so it was the wisdom of Cromwell that saw in them the great strength of the nation. Both these great men have in their own time suffered from the persecutions of their enemies, so that a future age only could do justice to their memories. Gorges, a devoted royalist, a persistent friend of the Stuart dynasty, has been as obnoxious to Puritan prejudice as were Cromwell and the Independents to that of the restored monarchy and its followers. But Gorges' fame shall yet eclipse that of any other name in our American annals. My native state has been remiss in the discharge of this duty; and supinely allowed the history of New England to cluster around the Rock of Plymouth, instead of standing clearly out in the earlier deeds of the great minds that saved New England and the continent from the grasp of the French. The high position and character of Gorges are vouched by his intimacy with the Chief-Justice of England, and the chief noblemen of the realm, whose confidence he enjoyed to the close of his long and illustrious life; and his entire freedom from intolerance is shown in every act. His ambition was to people these realms with the best countrymen of England, though he foresaw their early independence of the crown; and though a zealous Episcopalian, he gave equal encouragement to Puritan and Churchmen. If the greatness of an individual is to be measured by his influence on human affairs, the name of Gorges should be ranked with those of Cromwell and of Peter the Great of Russia, the men who have exerted most influence in shaping the history of modern times. The English, or Saxo-Norman, race, less than 5,000,000 in 1620, to-day is supreme on the ocean, and holds one sixth of the habitable globe. It governs one fourth part of the human race, four times in number the population of the Roman Empire when its eagles overshadowed the world.

The strength of a nation, like that of an individual, is its history; and while we recount with pride the deeds of the great men who have preceded us, we should reflect on the value to us of that larger theatre on which we are called to act; nor forget him whose genius and fidelity planted the English race in America. While the Saxo-Norman race learns more and more, and day by day to sympathize with whatever is good and true in old England, we find in

England's great men a corresponding sympathy with whatever is worthy of respect in the New England of our day; so well expressed by Mr. D'Israeli, in a speech at Aylesbury, in the last parliamentary election: "Whatever may be the fate of the England of the Old World," said D'Israeli, "all that she has accomplished for good, in art, science, or political economy, and all that is glorious in her history, her literature, or her institutions, is destined to still higher development in the hands of that race she has planted, springing from our loins, and enjoying a common ancestry with us, on the distant shores of New England and Australia."

THE FIRST COLONIZATION OF NEW ENG-
LAND.

ADDRESS DELIVERED AT FORT POPHAM, MAINE, 1862.

WE commemorate to-day the great event in American history. We are assembled on the spot that witnessed the first formal act of possession of New England, by a British colony, under the authority of a royal charter. We have come here, on the two hundred and fifty-fifth anniversary of that event, to rejoice in the manifold blessings that have flowed to us from that act,—to place on record a testimonial of our appreciation of the value of that day's work, —and to transmit to future generations an expression of our regard for the illustrious men who laid the foundation of England's title to the continent, and gave a new direction to the history of the world.

We meet under circumstances of deep and peculiar interest. The waters of the same broad Sagadahoc move onward in their majestic course to the ocean; the green summit of the beautiful Seguin still lifts itself in the distance, standing sentinel and breakwater to beat back the swelling surges of the sea; the flashing foam of the Atlantic still washes the rocky shores of the peninsula of Sabino, and the secure anchorage of this open bay receives the tempest-tost bark, as on the day that the *Gift of God*, the gallant fly-boat of George Popham, helped into port Raleigh Gilbert's good ship *Mary and John*, freighted with the hopes of a new empire. Behind us rises the green summit of yonder mount, around whose sides soon clustered the habitations of the intrepid Popham and his devoted companions; and the same rocky rampart that then encircled this proud bay stands unmoved amid the changes of two hundred and fifty-five years. All else is changed. The white sails of many a gallant ship now cover this broad expanse of water; a towering light-house rises high above the summit of Seguin, throwing the rays of its Fresnel lens far out into the darkness, and along these rocky shores; habitations of men dot every point of the surrounding landscape; while the stout steamer, unlike the ship of olden time, gladly encounters the rude waves of the ocean.

> " Against the wind, and against the tide,
> Still steady, with an upright keel."

But the heart of man has changed less than all, in these two hundred and fifty-five years. It still bows in submission to Almighty God, and lifts its voice in prayer and praise; as when, in the solemn service of his ritual, their pious preacher uttered these memorable words:

"At what time soever a sinner doth repent him of his sins from the bottom of his heart, I will blot all his wickedness out of my remembrance, saith the Lord."

"I will go to my Father, and say to him, Father,

I have sinned against heaven and against thee: I am no more worthy to be called thy son."[1]

All this was permanent and enduring. The same duty and the same dependence upon God, as then, are upon us all. We seem to see before us the faithful Richard Seymour, clad in the habiliments of the priesthood, as we hear the same accents of prayer and praise that he uttered,—when, before him knelt the faithful Popham and his hardy comrades, whose deep responses were borne upward to the mercy-seat. We listen to-day to the same strains of music and to the same lessons that first burst forth from human lips on the shores of this great continent! That same sense of sinfulness that then found utterance in the language of the liturgy, finds expression in our hearts to-day; and may it please the Father of mercies so to mould all hearts, that these words of penitential confession shall find willing utterance from all lips, and these words of prayer and praise, raised in devout aspiration from all hearts, be continued from generation to generation through all time, till there shall be one fold and one Shepherd, and this mortal reach immortality at the final consummation of all things.

The greatness of an event is to be measured by the influence it exerts over the destinies of mankind. Acts of sublime moral grandeur, essential to the education of the race, may surpass in real magnitude the most brilliant achievements of material success; and the silent eloquence of truth do more to conquer the fierce spirit of war, than the most imposing tri-

[1] King James' Liturgy of 1604.

umphs of warlike ambition. The ignominious execution of the teacher of our religion, in a remote and obscure province of the Roman Empire, was an event of so little interest at the time, as to be overlooked by the great writers of Roman history. The rise of the Christian sect in Judea was noticed by the younger Pliny in his letter to the Emperor Trajan within the next hundred years; but no human vision could then have foreseen that their despised doctrines would, within the next few hundred years, have become enthroned in the home of the Cæsars, and give law to the civilized world.

When Hannibal led his disciplined troops from the shores of Africa, through the perilous passes of the Pyrenees and across the Alps, into Italy, and slew more in number of the Roman youth than the entire force of his army, we instinctively honor this sublime exhibition of martial genius and energy. When at last he failed to conquer Rome, only from the lack of succor from his own countrymen; whose jealousy of his success destroyed their country, we respect that indignant sense of justice that bequeathed his bones to a foreign resting-place, lest his unworthy countrymen should in after times be honored by the homage done to his remains. We weep at every fresh recital of the splendor of his achievements, and the magnitude of his misfortunes (however much we may value the superior civilization of the Roman people over that of the Carthaginians), as we reflect that the history of future times hung suspended on the issue of that campaign. We are willing to rejoice that at last his ungrateful nation was blotted from the earth, and Carthage lives only as a dishonor to history, while his name stands foremost among warriors and heroes. When the brave and accomplished Champlain returned to France after an absence of three and a half years in Acadia,[1] having explored all these shores, and given them the names they now bear, and placed the symbols of the authority of his sovereign, from Cape Breton to Cape Cod, confidently anticipating the future greatness of his race and nation in this, their secure home in the finest portion of the New World, he found that the charter granted to De Monts, under which he held and occupied the country, had been revoked,[2] and that the most hopeful plan of empire ever revealed to human eyes had been marred, if not destroyed. With generous valor he sought a new home amid the snows of the St. Lawrence, and in 1608 planted the flag and the power of France upon the shores of that mighty river, where his bones now lie, in the midst of the race he there planted. But the folly of the great King Henry of Navarre could not be overcome by any heroism on his part; for the stronger foothold of Sir Ferdinando Gorges had meanwhile been planted on the shores of this open sea, from Sagadahoc to Plymouth; and the flag of France was compelled to withdraw across the Sagadahoc, never more to re-

---

[1] Champlain, with De Monts and his associates, sailed from St. Malo March 17, 1604, in two ships. They returned to St. Malo September 28, 1607. See Poor's "Vindication of Gorges," and the authorities there cited.

[2] "Champlain's Voyages," pp. 44, 45, 99 ed. 1632. L'Escarbot, p. 619, 2d edition, 1612.

turn thither after 1607, and finally to lay in the dust before that cross of St. George, which first floated from the rocky ramparts of Quebec on September 18, 1759,[1] when the power of France was swept from the continent forever. But all hearts instinctively honor the immortal Champlain. The sympathy of all generous minds ever flows forth at the utterance of his name. His monument still exists, in sight of an admiring posterity, more enduring than this stone we have this day raised in honor of another; and it shall forever remain in perpetual beauty, while the waters from the lofty summits of the Adirondack, mingling with those of the Green Mountains, shall fill the deep recesses of the lake that bears the honored name, *Champlain!*

Our duty to-day calls us to honor another, and a greater than Champlain; not greater in purpose, but in the results he achieved for humanity and his race, and more entitled to our sympathy from the blessings we owe to his labors,—the man that gave North America to his nation, and died without even the poor reward that followed his great rival. That colossal empire which Champlain planted on the St. Lawrence, and watched over till the close of his life,[2] which eventually held four fifths of the continent, was unable to regain its possession on these Atlantic shores: and from this cause alone, it finally fell beneath the power and sagacity of England's

---

[1] The battle was fought September 13, 1759; the surrender of Quebec was agreed on in the evening of the seventeenth, and the English flag raised on the morning of the eighteenth.

[2] Champlain died in the discharge of the duties of the office of Governor-General of Canada, at Quebec, December 25, 1635.

greatest war minister, Pitt; who gave to the heroic Wolfe, in his youthful prime, the noblest opportunity for fame that has yet fallen to a leader of armies. But the hero who gave the continent to England was neither Pitt nor Wolfe, but another and greater than either, the illustrious and sagacious Knight, whose manly daring and persevering energy upheld the drooping cause of colonization in its darkest hours against individual jealousy and parliamentary injustice; and saw, like Israel's great law-giver, from the top of the mountain, the goodly land that his countrymen should afterwards possess, though he was not allowed to enter it.[1] All honor, this day, to Sir Ferdinando Gorges. His praise is proclaimed by Puritan voices, after more than two hundred years of unjust reproach. His monument stands proudly erect among the nations, in that constitutional government of these United States which sheds blessings on the world.[2] His name, once perpetuated in our annals, was stricken from the records of the state, and no city, or town, or lake, or river, allowed to bear it to future times. But a returning sense of justice marks the American character, and two hundred years after his death it is heard once more in honorable renown. Busy hands, guided by consummate skill, are now shaping into beauty and order a work of enduring strength and national defence, that does honor to his name; and rising in sight of our chief commercial city, more beautiful in situation than

---

[1] See Poor's "Vindication of Gorges."
[2] Gorges foresaw and predicted the independence of the colonies of North America, of the British crown. "Briefe Narration," p. 51; vol. ii., "Maine Hist. Coll."; also Poor's "Vindication."

any that graces the Ægean coast, or smiles from the Adriatic shore,—the metropolis, too, of his ancient "Province of Mayne,"—proclaims Sir Ferdinando Gorges, *Father of English Colonization in America.*[1] And in after times, when his race shall become, not only masters of the continent, but of the earth, and his mother-tongue the universal language, History shall perpetuate the deeds of his genius, and Song shall make his name immortal.

The question that the European nations were called upon to solve, at the commencement of the seventeenth century, was, who should hereafter occupy and possess the broad belt of the temperate zone of the New World, from the Atlantic to the Pacific seas. All previous explorations were preliminary efforts towards this one great object, but the question remained open and undecided. The voyages of the Northmen to these shores, interesting to the curious, are of no historic value, because not connected with the colonization of the country—unless it shall hereafter appear that Columbus obtained from them information as to the extent of the Western Ocean. At the time of discovery by Columbus, the only races inhabiting the New World, north of Mexico, were tribes of wandering savages, incapable of accepting or acquiring habits of civilized life. An extinct race had left their mounds in the West, and their deposits of oyster-beds along the shores of

---

[1] FORT GORGES.—The new fort in Portland Harbor, has been named by the Secretary of War, FORT GORGES, in honor of Sir Ferdinando Gorges, "the original proprietor of the Province of Mayne and the Father of English Colonization in America."

the Atlantic, and passed from traditionary story. The adventurous Magellan in 1520 proved, by the first voyage round the world, the extent of the new continent; and in 1579, Sir Francis Drake, the first Englishman that circumnavigated the globe, in that daring voyage which excited the admiration of his countrymen, gave the name of New England to the Pacific shores of the continent; which name Captain John Smith afterwards, to strengthen the title to the country, affixed to the Atlantic slope.[1] But till the beginning of the seventeenth century, North America, north of Florida, remained unpeopled by Europeans. The Spaniards, the Portuguese, the French, the Dutch, and the English had all made voyages of discovery, and laid claims to the country. As early as 1542, it was parcelled off to the three powers first named: Florida, belonging to Spain, extending as far north as the thirty-third parallel of latitude; Verrazzan, or New France, from the thirty-third to the fiftieth parallel; and Terra Corterealis, northward to the Polar Ocean, thus named in honor of Gaspar Cortereal, a Portuguese, who explored the coast in the year 1500. The Spaniards were in pursuit of mines of gold and silver, the Portuguese in quest of slaves, and the French with hopes of profit in the fur trade, and crude but indefinite ideas of colonization.

Spain and Portugal originally claimed the New World by grant from the Pope.[2] England, practi-

---

[1] John Smith's "Description of New England," vol. ii., p. 2. Force's Tracts. "Mass. Historical Coll.," 3d series, vol. vi., p. 104.

[2] Bull of Pope Alexander VI., 1493.

cally abandoning all claim from the discoveries of Cabot on the Atlantic, and Drake on the Pacific coasts, laid down, in 1580, the broad doctrine, that prescription without occupation was of no avail; that possession of the country was essential to the maintenance of title. *Prescriptio sine possessione haud valeat.*[1]

Before this time the attention of England had been turned to the northern parts of America, with a view to colonization. As early as March 22, 1574, the queen had been petitioned to allow of the *discovery* of lands in America *"fatally reserved to England, and for the honor of Her Majesty."*[2] Sir Humphrey Gilbert's charter "for planting our people in America," was granted by Elizabeth, June 11, 1578; and in 1580 John Walker and his companions had discovered a silver mine in Norumbega. The explorations of Andrew Thevett, of John Barros, and John Walker, alluded to in the papers recently discovered in the British State-Paper Office, under date of 1580, we find nowhere else recorded. The possession of Newfoundland by Sir Humphrey Gilbert was abandoned on his loss at sea, and it was not till 1584 that the first charter to Sir Walter Raleigh was issued, by Elizabeth. Raleigh named the country VIRGINIA, in honor of his queen. Of the two colonies sent out by him, one returned, the other perished in the country, leaving no trace of its history and no record of its melancholy fate. Thus, at the period of Elizabeth's death, in 1603, England had not

---

[1] Camden's "Eliz. Annales," 1580. See Poor's "Vindication of Gorges."
[2] "Calendar of Colonial State Papers," edited by Sainsbury, vol. i., p. 1.

a colonial possession on the globe. Sir Richard Whitbourne had made voyages to Newfoundland in his own ship in 1588,[1] and in 1600 there was a proposition to the queen for planting a colony in *the Northwest of America*, in which can be unmistakably traced the agency of Sir Ferdinando Gorges; who it now appears was also concerned in the voyage of Gosnold in 1602, of Pring in 1603, and of George Weymouth in 1605, the earliest ones of which we have any authentic record.[2] That eloquent passage in Gorges' "Briefe Narration," in which he gives "the reasons and the means of renewing the undertaking of Plantations in America," deserves our highest praise; and it excites feelings of the warmest gratitude toward him, for it is a modest and touching statement of his own heroic efforts in the cause of American colonization.[3]

But the Hollanders and the French were equally aroused to the importance, and inflamed with the purpose, of seizing upon these shores. The vast wealth of the Dutch, their great commercial success prior to this time in both the East and West Indies, gave them the advantage. Champlain, with greater knowledge of North America than any of his rivals, had accompanied Pont Gravé to the St. Lawrence, by direction of the king, in 1603 : when, on his return to France, he found Acadia granted to De Monts, a Protestant and a member of the king's household, under date of November 8, 1603, extending across

---

[1] "Calendar of Col. State Papers," vol. i., p. 82.
[2] See Gorges' letter to Challons. Poor's " Vindication."
[3] Gorges' " Briefe Narration," p. 16.

the continent, between the fortieth and forty-sixth degrees of north latitude.[1]

In the spring of 1604, De Monts, accompanied by Champlain, Pont Gravé, Poutrincourt, and the learned and accomplished historian L'Escarbot, sailed from Dieppe for the occupation of the New World. They planted their colony at St. Croix, within the limits of our own State, in 1604,[2] and in the spring and summer of 1605, explored the coast under the lead of Champlain, from Campseau to Cape Malabar, twelve miles south of Cape Cod, "searching to the end of the bays," the same year that Weymouth explored this most excellent and beneficial river at Sagadahoc. To make sure of the country, Champlain, Champdoré, and L'Escarbot remained three and a half years, fishing, trading with the natives, and occupying at Boston, Piscadouet (Piscataqua), Marchin (Portland), Koskebee (Casco Bay), Kinnibequi (Kennebec), Pentagoet (Penobscot), and all east, to Campseau and Cape Breton. Returning to France in 1607, they found the charter of De Monts revoked,[3] on account of the jealousy of his rivals, and a small indemnity from the king as their only reward for these four years of sacrifice and unremitting toil. This shortsightedness of the great Henry of Navarre cost France the dominion of the New World. For on the return of Weymouth to Plymouth, in 1605, with five savages from Pemaquid, Sir Ferdinando Gorges gathered from them full particulars of this

---

[1] L'Escarbot, p. 432, 2d edition, 1612.
[2] See Poor's "Vindication of Gorges."
[3] L'Escarbot, p. 460, 2d edition, 1612; Champlain, pp. 44, 45, 99.

whole region, its harbors, rivers, natural characteristics and features, its people and mode of government.[1]

Associating himself with the Earl of Southampton, Gorges, relying upon these circumstances as a
means of inflaming the imagination of his countrymen, petitioned the king for a charter,[2] which he
obtained, under date of April 10, 1606; granting to
George Popham, and seven others, the continent of
North America, from the thirty-fourth to the forty-
fifth degrees of north latitude, extending one hundred
miles into the mainland, and including all islands of
the sea within one hundred miles of the shore. *This
charter is the basis on which rests the title of our
race to the New World.* It provided for a local
government at home, intrusted to a Council of
Thirteen; with two companies, one of North, and the
other of South Virginia, for carrying into execution
the plans of colonization in the country.[3] The venerable Sir John Popham,[4] Chief-Justice of England
by the appointment of Elizabeth, a man of vast
wealth and influence, became the patron of the company; and his son, Sir Francis Popham, was appointed
by the king, with Sir Ferdinando Gorges, one of the
Council of Thirteen, under whom, as the Council of
Virginia, the work of colonization was to be carried

[1] Gorges' "Briefe Narration"; "Maine Historical Collections," vol. ii., p. 19.
[2] Strachey's "Travaile into Virginia," p. 161.
[3] The Council of Virginia, appointed by King James, November 20, 1606, consisted of *fourteen* persons instead of thirteen.
[4] The fact of his appointment as Chief-Justice by Elizabeth, in the later years of her life, proves him to have been a great lawyer. Elizabeth appointed the ablest men she could find to public office.

forward. From the great fame of Chief-Justice Popham, and his interest in the matter, the colony sent by the North Virginia Company was popularly known as Popham's Colony, though his name was not in the charter, or included among the council. "The planting of New England in the North, was by Chief-Justice Popham," said the Scotch adventurers, in their address to the king, September 9, 1630, recently brought to our notice from the British State-Paper Office.[1] In a work entitled "Encouragement to Colonies," by William Alexander, Knight, in 1625, he says: "Sir John Popham sent the first colony that went, of purpose to inhabit there near to Sagadahoc."[2] But until the comparatively recent publication of Strachey, the history of this colony was almost unknown. Two unsuccessful attempts at planting a colony were made in 1606.[3]

On May 31, 1607, the first colony to New England sailed from Plymouth for the Sagadahoc, in two ships—one called the *Gift of God*, whereof George Popham, brother of the Chief-Justice,[4] was commander, and the other, the *Mary and John*, commanded by Raleigh Gilbert—on board which ships were one hundred and twenty persons, for planters. They came to anchor under an island, supposed to be Monhegan, July 31. After exploring the coast

---

[1] This paper is now printed for the first time in the appendix.

[2] A copy of this rare work is in the possession of General Peter Force, of Washington City.

[3] See Poor's "Vindication."

[4] Note by R. H. Major, editor of Strachey's "Travaile into Virginia," p. 27, published by the Hakluyt Society—one of the volumes of its series. Hubbard's "History of Massachusetts Bay," p. 10.

and islands, on Sunday, August 9, 1607, they landed on an island they called St. George; where they heard a sermon, delivered unto them by Mr. Seymour, their preacher, and so returned aboard again. On August 15 they anchored under Seguin, and on that day the *Gift of God* got into the river of Sagadahoc. August 16, after a severe storm, both ships got safely in and came to anchor. The seventeenth, in two boats, they sailed up the river—Captain Popham in his pinnace, with thirty persons, and Captain Gilbert in his long-boat, with eighteen persons, and "found it a very gallant river; many good islands therein, and many branches of other small rivers falling into it," and returned. The "next day they all went ashore, and there made a choice of a place for their plantation, at the mouth or entry of the river, on the west side, (for the river bendeth itself towards the nor-east and by east,) being almost an island, of good bigness, in a province called by the Indians, 'Sabino'—so called of a Sagamo, or chief commander, under the grand bashaba." The nineteenth they all went ashore where they had made choice of their plantation, and where they had a sermon delivered unto them by their preacher, and after the sermon the president's commission was read, with the patent,[1] and the laws to be observed and kept.[2]

"George Popham, gent., was nominated President. Captain Raleigh Gilbert, James Davies, Richard

[1] By the original charter, the company had the right to sell lands, work mines, coin money, transport thither colonists, expel by force all intruders, raise a revenue by imposts, carry out goods free of duty to the crown, for seven years, with a denization of all persons born or residing in the country.

[2] A constituent code of laws was prepared, and signed by King James, in

Seymour Preacher, Captain Richard Davies, Captain Harlowe, were all sworn assistants; and so they returned back again."

Thus commenced the first occupation and settlement of New England.

accordance with the provision to this effect set forth in the seventh section of the charter of April 10, 1606. Lucas' "Charters of the Old English Colonies," p. 4.

This constituent code is contained in two ordinances, or articles of instructions, from the king, namely:

I. Ordinance dated November 20, 1606, appointing

Sir William Wade,	Thomas Warr, Esq.,	Sir Henry Montague,
Sir Walter Cope,	Thomas James, Esq.,	John Doddridge, Esq.,
Sir Francis Popham,	Sir Ferdinando Gorges,	John Eldred, Esq.,
Sir John Trevor,	Sir George More,	James Bagg, Esq.,
Sir William Romney,	Sir Thomas Smith.	

as the Council of Virginia.

This ordinance provided that:

1. Each colony may elect associates, and annually elect a president for one year, and assistants or councillors for the same time.

2. The Christian religion shall be preached and observed as established in the realm of England.

3. Lands shall descend to heirs as provided by law in England.

4. Trial by jury of twelve men in all criminal cases. Tumults, rebellion, conspiracy, mutiny and sedition, murder, manslaughter, incest, rape, and adultery only are capital offences.

5. In civil causes, the president and council shall determine. They may punish excesses in drunkenness, vagrancy, etc.

6. All produce or goods imported to be stored in the magazine of the Company.

7. They shall elect a clerk and treasurer, or cape-merchant.

8. May make laws needful and proper, *consonant with the laws of England*.

9. Indians to be civilized and taught the Christian religion.

10. All offenders to be tried in the colony.

11. Oath of obedience to be taken.

12. Records of all proceedings and judgments fully set forth and preserved, implying a right of appeal. In all criminal cases, magistrates to suspend sentence till opportunity of pardon is had by the king.

These were the laws "to be observed and kept."

II. Ordinance, dated March 9, 1607.

On the recommendation or nomination of the *Southern* Company, additional members of the Council of Virginia were appointed.

FIRST COLONIZATION OF NEW ENGLAND. 369

On a careful examination of this patent of King James, and of the articles, instructions, and orders by him set down for the government of these colonies, we are struck with the sagacity and statesmanship everywhere evinced by the monarch. He rose superior to the notions of his times, reduced the number of capital offences to ten, and declared none should be capital but the more gross of political and the more heinous of moral crimes. He gave them all the liberties they could desire. In the subsequent charters for Virginia and New England, the same broad principles of self-government were in the main re-enacted. In the contests with the king and Parliament of England, one hundred and fifty years later, the colonists only demanded their *ancient rights*, as subjects of the British crown. From August 19, O. S., 1607, the title of England to the New World was maintained. At this place they opened a friendly trade with the natives, put up houses, and built a small vessel during the autumn and winter.

Richard Bloome, in his "History of the Present State of the Territories in America," printed in London, 1687, says:

"In the year 1607, Sir John Popham and others settled a plantation at the mouth of the river Sagadahoc. But Capt. James Davis chose a small place, almost an Island, to sit down in, when, having heard a sermon, read the patent and laws ; and after he had built a fort, sailed further up the river. They call the fort St. George, Capt. George Popham being President ; and the people (savages) seemed to be much affected with our men's devotion, and would say King James is a good King, and his God a good God ; but our God, *Tanto*, is a naughty

God. In January, in the space of seven hours, they had thunder, lightning, rain, frost, and snow all in very great abundance."

On the 5th of February, 1608, George Popham died,[1] and his remains were deposited within the wall of his fort, which was named Fort St. George. It is well known that the Popham Colony, or a portion of them, returned to England in 1608, with the ship they had built on this peninsula, the first specimen of naval architecture constructed on this continent, named the *Virginia of Sagadahoc*.

But this possession of the Popham Colony proved sufficient to establish the title. The revocation of the charter to De Monts gave priority to the grant of King James, covering the same territory, and this formal act of possession was ever after upheld, by an assertion of the title by Gorges. It was sufficient, effectually, to hold the country against the French and Spaniards alike.[2] When Argall, in

---

[1] Prince's "New England Chronology," p. 118; Brodhead's "History of New York."

[2] The Spanish Secretary of State in 1612 and 1613 complained to King James for allowing his subjects to plant in Virginia and Bermuda, as the country belonged to Spain, by the conquest of Castile, who acquired it by the discovery of Columbus, and the Pope's donation; to which Sir Dudley Carleton, Secretary of State, by order of King James made answer: "Spain has no *possessions* north of Florida. They belong to the crown of England by right of discovery and actual possession by *the two English colonies thither deducted, whereof the latter is yet there remaining*. These countries should not be given over to the Spaniards."

"Cal. of Col. State Papers," vol. i., p. 14, Nos. 28 and 29; also page 16, Nos, 31 and 32.

In the memorials of the English and French Commission concerning the limits of Nova Scotia or Acadia, under the Treaty of Utrecht, the French Commissioners say: "The Court of France adjudged that they had the right te extend the western limits of Acadia as far as the River Kinnibequi " (p. 39). On page 98 of the same collections it says: "Chief-Justice Popham planted the colony of Sagadahoc."

1613, destroyed the French settlement at Mount Desert,[1] the French Minister demanded satisfaction at the hands of the British nation.[2] But no notice was taken of this demand, because the French could show no claim of title. Again in 1624, M. Tillieres, the French ambassador, claimed the territory of New England as a portion of New France, and proposed to yield all claim to Virginia, and the country as far south as the Gulf of Mexico; overlooking entirely the title of Spain to Florida, which had always been recognized as extending to the thirty-third parallel of north latitude. France had at this time become aware of the importance of securing the

[1] Mount Desert was so named by Champlain in 1605. The English named it Mount Mansell, in honor of Sir Robert Mansell, the highest naval officer of England, one of the grantees of the Virginia Company of 1609, and of the New England Company in 1620. But it has retained the name of Mount Desert. It has always been celebrated for the excellence of its harbor and the boldness of its shores. It is the most celebrated locality on the Atlantic coast, and one of the three great harbors of the continent. The French Jesuits, who settled there in 1613, called it St. Saviour. Their precise place of settlement is described in the " Relations of the Jesuits," vol. i., pp. 44, 46.

What is of still more interest is the fact that this was the easternmost limits of Mavosheen, or of the English discoveries up to 1609. See Purchase, vol. iv., p. 1873. L'Escarbot, the historian of New France and of De Monts' expedition, says the Sagamo Marchin was residing at their next place west of Kinnibepui, and they named the place Marchin, (Portland), in honor of him. Marchin was slain in 1607, and Bessabes was chosen captain in his place. Bessabes was slain also, and then Asticou was chosen in his stead. According to the statement of Purchase, vol. iv., pp. 1573-4, at the easternmost part of Mavosheen, at the river of Quibiquesson, dwelt Asticou. In 1613, Asticou was dwelling at Mount Desert, and the assurance given by his followers to Fathers Biard and Masse of his being sick and desirous of baptism at their hands, led them to go thither, and finally to yield to entreaties for making their settlement there, instead of at Kadesquit (Kenduskeag,) Bangor, on the Penobscot, as they had agreed in 1611. It would seem from these facts that the authority of Asticou extended from Mount Desert to the Saco, the river of the Sagamo Olmouchin.

[2] " Calendar of Colonial State Papers," vol i., p. 15.

title and possession of these shores.[1] King James called on Sir Ferdinando Gorges to prepare a reply to the claims of the French monarch. "Whereunto," says Gorges, "I made so full a reply (as it seems) there was no more heard of their claim."[2] From the abstract of this reply, recently printed in the Calendar of British State Papers, it would seem that no notice was taken of the Leyden flock, who were then at Plymouth; but Sir Ferdinando Gorges based the claim of his government on the ground of the charter of 1606, and the formal occupation of the country under it, with a continued claim of title.

In 1631, Champlain,—the greatest mind of his nation ever engaged in colonial enterprise, the boldest and most wary of all his countrymen, second only to Gorges in the results he achieved,—in his memoir to his sovereign, as to the title of the two nations, says: "King James issued his charter twenty-four years ago, for the country from the thirty-third to the forty-fifth degree. England seized the coast of New France, where lies Acadia, on which they imposed the name of New England."[3]

The Dutch West India Company, in their address to the States General, 1632, say: "In the year 1606, his Majesty of Great Britain granted to his subjects, under the names of New England and Virginia, north and south of the river (Manhattoes), on express condition that the companies should remain one hundred miles apart. Whereupon the English be-

---

[1] "Cal. of Col. State Papers," vol. i., p. 60.
[2] Gorges' "Briefe Narration," p. 40.
[3] "N. Y. Doc. Hist.," vol. ix., p. 112.

gan, about the year 1607, to settle by the river of Sagadahoc. The English place New England between the forty-first and forty-fifth degrees of north latitude." [1]

In Garneau's History of Canada, speaking of the destruction of Mount Desert and Port Royal in 1613, he says: "England claimed the territory to the forty-fifth degree of north latitude." This was seven years before the date of the New England charter. This claim was founded on possession; for Old England stoutly maintained, from the time of Elizabeth onward, that without possession there was no valid title to a newly discovered country.

This view of history is overlooked by Puritan writers, and those who follow their authority. That protection of the British nation which enabled the Puritans of Massachusetts Bay, and the humble followers of Robinson, to establish, unmolested, homes in the New World, under organized forms of government, was grudgingly acknowledged by them; and the man who secured to them these blessings, and watched over them with the same jealous care as of his own colony, they always stigmatized as their great enemy; [2] because, among other acts of humanity, he allowed the mild and conscientious men, who could not yield implicit obedience to their fierce doctrines and more barbarous laws, [3] to escape into Maine, and

[1] "Holland Doc. N. Y.," p. 61.
[2] Winthrop, vol. ii., p. 14; Bradford's "History of Plymouth," p. 328.
[3] None but church members shall be allowed the privileges of freemen. —Statute of 1631, "Massachusetts Colony Laws," p. 117.
Any attempt to change the form of government is punishable with death. —Statute of 1641, "Col. Laws," p. 59.

there remain unharmed. When Cromwell granted to Sir Thomas Temple the country east of the Sagadahoc, at the time that the persecution of the Quakers was at its greatest height, with the design of affording them a place of refuge beyond the limits even of the Province of Maine,[1] which had just been conquered by violence; the anger of Massachusetts Puritans fell upon the head of the Protector, himself a Puritan, and an Independent of the strictest sect at home. But time allows no allusion to-day to historic details, except what is essential to the vindication of the truth of history. The fact that August 19, Old Style, is the true date of the foundation of England's title to the continent, is all we are called upon to establish.

It may be said that, in giving this prominence to the occupation of the country by the colony of Popham, we overlook other events of importance in establishing the English title—the possession of the

---

Absence from meeting on Sunday, fast, or thanksgiving, subjected the offender to a fine.—"Col. Laws," p. 103.

Keeping or observing Christmas was punishable by fine.—"Col. Laws," p. 119.

Wages to be regulated in each town by vote of the freemen of each.—"Col. Laws," p. 156.

Baptists are to be punished by banishment.—"Col. Laws," 1646, p. 120.

Quakers to be imprisoned and then banished, on pain of death if they returned.—"Col. Laws," 1658, p. 123.

Witches shall be put to death.—"Col. Laws," 1641, p. 59.

Magistrates shall issue warrants to a constable, and in his absence to any person, to cause Quakers to be stripped naked from the middle upward, tied to a cart's tail, and whipped from town to town till conveyed out of our jurisdiction.—"Col. Laws," p. 125.

Under these laws Baptists had their ears cropped in Boston as late as 1658, and Quakers were put to death.

[1] "N. Y. Doc. Hist.," vol. ix., pp. 71, 75.

Elizabeth Isles by Gosnold in 1602, and the settlement of Jamestown May 13, 1607, prior to the landing of the Popham Colony at Sagadahoc. In reference to the occupation of Elizabeth Isles by Gosnold, it is sufficient to say, that it was prior to the date of the Royal Charter, and consequently of no legal effect in establishing title. As to the settlement of Jamestown, it was south of the fortieth parallel of latitude, and therefore did not come in conflict with the French king's prior charter to De Monts. The territory between the fortieth and the forty-fifth degrees only was in dispute. Although the maps of the time made New France to extend from the thirty-third to the fiftieth degree of north latitude, France practically abandoned the country south of the fortieth degree from the time of the grant of the charter to De Monts; so that below that line south it was open to any people who might have the courage to possess it; this south line of De Monts' grant, intersecting what is now Pennsylvania, just north of the city of Philadelphia, cuts Ohio, Indiana, and Illinois very nearly in their centre. Had there been no English settlement or occupancy north of the fortieth parallel of latitude prior to 1610, when Poutrincourt obtained a new grant of Acadia, the whole country north of that line must have fallen into the hands of the French.

The reason, undoubtedly, why France at this time extended her claims no further south than the fortieth parallel was a fear of exciting the jealousy and hostility of the Spaniards. In 1562, when Ribaut and Laudonnière planted at Port Royal, Spain looked upon it as an invasion of her just domain, and promptly expelled the French invaders. Recent discoveries show that she watched with a most jealous eye the fate of the earlier voyages of Cartier from 1534 to 1541. Spain, at that time, was the great military and naval power of Europe. There can be no doubt that the limiting of De Monts' charter to the fortieth parallel of latitude, seven degrees short of all her previous claims, was induced by a dread of Spanish interference. Spanish jealousy showed itself equally in opposition to the English occupation of the country; but the prompt assertion in 1613 of their title, averring the actual occupation of the country; and the denial, on the part of King James, of any validity in the bull of the Pope, upheld the right of England. It was not Spain, however, but France that became the actual competitor of England in the struggle for the new dominion. The relations of Spain and France were friendly. Between Spain and England there were many irritations, and so far had this ill-feeling grown, that the capture of English ships by Spanish cruisers was not an uncommon occurrence, as in the case of Challons, and others bound to New England for purposes of colonization. The French, therefore, made no claim to that Virginia occupied by the colony at Jamestown, while Spain claimed the whole country. French plans of empire looked northward and westward; resting their base on the great inland sea, or gulf lying inside Cape Sable and Cape Cod, where, for a whole century previous, from 1504, and onward, their fishermen had found the choicest treasures of the ocean. Whoever held this region, as all now see, must eventually become the dominant power of the New World.

The national feeling was not fully aroused in either country to the greatness of the prize at stake. Champlain comprehended the true measure of the occasion, and its importance to his country; while Sir Ferdinando Gorges, with equal grasp of intellect, rested on a more secure foundation—the confidence of his sovereign. But the people of England were incapable of estimating the value of the prize, or doing justice to the man who secured it. In the debate in the House of Commons, in 1621 and 1622, on the bill to abrogate or annul the New England charter, and throw open the fisheries, briefly reported in the parliamentary journals, the issue was: "*Which is of most value, fishing or plantations?*" and the result showed that the enemies of colonization were in the ascendant, and a bill to this effect passed the House. By the influence of the King acting with the Lords, it was prevented from becoming a law.[1]

From the time of the first conflict at Mount Desert, where Father Du Thet was killed in defending his home, in 1613—the first shedding of blood between the French and English on this continent,—till the

---

[1] April 19, 1621, "Mr. Neale said three hundred ships, at least, had gone this year from these ports," p. 591. November 20, 1621, "Mr. Glanville moved to speed the bill," etc. "Sir Ferdinando Gorges hath exhibited patent," etc. "Friday next Sir F. G. to be heard," p. 640. December 1, 1621, bill under consideration. "Mr. Guy moves a provision; debate by Mr. Neale, Mr. Secretary, Dr. Gooch, Sir Edward Gyles, Mr. Guy, and Shewell, which is of most value, fishing or plantations?" £120,000 brought in annually by fishing." "Provision lost. Bill passed, p. 654.—Extracts from the "Journal of the Commons."

fall of Quebec, in 1759, and the Treaty of Peace consequent thereon, in 1763, surrendering New France to Great Britain, there was a strife of races, of nationalities, and of religion for the territory of New England; while Virginia, along the Atlantic slope, was never molested by the French. The western boundary of Virginia was the Pacific Ocean, and she came into conflict with France when she crossed the Alleghanies and descended into the Mississippi basin, and there met the French settlers, who had seized upon the western waters, claiming a continuous possession of the entire regions drained by the waters of the Mississippi and the St. Lawrence. Had England acquired nothing in the way of title in the New World north of the fortieth parallel prior to the Plymouth Plantation in 1620, there is no reason to doubt that France would have swept the British power from the continent at the first clash of arms with Great Britain. It was this possession of the shores of the Atlantic Ocean, within the limits of the fortieth and forty-fifth degrees of north latitude, prior to 1610, that settled the future destiny of the continent of North America. The consummation of title, therefore, perfected by the act of possession of August 19, O. S., 1607, by the Popham Colony (whose two hundred and fifty-fifth anniversary we this day celebrate), must, if these premises are admitted, forever remain the great fact in the history of the New World.

The Maine Historical Society, whose duty it is made, by the charter establishing it, " to collect and preserve whatever may tend to explain and illustrate the civil, ecclesiastical, and natural history of this State and the United States," was pleased to approve of the act of two of its members, then in the service of the state, who petitioned the authorities of the general government, that this great work of national defence, then about to be undertaken, should be named Fort Popham, in honor of George Popham, the governor, who led the first British colony into New England, under the charter of April 10, 1606; and who, discharging the duties of his office as president, and presenting a report, in the form of a letter, to the king, dated at Fort St. George, December 13, 1607,[1] here laid down his life—the first man of the English race whose bones were laid beneath the soil of New England. The venerable Chief of the Engineer Bureau of the United States Army, to whom this petition was referred, ever jealous of the honor of his country, not only as to the character of its military structures, but as to the names to whose honor they should attest, promptly endorsed the application; and it met the ready approval of the Secretary of War. To mark, with greater distinctness, the event thus commemorated, the Maine Historical Society asked permission to place within the walls of this fort a memorial stone, bearing on its face an appropriate inscription of the event; and a tablet, in memory of George Popham, so honorably associated with the great event of that period.

By the favor of the government we have this day performed that duty, with appropriate form and ceremony. The learned president of the Maine

[1] Popham's letter in the "Maine Hist. Coll.," vol. v., p. 341.

Historical Society has announced the historic facts on which this somewhat novel proceeding has taken place. The accomplished and honored chief magistrate of the state has given to the occasion the influence of his official station, and the more acceptable service of eloquent words, proclaiming the importance of the event commemorated, upon the history of the country and the world; while the Episcopal bishop of the diocese of Maine, and the president of our oldest seminary of learning, as chairman of the Standing Committee of the Maine Historical Society, have jointly participated in the appropriate services of this occasion; and that most ancient, the Masonic Fraternity, has lent to the celebration whatever of dignity or grace the wisest of their Order have been able to embody in artistic form and expression. With the consent of the government, these imposing ceremonies have proceeded, and finally the skilful hand of him who is charged with the construction of this fort, will place this stone in its final resting-place; for the information of those who come after us, proclaiming to future times, in the simple eloquence of truthful words, that

The First Colony
On the Shores of New England
Was Founded Here,
August 19, O. S., 1607,
under
George Popham.

It would ill comport with the dignity of this occasion to fail to speak of him whose name is thus imperishably connected with the history of our state and nation. To his family and the events of his life others may more appropriately refer. We allude to him as a public man, and to his claims to public gratitude and respect. His chief distinction is, that he was one of the eight persons named in the great charter of April 10, 1606; and that he led to these shores the first colony under that charter. In it he is styled *gentleman*, and he must have been a man of consequence and position, from the fact that he was one of its grantees. After his death, Gorges in a few beautiful lines thus sums up his character: "He was well stricken in years, and had long been an infirm man. Howsoever, heartened by hopes, willing he was to die in acting something that might be serviceable to God, and honorable to his country."[1] A glorious consummation of a long life, devoted to duty, to his country, and his God.

Inside the walls of this fort, and as a companion-piece to the memorial stone which records the historic fact of this day's celebration, the Maine Historical Society will place a tablet in memory of George Popham; expressing, in that sonorous Latin language which he employed in his communication to the king, and which was at that time used by all who wrote for enduring fame, these words:

In Memoriam
GEORGII POPHAM,
Angliæ qui primus ab oris
Coloniam collocavit in Nov. Angliæ terris,
Augusti mense annoque MDCVII.
Leges literasque Anglicanas
Et fidem ecclesiamque Christi

[1] Gorges' "Briefe Narration," p. 22; vol. ii., "Maine Hist. Coll."

In has sylvas duxit.
Solus ex colonis atque senex obiit
Nonis Februariis sequentibus,
Et juxta hunc locum est sepultus.

Societate Historica Mainensi auspicante,
In præsidio ejus nomen ferente,
Quarto die ante calendas Septembres
Annoque MDCCCLXII.
Multis civibus intuentibus,
Hic lapis positus est.

[TRANSLATION.]

IN MEMORY OF
GEORGE POPHAM,
Who first from the shores of England
Founded a colony in New England,
August, 1607.
He brought into these wilds
English laws and learning
And the faith and the Church of Christ.
He only of the colonists, and in his old age, died
On the fifth of the following February,
And was buried near this spot.

Under the auspices of the Maine Historical Society,
In the fort bearing his name,
August 29, 1862,
In the presence of many citizens,
This stone was placed.

This fort, so conspicuously placed, bearing these appropriate testimonials, thus becomes a fitting monument to perpetuate the events of the early history of New England; and to transmit to future times the memory of those illustrious men who laid the foundation of English colonies in America; to which the laws, the institutions, and civilization of

England were transferred, and from which has sprung the glorious fabric of American constitutional government.

Standing here to-day, in sight of the spot where Popham, two hundred and fifty-five years ago, took upon himself the office of president, and near the place where, on the fifth of February following, he died; it seems our privilege to be admitted into his presence-chamber, as for the last time he had summoned around him his faithful assistants and companions, and gave commands for the future. The scene is worthy of a painter's pencil and a poet's pen. The ever-faithful and heroic Raleigh Gilbert, "a man," says Gorges, "worthy to be beloved of them for his industry and care for their well-being," —the future president of the colony,—is by his side. The pious Richard Seymour administers to him words of comfort and consolation. Captain Richard Davies only, of all his assistants, was absent in England. His devoted companions stand around their dying chief, when, in the language of Israel's great law-giver, laying the burden of the government on Joshua, he might well say to Raleigh Gilbert: "Be strong and of good courage, for thou must go with this people into the land which the Lord hath sworn unto their fathers to give them: and thou shalt cause them to inherit it. And the Lord he it is that doth go before thee; he will be with thee, he will not fail thee, neither forsake thee: fear not, neither be dismayed."

"So Moses, the servant of the Lord, died there, in the land of Moab, according to the word of the Lord.

And he buried him in a valley in the land of Moab, over against Bethpeor; but no man knoweth of his sepulchre unto this day."

In the far-distant future, not two hundred and fifty-five years from this day, the period of time that has intervened since his death, but in that period of more than three thousand years to come, like that from the death of Israel's law-giver to that of Popham, these stones which are here builded, shall mark the place of his sepulture; and the myriads of thronging pilgrims, led by eager curiosity to tread the soil of this peninsula of Sabino, hereafter made classic by song and story, shall pause and read, on that memorial stone, the record of his great work; and when we who are now here shall have passed away and beyond the reach of story or tradition, Popham's name shall live in the history of the mighty race who have changed this continent from one vast wilderness to a marvel of refinement and beauty fitted for the enjoyment of civilized man.

His sagacity and ability are best evidenced by the fact that, after the experience of two hundred and fifty-five years, the highest military skill has confirmed the wisdom of his choice of a place of settlement, by the adoption of it as the proper site of the great work of defence for the Kennebec River. To this spot multitudes shall annually repair; for this region will continue to be—what it ever was to the early navigators and colonists of both France and England—a chief point of interest. The French historian L'Escarbot, speaking of this river, says "*it shortened the way*" to the great river of Canada.[1]

---

[1] L'Escarbot, p. 497.

Gosnold's landfall, in 1602, was at Sagadahoc.[1] Pring, in 1603, made it the chief point of his discoveries; and the great voyage of Weymouth was to "the most excellent and beneficyall river of Sagadahoc."[2] Here the English remained in 1608 and 1609, as related by the French Jesuits.[3] Here Vines pursued his vocation,[4] and hither all the fishing vessels came, because the finest fish were taken in this region. The salmon of the Kennebec are to this day known in all our cities.

The Council of New England, on July 24, 1622, set apart "two great islands in the river of Sagadahoc to be reserved for the public plantation," and "a place between the branches of the two rivers *for a public city*."[5] Though the strife of races and of nationalities has kept back the settlement of this whole region, and the still more disastrous conflicts of rival grants and hostile occupation destroyed for

[1] Strachey, Hakluyt Society edition, p. 155; caption at the head of the chapter. See Poor's "Vindication of Gorges."

[2] Much controversy and discussion have arisen as to the route of Weymouth, and as to the river he explored. I find in Purchase a fact, not alluded to by any of these writers, that may aid in solving the difficulty. John Stoneman, of Plymouth, who went out with Weymouth, in 1605, sailed as pilot in the ship *Richard*, of Plymouth, in charge of Henry Challons, commander, in Gorges' employ, to found the colony at Sagadahoc, in 1606. Nicholas Hine, of Cockington, near Dartmouth, was master. Although Challons failed of his object, by disregarding his instructions, and was taken captive by the Spaniards, his purpose of going to Sagadahoc is expressly stated, and his pilot was of Weymouth's party in 1605. This discovery of the name of *Hine*, as master under Challons, also relieves us of the difficulty in the apparent contradiction between Gorges and Strachey; the former using the name of Challons as master, the latter calling the master's name Haines, leading us to suppose there were two several voyages, instead of one in fact.

[3] "Relations des Jesuites," vol. i., p. 36.

[4] Gorges' "Briefe Narration," p. 24.

[5] Minutes of the Council of New England, July 24, 1622.—"Calendar of Colonial State Papers," vol. i., p. 32.

generations all plans of improvement, who shall dare to say that these plans shall not be realized? When this Acadian peninsula, with its one hundred and fifty thousand square miles of territory and its abundant resources, shall contain a population equal to that now peopling the British Isles, this magnificent estuary, with its deep-sea soundings, discharging a larger volume of water than any river of the Atlantic coast between the St. John and the Mississippi, may become the chief seat of wealth and power of the mighty race who inhabit the continent,—why then *may* not the history of other lands become ours, and another Liverpool here rival the great commercial city of England; and Boston become to the city of the Sagadahoc, what Bristol is to the great shipping port of the Mersey?[1]

We must not, in this connection, forget our obligations to the people of the colony of Massachusetts, and the early settlers of Plymouth, for their share in conquering the continent for our race, though dealing harshly with Maine.[2] These Massachusetts Puritans of the Saxon type, inheriting all the gloomy errors of a cruel and bloody period, under the iron rule of the Tudors, were ready to demand of Elizabeth the enforcement of the Act of Uniformity against Papists, but refused obedience to it themselves. Nor would they yield to the decision of a majority of the clergy,

[1] The extraordinary advantages of Bath for a naval and military depôt, are admitted by all military engineers, but no effort adequate to such a consummation has yet been made.

[2] See petition of Edward Godfrey and other inhabitants of Maine, to the Parliament of the Commonwealth.—" Cal. Col. State Papers," vol. i., p. 479. Also, Godfrey's letters in Mr. Geo. Folsom's " Catalogue of Papers in the English State-Paper Office in Relation to Maine," pp. 52, 54.

who in 1562, in full convention, voted to retain the priestly vestments and the forms of liturgy. While agreeing to all the doctrines of its creed, they grew restless under the forms of the church service, elevated non-essentials into the dignity of principles, and stigmatized the Prayer-book and the priestly robes as badges of Popery.

They imagined that by a severe austerity they secured the favor of God, and became his chosen people. They mistook their hatred of others for hatred of sin. They set up their own morbid convictions as the standard of right; and rather than submit to the laws of their own land, they endured the penalties, or sought escape from them by expatriation. Once planted on the shores of New England, the Puritans of Massachusetts Bay endeavored to exterminate every thing that stood in the way of their ambition.[1] Hence, after their conquest of Maine,

[1] The charter of the Massachusetts Company of March 4, 1629, authorized them to make laws and ordinances for their government, "*not contrary to the laws of England.*" Notwithstanding this they proceeded at once to frame a code of laws designed for the purpose, abrogating the laws of England whenever they stood in the way of their own wishes. The obvious purpose of the charter was to allow such minor regulations to be made as might meet the peculiar wants of the local population. A similar provision is inserted in charters in modern times, designed to allow the recipients of such grants to exercise their rights in any way they choose, not infringing any of the general laws of the state. These Puritans construed their grant differently from all others, because they designed to establish a religious community on a plan of their own, discarding all portions of the English law, unless re-enacted by themselves. Their be-praised Body of Liberties, enacted in 1641, but not printed till within about thirty years, virtually abrogated the laws of England.

Equally striking was their claim to the territory of Maine. The political troubles at home, from 1637 to the restoration of Charles II. in 1660, withdrew public attention almost entirely from America, and it was not till 1676 that the heirs of Gorges, nearly worn out in the controversy, obtained a decision

they gloried in extirpating every trace of title granted to others, making war on whatever was opposed to them, aiming at unlimited despotism. True, they planted other men's fields, instead of devastating them, and seized upon the territory of others by the same authority and in the same spirit as the Israelites drove out the tribes that formerly possessed the valley of the Jordan.

It is hardly necessary to remind the student of American history that, at the close of the seventeenth century, as at the beginning, the two great geographical divisions of English dominion on this continent north of the Delaware, were "the Provinces of New York and Sagadahoc." Such are the definitions employed in the grant of that dominion by King Charles II. to his brother, the Duke of York; and such are the titles under which the Duke of York when he ascended the throne as James II., commissioned his governor, Col. Thomas Dongan, afterwards Earl of Limerick, to exercise authority over these countries. In England, a country of precedents, where the law advisers of the crown always scrupulously adhered to ancient records in the preparation of official documents, such recognition. eighty years after the death of George Pop-

in their favor against usurpations. Thereupon March 13, 1677, for £1,250 the Puritans purchased the title of Gorges' heirs. Finally in 1684, on *scire facias*, the Court of Chancery declared their charter forfeited, and thereby put an end to the Massachusetts theocracy.

A new charter, protecting all Protestant Christians in the exercise of their religion, was granted by William and Mary, in 1691, including the Colony of Plymouth and of Massachusetts, the Province of Maine, and Sagadahoc, under one government, and Sir William Phipps, a native of Maine, was appointed Governor.

ham, is another proof, if any were wanting, of the legal establishment of England's claims in these latitudes being inseparable from the foundation of the first settlement, which to-day we commemorate.

To review, in the most hurried manner, the events affecting our race, that have transpired within the two hundred and fifty-five years since it was planted here, would transcend the proper limits of this occasion. Less than five millions of people, at that time engaged in the ruder forms of labor, were shut up in the narrow limits of the British Isles; those who speak the English language to-day in the two hemispheres, hold dominion over one fifth of the earth's surface, and govern one fourth of the human species. Their material greatness commenced with colonizing North America. Slowly, patiently, and in much suffering our fathers gained possession of this soil. The title was secured by the act of possession of the Popham Colony. Others came in to help to hold it; political troubles at home favored emigration hither; and one hundred years after Popham, three hundred thousand people of the Saxo-Norman race inhabited the then eleven existing colonies. During the next sixty years they had mastered the French, and gained the Atlantic slope from the St. Lawrence to Florida. Before the end of the next one hundred years the same people had grown into the colossal Empire of the West, embracing thirty-four states, and regions yet unpeopled of still greater extent, including, in all their dominions, a territory equal to the continent of Europe, inhabited by more than thirty millions of human beings, speaking one language; while a new power has arisen in North America, the Colonial Empire of Great Britain, extending over a larger but less valuable territory than the United States, and containing more than three millions of inhabitants.

Temporary differences and periods of alienated feeling will from time to time arise, but nothing can prevent the gradual and cordial union of the English-speaking people of this continent in every thing essential to their highest welfare. Though divided into various governments, each pursuing its own lawful ends, in obedience to that principle of political harmony, that allows each to revolve, in its own appropriate orbit, around its common centre; an enlightened sense of justice, and obedience to the divine law, as the highest of all good to communities and states, is the daily lesson of their life. Let, then, each returning anniversary of this day's commemoration draw closer and closer the bonds of fraternal fellowship; and strengthen those ties of lineage that shall gradually encircle the earth, and constitute all mankind, of various races and nationalities, one final brotherhood of nations.

Two hundred and fifty-five years have sufficed to change this wilderness continent, as if by enchantment, into the home of a refined civilization. Cultivated fields, clustering villages, the refinements of city life, rise to our immediate view; stretching from this point eastward to Ascension Bay, northward to the Laurentian Hills, southward to the Gulf of Mexico, and westward to the Pacific seas; where San Francisco, at the Golden Gate, at the touch of the telegraph, sends to us kindly greetings for this hour. The improvement in agricultural implements, the wonders of the power-loom and the spinning-jenny, the marvels of the steamship, the mysteries of the photograph, the magic of the telegraph, and the omnipotent power of the locomotive railway, have since been made our ever-willing ministers; so that man seems almost invested with ubiquity and omnipotence; yet each revolving year brings forth new marvels, till the finite mind is overwhelmed at any attempt to forecast the future. And the historian of our race traces back this development to the two first acts in the great drama of American history by which the title of England to the continent was established: the first, closing with the grant of the Great Charter of April 10, 1606; the second, with the formal act of possession of the New World under it, August 19, O. S., 1607, thereby making the title forever clear and unquestionable.

On that day, and upon this peninsula of Sabino, was unfurled that proud flag that had so long braved the battle and the breeze; then our fathers' flag—and now the flag of the Fatherland,—and beneath its waving folds were proclaimed, for the first time, the political principles which lie at the foundation of free government, in ever memorable words.

"I give," said King James, "to my loving subjects, liberty to settle Virginia, in the north of America, between the thirty-fourth and forty-fifth degrees of north latitude. I authorize them to transport thither any of my own people, or those of other lands, and appoint over them a government of their own choice, subject to my approval, according to the laws of this kingdom. I authorize them to work mines, coin money, collect duties by imposts, and to expel all intruders therefrom by military force; and I declare, that all children born therein, and all persons residing therein, are, and shall always remain, citizens, entitled to all the rights, privileges, and immunities of the loyal subjects of the British realm. And I do further declare, that these, my loving subjects, shall have the right annually to elect a President, and other officers; that the Christian religion, established in this our kingdom, shall be therein preached and observed; that lands shall descend to heirs, according to the provisions of our ancient laws; that trial by jury of twelve men is established in all criminal cases, with a right of pardon by the King; that in civil causes the President and Council shall determine between party and party, keeping full records of all proceedings and judgments, with a right of appeal to the King in Council; that no man shall be tried as an offender outside of the colony where the alleged offence was committed; and no offences shall be capital except tumult, rebellion, conspiracy, mutiny and sedition, murder, manslaughter, incest, rape, and adultery. And I do further declare, and ordain, that my loving subjects in America shall forever possess and enjoy the right to make all needful laws for their own government, provided only, that they be consonant to the laws of England. And these, my loving subjects, shall be, and forever remain, entitled to the protection of the British crown, and I establish over them the government of the King of Great Britain, France, and Ireland."

This charter of liberties was never revoked. It was a decree of universal emancipation, and every man of any color, from any clime, was by this act of King James redeemed, regenerated, disenthralled, the moment he touched the soil of America, between the thirty-fourth and forty-fifth degrees of north latitude, and he at once became entitled to all the rights of citizenship—one hundred and fifty years before the decree of Lord Mansfield struck off the chains and fetters from the African in England. This ordinance also established the right of the people to self-government, subject only to the paramount authority of the crown and laws of England. These solemn formalities, unknown to any other of the early colonies, counselled by the Lord Chief-Justice of England, whose brother, as president of the infant commonwealth, planted on these shores the emblems of the authority of his nation; proclaimed in no doubtful accents to all other nations, that here the title of England was established. That pledge of the protection of his government, which every Englishman has always felt when he planted his foot on any portion of the empire of his sovereign, gave strength and courage to this colony; and when the humble settlers of Plymouth, thirteen years later, impressed with their feet the sandy shores of Cape Cod, the claim of England to the country had been vindicated and established against the asserted claims of both Spain and France.

The power of England remained undisturbed west

of Sagadahoc, and southward, till it was finally yielded on September 3, 1783,—one hundred and seventy-six years from the time it was first planted, —when all political connection with Great Britain was dissolved, on the conclusion of the definitive treaty of peace. In announcing that fact, King George the Third said: "In thus admitting their separation from the Crown of these kingdoms, I have sacrificed every consideration of my own to the wishes and opinions of my people. I make it my humble and earnest prayer to Almighty God, that Great Britain may not feel the evils which might result from so great a dismemberment of the empire; and that America may be free from the calamities which have formerly proved, in the mother country, how essential monarchy is to the enjoyment of constitutional liberty. Religion, language, interest, affections may, and I hope will, yet prove a bond of permanent union between the two countries. To this end neither attention nor disposition on my part shall be wanting." Memorable words, for they admit the national error.

But the repentance of the king had come too late. The loyal subjects of King James had planted on these shores the principles of civil and religious liberty, under his guidance and his express authority; and it was not in the power of King or Parliament, after one hundred and seventy-six years of the exercise of these rights, to reclaim them by force of arms. It was in defence of rights granted by King James, that our fathers took up arms against the arbitrary nactments of King George the Third and his Parliament, under the lead of Sir George Grenville, then First Minister of the Crown. They defended a principle since made universal in its application in every part of the British Colonial Empire. They claimed only their rights as loyal subjects of Great Britain. Our fathers charged the acts of oppression, commencing in 1763, and ending in the Revolution of 1776, on the King, as the responsible head of the British government; but the exact truth has remained obscured, from want of public access, till a recent date, to the state papers of that period. If the odium of these acts shall justly fall on the head of the minister rather than on the King, to what an eminence of guilt did Sir George Grenville attain; and how different the award of future over cotemporary times and opinions, as to the claims to veneration of the two men of England most intimately associated with American affairs; Sir Ferdinando Gorges, the father of English colonization in America, a private citizen, and Sir George Grenville, the highest officer of state.

The mind of each one present instinctively turns back to-day, over this long line of history, pausing to survey, in this broad sweep, the great epochs that mark its progress. It lingers longest in contemplating the initiatory steps that gave title and possession to the country,—and delights to loiter here, around this cherished spot, and recall to present view the deeds of Gorges and Popham, and those who assisted them to transport hither the Saxon Norman race; for that race, planted on this new continent, has favored and illustrated every thing that tends to the advancement of freedom and humanity, whatever may have been its occasional errors. We have established our power as a people, developed the natural resources of our country, and demonstrated the ability of our government to resist foreign aggression. One further duty remains—the vindication of its principles in reference to ourselves. Can a government, resting for its strength and support on the consent of the governed, so far maintain its power as to suppress insurrection without weakening the safeguards to personal liberty? Can popular elections fill the highest offices of the state, and insure that strength and stability to the government that can vindicate its power in times of domestic insurrection, or open rebellion, like that now shaking it to its foundations?

Putting our trust in that Power that alone can save us, invoking that Arm that can alone be stretched forth for our deliverance, we bow our wills to the Divine teaching. What though at this hour clouds and darkness hang like a thick pall over our country, and in the excess of our marvellous prosperity we are called for a time to self-abasement and trial, the race shall survive all shocks of civil strife and of foreign invasion, and rise superior to both; this free government emerge into the full strength and measure of its giant proportions; and "the gorgeous ensign of the Republic," known and honored throughout the earth, shall once more float full and free, as in former days, over a united and prosperous people.

APPENDIX.

In another place, reference is made to a paper addressed to the King, by the Scotch adventurers, REASONS ALLEDGED FOR HOLDING PORT ROYAL, which is of so much historic interest and value that we give the same in full, copied from the British State-Paper Office, and not heretofore published. (1862.)

PUBLIC RECORD OFFICE, LONDON.

COLONIAL, VOL. 5. No. 102. T.

Immediately about the time that Columbus discovered the Isle of Cuba, Sebastian Chabot set out from England by Henrie the seuenth did first discouer the continent of America, beginning at the Newfoundland, and thereafter going to the Gulph of Canada and from thence hauing seene Cap Bretton all along the Coast to Florida, By which discouery his Matie hath the title to Virginia, New England and New Scotland, as being then first discouered by Chabot at the charges of the K of England.

The French after this neglecting the knowledge they had thereafter by Jaquef Cartier of the riuer of Canada as a cold climate, or as it may bee in regard it was challenged as first discouered by the English, having a great desire to possesse themselues in some part of America, they planted first a Colony vnder the charge of Monsr Villegas now in Brasill, and an other vnder the charge of Monsr Laudoniere in Florida, from both which they were expelled by the Spaniards.

Then giving ouer all hope of attempting anything that was belonging to the Spaniards and pressing by all meanes to have some interest in America, notwithstanding that the English (though they were not able to possesse the whole at first) had possessed themselves of that continent, discouered by them, by a Colonie in the South part thereof now called Virginia, and by an other in the North part thereof now called New England and New Scotland planted by Justice Popham.

The French in the time of Henry the Fourth vnder the charge of Monsr Poutrincourt hauing seene all the coasts of Newengland and Newscotland to both which parts they did then beginne to claime right. They seated themselues in Port Royal, out of which soone as it was made knowne to the English they were displanted by S^r. Samuel Argall, as having wrongfully intruded themselues within those bounds, which did belong to this Crowne, both by discouery and possession.

The remainder of this French Collony not hauing occasion to bee transported to France, stayed still in the Countrie, yet they were so neglected by the State, not owning them any more and hardly supplied in that which was necessary for them by voluntary adventurers, who came to trade in hope of their commodities in exchange of what they brought, and during the time of King James there was no complaint made vpon S^r. Samuel Argall for hauing displanted them, and they were now lately glad to demand that protection from his Ma^{te} which was not afforded them from any other. Whereby it may euidently appeare that his Maties title was thought good. Otherwise it is likely that the French King, if any wrong had beene done unto him, would haue sought to haue had the same repaired, either by Treatie or otherwise. But without making either any priuat complaint, or yet doing any publick Act against the same, They went next and seated themselues vpon the Northside of the river of Canada at Kebeck, a place whereunto the English by a preceding title might likewise haue claimed right. But small notice was taken thereof till during the time of the late warre, a Commission was giuen by his Matie to remoue them from thence, which was accordingly performed, the place being taken a little after the peace was concluded, which at that time had not come to the takers knowledge, and a Colonie of Scottish was planted at Port Royal, which had neuer beene repossessed nor claimed by the French since they were first remoued from the same.

This businesse of Port Royal cannot be made lyable to the articles of the peace, seeing there was no Act of hostilities comitted thereby, a Colonny onely beeing planted vpon his Ma:tie owne ground, according to a patent granted by his Ma:tie late deare father and his Ma:tie self, hauing as good right thereunto as to any part of that Continent, and both the patent and possession taken thereupon was in the time of his Ma:tie late deare father, as is set downe at length in the voyages written by Purchas. But neither by that possession nor by the subsequent plata'on hath any thing beene taken from the French whereof they had any right at all, or yet any possession for the time, and what might haue beene done either before the warre or since the warre without a breach of peace, cannot bee justly complained vpon for being done at that time.

After that the Scottish Colony was planted at Port Royal, they and the French who dwelled there hauing met with the Commanders of the Natives, called by them Sagamoes did make choice of one of the cheefe of them called Sagamo Sigipt to come in name of the rest to his Ma:tie for acknowledging of his title, and to become his Ma:tie subjects, crauing onely to bee protected by his Ma:tie against their enemies, which demand of his was accepted by his Ma:tie who did promise to protect them as he reported to the rest at his returne.

Mons:r. La Tour, who was cheefe comand:r of the few French in that countrie beeing neglected (as is said) by his owne Countriemen, and finding his Ma:ties title not so much as questioned after theyr beeing expelled from Port Royall and the coming in of the Scottish necessary for his securitie did come along with the same Sagamo offring and demanding the like in name of the French who liue there, so that his Ma:tie hath a good right to New Scotland by discouere by possession of his Ma:tie subjects by remouing of the French who had seated themselues at Port Royall and by Mons. La Tour the comander of them there his turning Tenant and by the volontarie turning tenants of the rest to his Ma:tie. And that no obstacle might remaine the very Sauages by their Commissioner willingly offering their obedience vnto his Ma:tie so that his Ma:tie now is bound to maintaine them both in regard of his subjects that have planted there vpon his warrant and of the promise that he made to the Commissioner of the Natiues that came to him from thence, as he promised to the Commissioner of the Natiues, and as all the subjects of his Ma^{ts} ancient Kingdome of Scotland did humbly entreat at their last conuention, as may appeare by a letter to his Ma^{ie} from his Counsel to that effect.

 indorsed. Reasons alleaged by the Scottish adventurers for the holding of Port Royal

Discours

Concerning his Ma^{ts} right and title to the port Royall and whole Canada, &c. 9 Sept^e 1630.

Canada.

END.

www.ingramcontent.com/pod-product-compliance
Lightning Source LLC
Chambersburg PA
CBHW022121290426
44112CB00008B/762